TEN YEARS
OF EXILE

TEN YEARS OF EXILE

Madame de Staël

TRANSLATED BY

DORIS BEIK

With an Introduction by Peter Gay

Saturday Review Press

NEW YORK

Published simultaneously in Canada by
Doubleday Canada Ltd., Toronto

Library of Congress Catalog Card Number: 72–79117

ISBN 0–8415–0204–8

Saturday Review Press
380 Madison Avenue
New York, New York 10017

PRINTED IN THE UNITED STATES OF AMERICA

Design by Tere LoPrete

Contents

PART TWO

List of Illustrations

(Illustrations appear after page 124)

1. Madame de Staël
2. Auguste de Staël, Madame de Staël's son (*From a portrait by Anne Louis Girodet de Roucy Trioson. Reproduced by kind permission of the Château de Coppet.*)
3. The Morning of 18 Brumaire (*Engraving from a painting by Schopin*)
4. Napoleon Bonaparte
5. Benjamin Constant
6. Joseph Fouché (*Engraving after a painting by Claude-Marie Dubufe*)
7. Charles Maurice de Talleyrand (*Engraving after a portrait by François Gérard*)
8. Jacques Necker, Madame de Staël's father (*From a contemporary lithograph*)
9. Lucien Bonaparte (*From a contemporary lithograph*)
10. Madame Juliette Récamier (*From a painting by David*)
11. Church square in St. Petersburg
12. Harbor of St. Petersburg
13. Alexander I, Emperor of Russia
14. Merchants of St. Petersburg

Translator's Foreword

This translation was made from the Paul Gautier edition of
1904.* The Baron de Staël had published an earlier edition in
1821 in which he omitted certain passages and anecdotes for the
sake of propriety, such as the remarkable portrait of Talleyrand
(Part I, Chapter 3), the description of Empress Marie Louise
(Part II, Chapter 7), and the comments on educational reform
under the Consulate (Part I, Chapter 9). In addition, he replaced
a great number of proper names either by asterisks or by desig-
nations such as "a minister" or "a general." The 1904 text re-
establishes Madame de Staël's original manuscript, to which
Gautier had access in the Château de Coppet.

The footnotes cited are also from the 1904 edition, although
Gautier took many of them from Auguste de Staël's earlier edition; they are included because they supplement the narrative. The
Baron de Staël was responsible for the division of the work into
chapters; according to Gautier, the original manuscript had neither chapter divisions nor punctuation, and both were supplied
by Madame de Staël's son.

---

* Staël, Mme de. *Dix années d'exil. Edition nouvelle, d'après les manuscrits,
avec une introduction, des notes et un appendice par Paul Gautier.* Paris, Plon-
Nourrit et Cie, 1904.

Chronology

1766 Anne Louise Germaine Necker born in Paris on April 22.

1777 Jacques Necker, her father, appointed Minister of Finance for Louis XVI.

1781 Dismissal of Necker after his *Compte rendu au Roi sur l'état des finances*. Exiled to Switzerland.

1784 Purchase by Necker of the baronetcy and Château of Coppet in the province of Vaud in Switzerland.

1786 Marriage of Germaine in Paris to Eric Magnus de Staël-Holstein, Swedish ambassador to France.

1787 Birth of daughter Gustavine de Staël.

1788 Publication of Madame de Staël's *Lettres sur les ouvrages et le caractère de J. J. Rousseau*.

Her liaison with Narbonne, a noble who was to become Minister of War in 1791.

Necker recalled as Minister of Finance as a result of the crisis over French finances.

1789 Death of Gustavine de Staël.

Meeting of the Estates General at Versailles.

Fall of the Bastille.

1790 Birth of Auguste de Staël.

Resignation of Necker and his return to Coppet.

1792 Dismissal of Narbonne.

Downfall of the Monarchy.

Madame de Staël's flight to Coppet.

Birth of Albert de Staël at Coppet.

1793 Louis XVI guillotined.

Reign of Terror.

      Napoleon Bonaparte gains prominence in defeat of English at Toulon.

1794   Overthrow and execution of Robespierre. End of Reign of Terror.

      Madame de Staël's first meeting with Benjamin Constant.

1795   Return to Paris with Constant; influential salon in the rue du Bac; exiled from Paris at end of the year by the Directory, the new Republican government.

1796   Publication of Madame de Staël's *De l'influence des passions*.

      Napoleon's victories in Italy.

1797   Madame de Staël in Paris again with Benjamin Constant.

      Birth of Albertine de Staël.

1799   Napoleon's return from Egypt.

      Coup d'état of 18 Brumaire.

1800   Napoleon's passage through St. Bernard Pass on way to campaign in Italy.

      Battle of Marengo.

      Attempt on Napoleon's life in rue Saint-Nicaise.

      Publication of *De la littérature*.

      Madame de Staël's separation from Eric de Staël.

1802   Death of Eric de Staël.

      Publication of *Delphine*.

      Peace of Amiens with English.

      Bonaparte becomes consul for life.

1803   Renewal of war with England.

      Madame de Staël's exile from France and departure for Germany.

1804   Visits to Weimar, Berlin.

      Death of Necker.

      Madame de Staël's trip to Italy.

      Arrests of Moreau, Pichegru, Cadoudal.

      Execution of the Duke d'Enghien.

      Napoleon crowned Emperor by Pope Pius VII in Paris.

1805   Napoleon crowned King of Italy.

      Nelson's victory over the French fleet at Trafalgar.

Napoleon's victory over the Austrians and Russians at Austerlitz.

1806   Madame de Staël's sojourns in Auxerre, Rouen, Meulan.

1807   Madame de Staël's exile to Coppet.

Publication of *Corinne*.

Treaty of Tilsit between France and Russia, following Napoleon's interview with Emperor Alexander I.

1808   French take Madrid.

Joseph Bonaparte made King of Spain.

1810   Dissolution of Napoleon's religious marriage to Josephine.

His marriage with Marie Louise.

Madame de Staël's brief return to France, to Blois and Fossé.

Her first vesion of *De l'Allemagne* seized and destroyed.

She receives her order of exile to Coppet.

Her meeting with John Rocca.

1812   Secret birth of Madame de Staël's son, Louis Alphonse Rocca.

May 23   Madame de Staël leaves Coppet.

June 22   She leaves Vienna.

France declares war on Russia.

June 24   The French Grand Army crosses Niemen River on way into Russia.

June 26   The French reach Vilna.

July 1   Madame de Staël leaves Brünn.

July 10   She passes through Lemberg.

July 14   She enters Russia.

August 2   She reaches Moscow, by way of Zhitomir, Kiev, Orel, Toula.

August 7   She leaves Moscow.

August 13   She arrives in St. Petersburg.

August 18   The French enter Smolensk.

September 5–7   Battle of the Moskva (Borodino).

September 7   Madame de Staël leaves St. Petersburg.

September 14   Napoleon's entry into Moscow.

September 15   Madame de Staël's arrival at Abo, point

of embarkation for Sweden, after stopping at Viborg
and Helsinki.

September 24   Madame de Staël's arrival in Stockholm.

October 19   Napoleon's retreat from Moscow.

1813   Madame de Staël in London.

Death of Albert de Staël in a duel.

Publication of *De l'Allemagne* and *Réflexions sur le suicide*.

1814   Napoleon's abdication.

Madame de Staël's return from London to Paris; summer
at Coppet.

The Bourbons repay her father's loan.

1815   Napoleon's escape from Elba.

Battle of Waterloo; end of Napoleon's Hundred Days.

Madame de Staël's departure from Paris during the Hundred Days; summer at Coppet; winter of 1815–1816
in Italy.

1816   Marriage of Albertine de Staël and Victor de Broglie in
Italy.

Marriage of Madame de Staël to John Rocca.

1817   Madame de Staël's death on July 14 in Paris.

Introduction

Anne Louise Germaine Necker, Baronne de Staël-Holstein, was the most intelligent woman of her time. She was also the most interesting. Novelist, critic, political thinker, sociologist of literature, and autobiographer, courageous in politics and self-indulgent in love, Madame de Staël attracted men of wit and power to her salon and to her bed; she alone could have inspired Benjamin Constant and defied Napoleon Bonaparte. J. Christopher Herold, whose biography of her is justly popular, called her, in a suitably ambiguous phrase, "Mistress to an Age." It is a title she eminently deserved, however it may be interpreted.*

Her autobiography, *Ten Years of Exile*, is vintage de Staël, but since it covers only a portion of her later life, it does not entirely clarify why the great should have loved and feared her, and why the best of her work has always had its admirers.

Madame de Staël's parentage is as remarkable as her career. Her mother was Suzanne Curchod, an educated and handsome Swiss girl from Lausanne, in whom the young Gibbon had at one time been romantically interested. When his father forbade the match, Gibbon accepted the parental verdict with resigned passivity. "I sighed as a lover," he recorded in his *Autobiography*, "I obeyed as a son." The sigh, we can sense, was a sigh of relief; for Gibbon, women were not nearly so interesting as books. Perhaps it was just as well for Mademoiselle Curchod; in any event she consoled herself with the Genevan financier, Jacques Necker,

---

* Anyone familiar with *Mistress to An Age: A Life of Madame de Staël* (Indianapolis: Bobbs-Merrill, 1958) will recognize how close my interpretation is to Christopher Herold's, and how much I owe to his book.

whose career is irrevocably linked with the history of France during the reign of Louis XVI, and during the Revolution.

When Anne Louise Germaine Necker was born in 1766, her father had been living in Paris for nearly twenty years. A Swiss Protestant eminently at home in Catholic France, he had risen to prosperity and prominence as a banker and as a director of the French East India Company. In 1767 he was appointed minister of the Genevan Republic to the Court of Versailles, a minor post which he used as a springboard for positions of great authority. Necker was always a charmer and was always admired more than he deserved—Germaine, his only daughter, loved him passionately.

Germaine's feelings about her mother, a cool if cultivated preceptor, were far less positive. Madame Necker, something of a writer herself, presided over an articulate Parisian salon, resonant with free conversation and advanced ideas. It was quite a household for a child as perceptive and precocious as Germaine, and she took advantage of her opportunities there. As a little girl, perhaps no more than ten years old, she would participate in her mother's Friday receptions, taking it all in, perched on her stool and listening intently. Her mother raised her, teaching her languages and extolling the life of the mind, to the exclusion of nature and the emotions. When she was older, Germaine reversed the direction of her education; without neglecting her mind, she developed a romantic interest in nature and gave full rights to physical pleasures.

Her chance for escape came soon enough, through marriage. In 1786 she married a young Swedish nobleman who was ambassador from his country to France. Unfortunately—at least as far as his relations with his wife were concerned—he had acquired his position through his connections rather than his abilities. Germaine, at twenty, was naïve; her knowledge of books was vast, but her ignorance of life was total. She soon learned. She wanted to give love, but she could not love unless she could admire. De Staël was charming, handsome, and complaisant, yet he barely interested her. Germaine de Staël, a spirited young woman, did not resign herself to her situation; she demanded equal rights with her husband, and sought emotional consolation with other men. The roster of her lovers reads like a Who's Who of the age: the statesman Talleyrand, the diplomat Louis de Narbonne, the novelist Benjamin Constant, the historian Simonde de Sismondi, the critic and poet August Wilhelm von Schlegel, to mention the most famous ones.

The first of her extra-marital consolations was probably Talleyrand, whom she met in 1788–1789 in Paris, a turbulent city hovering nervously on the edge of great events. Talleyrand was still a bishop but then, as throughout all his life, he was also a cynic; he was on his way to power, to becoming the architect of French foreign policy at a critical moment in the country's history. He was a man of enormous suppleness and irresistible charm who managed to survive the regimes of the French Revolution, of the Directory, and even of Napoleon, and to play significant roles in each. His malicious wit was unsurpassed; this was one of his virtues. When, some years after their break, Madame de Staël drew a most unflattering portrait of him as the character of Madame de Vernon in her novel *Delphine* (1802), the victim protested: "They say that Madame de Staël has portrayed us, herself and me, *disguised as women.*" With later lovers, Germaine's relations were perhaps more turbulent, but also more satisfactory: her association with Constant, romantic novelist and liberal political thinker, which began in 1794 and ended, after some tempestuous interludes, in 1809, was marked by the intense discussion of every possible topic. While it is impossible to discern any mark she might have left on Talleyrand, Madame de Staël's influence on Constant was prolonged and far-reaching. She had important discussions with all of her famous lovers: she talked politics with Constant, history with Sismondi, Romanticism with Schlegel, and her talk was certainly never on the level of gossip.

Madame de Staël's life was unsettled for political as well as for erotic reasons. The outbreak of the French Revolution in 1789 found her in Paris. Her father, with whom her relationship continued to be close, had been France's Director General of Finance from 1776 to 1781 and after his resignation he had left behind an adroit account of his stewardship. This famous self-serving *Compte rendu* made his labors, and French finances, appear far sounder than both in fact were. His reputation as a miracle-man survived his administration, and in 1788 the desperate Louis XVI recalled the "wizard" to rescue France from bankruptcy. Necker failed, but the French people never blamed him for his failure; when the king dismissed him in early July, 1789, the act was one of the causes for the storming of the Bastille on July 14. Once again, Necker, hero of the populace, was called into office, but this time it became obvious to his most infatuated supporters that his financial expedients, even when coupled with his confident presence, would not save the country. In 1790 he was forced to resign, and in September he returned to Switzerland.

Two years later his daughter followed him. In the early 1780s Necker had bought the territory of Coppet on the lake of Geneva, and restored its old château on the property. Germaine de Staël joined her father at Coppet in September, 1792. A vigorous supporter of the Revolution, she had been close to those who wrote France's first modern Constitution of 1791, and who also made the policies leading to war with Europe in early 1792. But then, on August 10, 1792, there was a "second Revolution" which radicalized the country, and which led to the arrest and exile of Germaine's friends. In early September, while allied troops were threatening Paris, popular hysteria, fanned by deliberate incitement, set off the notorious prison massacres. Mobs stormed the prisons in Paris and some provincial towns, murdering most of their inmates. Germaine was enraged mainly for political reasons: she was a consistent liberal and principled constitutionalist who hated mob rule and the casual employment of violence as an instrument of policy.

Between 1792 and 1795, Germaine lived in Switzerland. She watched the stirring and terrible events in her native France with fascinated interest: the trial and execution of the royal family, the mobilization of the country for war, the reign of the Jacobins, the internecine struggle among the revolutionaries which culminated in the end of Jacobin domination in July, 1794, the victory of the French military and, in 1795, the establishment of the Directory.

The Directory, which promised stability for the country without jeopardizing the gains of the Revolution, gave Madame de Staël the opportunity she had been waiting for: she returned to Paris, to the center of things, to get back into politics. But she had too many enemies in high places, and in 1796 she briefly returned to Coppet, in voluntary, though temporary, exile. During the next few years, her life situation swung back and forth like a pendulum: she was in Paris one week, advising the great; she was in Coppet the next, chafing at her remoteness from events. In 1803, finally, she was forced to leave Paris for a long time; she had aroused the enmity of a formidable opponent, Bonaparte, and there was nothing she could do but yield to his demands.

Madame de Staël had first encountered Napoleon Bonaparte late in December, 1797, on his return to Paris from his stunning victories in Italy. General Bonaparte was the hero of the hour. Germaine de Staël, like everyone else, felt his power, and for some time she boldly curried favor with him. Too boldly, it seems: when she hinted that the two might be equal partners, ruling France, Bonaparte would have none of it. He needed no partners, and certainly not a forward woman. By 1800, after he had become First Consul, the two were enemies; Madame de Staël found herself reduced to placating him. This was not a role she enjoyed since she could not play it while retaining her own self-respect. Late that year she persuaded Constant to make an anti-Bonapartist speech in the Tribunate—another stay at Coppet followed. Her relationship with Napoleon could only end badly: Bonaparte was too single-minded and temperamental to bear the kind of clever opposition Germaine displayed in her drawing room; Madame de Staël was too active, too proud, and too talkative to keep silent. And she did not like tyrants, no matter how impressive they might be. The exile into which Bonaparte forced her in 1803, when he was Consul for Life, lasted for many years. And when Bonaparte, then Consul, made himself Napoleon I, Emperor in 1804, he was not inclined to reverse himself on that point.

If anything, he became more implacable. While Germaine de Staël continued her peripatetic life, Coppet was her permanent base. Her husband, of whom she was moderately fond, had died in 1802; her father, for whom her passion never cooled, died in 1804. Germaine learned to deal with her grief although she was miserable; she made Coppet into a salon and a refuge, filled with talk of politics and literature. "Her house at Coppet," Napoleon later said at St. Helena, "became a veritable arsenal against me." For six years, exiled politicians and aspiring Romantics found hospitality inside its doors. Germaine was not always there: she traveled continuously, to Geneva, to Lausanne, to Italy, to Germany. But Coppet was the place to which she returned, and from which she drew strength.

Eventually, she was driven from her home by the repressive measures of the vindictive Emperor. In 1810, Madame de Staël had completed a three-volume work, *De l'Allemagne;* the first two volumes had passed the French censorship with little difficulty, but the third aroused the censors and infuriated the Emperor because of its favorable report on Germany. The proofs and the plates were seized, and, consequently, *De l'Allemagne* was not published until 1813—and then, significantly, it was published in London. By that time Germaine de Staël had fled from Coppet, visiting Russia and England. She did not return to Paris until 1814, in the wake of the Allies, and she arrived at Coppet later in the same year. Napoleon's definitive defeat in 1815 gave her security and freedom at last, but she enjoyed very little of it; in 1817 she died, her search for love unsatisfied.

This straightforward summary of Madame de Staël's life might suggest that she was an amorous dilettante, more interested in sex than in ideas. But that would be grossly unjust. The men she loved were extraordinarily intelligent, and besides, the body of her work testifies to gifts of concentration, unremitting diligence, and a powerful interest in the life of the mind. Napoleon would not have been aroused by a trivial woman or by trivial books.

The best way to suggest the reasons for the enduring interest in her is to turn directly to these books, and to single out three of them, each of which illuminates one facet of her complex being: *De la littérature*, published in 1800, for her sociology; *Corinne* of 1807, for her Romanticism; and *De l'Allemagne*, for her politics. These categories, as we shall see, are artificial: in the eighteenth century everything was connected with politics, and in Madame de Staël's mind everything was touched by Romanticism.

The very title of her book on literature marks an original departure from the past; it reads, in its entirety, *De la littérature considerée dans ses rapports avec les institutions.* The metaphor of society as an organism in which one part affects all others was popular in the late eighteenth century. While the word "sociology" had not yet been invented, sociology had been practiced since Montesquieu had published his *De l'esprit des lois* in 1748. In that sprawling, ill-organized masterpiece, Montesquieu had sought to show that forms of government and styles of life are intimately bound up with geographic and climatic conditions. Montesquieu had moved beyond the formal considerations traditionally used to analyze forms of government to substantive questions concerning the interaction of ways of thought, moral codes, and political organization. The Scottish school of social scientists, notably Adam Ferguson, Adam Smith, and John Millar, had applied Montesquieu's "sociology" to the origin of classes, the function of conflict, and the consequences of industrialization. The pioneer of modern art history, Johann Joachim Winckelmann, had made a tentative beginning of a sociology of art in his *History of Art in Antiquity* (1764), in which he had traced the achievements of Greek sculpture to Greek freedom and even to the Greek climate. Madame de Staël's *De la littérature* applied some of these ideas to literature. Each age, each climate, each political system, she argued, calls forth its appropriate literature. The North, given to innovation and melancholy, is Romantic; the South, intent on form, and illuminated by the clear Mediterranean light, is Classical.

This was a suggestive and novel point of view; although *De la littérature* is often incorrect in its details, although it betrays the superficiality of Madame de Staël's learning and suffers from her hasty generalizations, it points the way to a social history of literature and a literary history of society. Beyond this, the book is deeply political; it has justly been called a tract and a manifesto. *De la littérature* proclaims the superiority of reason over illusion, enlightenment over obscurantism; it stresses Madame de Staël's unquenchable belief in progress, and in a new, more democratic literature. Why had the French Revolution, so necessary in its origins and beneficent in its legislation, produced the bloody interlude of the Terror? Because the masses had been kept in helpless ignorance; they had been brutal with their victims because the educational system of the Old Regime had brutalized them. Such preachments, which seemed to express the belief that the most hopeful visions of the Enlightenment could become authentic possibilities for the future, were scarcely calculated to ingratiate Madame de Staël with Bonaparte, whose main concern in 1800 was not so much progress as stability—above all, his stability in power.

Madame de Staël's Romanticism seems rather less political than her sociology at first glance. Her novel *Delphine*, published in 1802, employed the traditional epistolary form used by Richardson in *Clarissa*, by Rousseau in *La Nouvelle Héloïse*, and by Goethe in *Werther*. Delphine, the heroine, is a superior woman who dies by taking poison at the moment her lover is shot. But while Delphine's love seems an obviously unpolitical theme, and while Madame de Staël assiduously avoided allusions to current affairs by having the book take place a decade earlier, the novel has its political message: it is, in its way, an early feminist tract. And it is more: "the book," in Christopher Herold's summation, "is a ferocious attack on marriage unsanctified by love, a satire on Catholic bigotry, a brief for divorce, and a plea for the rights of women." Once again, Madame de Staël managed to anger Bonaparte, whose views on these questions were precisely opposite to hers.

Corinne, her most widely read book, is also a novel with a thesis. The book is a kind of internal dialogue and came out of an Italian voyage she undertook in the company of Schlegel and

Sismondi. The dramatic scene is based in Italy, the home of Southern literature, but its hero represents the North: he is a melancholy Scot. And its heroine, palpably an idealized portrait of the author, is half English, half Italian, an enthusiast, a poet given to brilliant improvisations. The story is unimportant; what is crucial here is the author's inner struggle: in the combat between coldness and passion, the latter must win, though the attributes of both North and South have their value and may complement each other—is not Corinne, in herself, a combination of the two? Stendhal, a Romantic endowed with detachment and ironic humor, disliked the book intensely. "Mme. de Staël (*Corinne*) makes me sick," he wrote into his journal. "That stilted style, the least fault of which is to strive to command admiration continually, that wit which lays claim to the honors of genius and doesn't realize that the latter's most salient quality (naturalness) is entirely lacking in it, that farce which ridicules what I love most, makes me acutely ill."

We can see what he means. And yet, no matter how unsatisfactory *Corinne* may seem today, it was an early example of the novel of ideas, an authentically cosmopolitan novel, and a passionate treatment of the place of the intelligent woman in a man's world—this last is one of Madame de Staël's most personal and most poignant themes. Besides, though Madame de Staël lacked the talent to make *Corinne* a memorable novel, she really wrote it as part of a voyage of discovery. And *De l'Allemagne* was the greatest booty she brought back from that voyage. Madame de Staël had traveled in Germany in 1804, and then again, after publishing *Corinne*, in 1808. She composed an exhaustive and subjective survey of German customs, literature, philosophy, ethics, and religion from her impressions of the country. She spoke little German and knew few Germans; readers complained that much of her exposition, as well as her sections on philosophy, was unrevealing or imprecise. But the book put German thought and German literature on the map of Europe, and it popularized the distinction between Classical and Romantic that was still little known, or largely confined to the intellectual circles around the Schlegels. In this instance, as in so many others, Madame de

Staël's quick perception made use of whom she knew rather than what she knew. And, once again, literature became political. By praising Germany, Madame de Staël was covertly criticizing France; *De l'Allemagne* stands in the great Enlightenment tradition of Montesquieu's *Persian Letters* and Voltaire's *English Letters*, two masterly attacks on the Old Regime in France. Both depended on the favorable presentation of foreign institutions, and the naïve comments on France by foreign visitors for their effectiveness. Madame de Staël was suggesting that France needed foreign ideas and needed freedom. The political application of these hints would not be lost on Napoleon Bonaparte.

This, then, is the context in which we must read *Ten Years of Exile*. I shall say nothing of its apt character sketches and its brilliant recital of events—those are obvious. What is perhaps less obvious is that the book is, throughout, a hymn to freedom coupled with a hard-headed understanding of what makes freedom possible. "Public opinion!" Madame de Staël exclaims, "what is it, without the authority of the law? What is it, without independent organs to express it?" The protagonist, though hardly the hero, of this autobiography is Napoleon Bonaparte. And the dominance of this character raises *Ten Years in Exile* from the category of autobiography to that of a valuable political document.

For the verdict of history on Napoleon remains a difficult task. Twentieth-century tyrants have made it no easier. Their sanguinary careers have produced two extreme responses in the student of Napoleon, neither of them wholly just. Some historians, repelled by the mass murder that was standard policy in Nazi Germany and Soviet Russia, have taken pains to deny all resemblance between Napoleon on the one hand, Hitler and Stalin on the other. They point to the unflagging admiration for Napoleon's work of good Europeans like Stendhal or Heine. The opposite response has been to treat Napoleon as the ancestor, and twentieth-century dictators as his logical successors in the craft of tyranny. Yet neither of these judgments will do. Our verdict on Napoleon, his intentions, actions, and consequences, must always be far more complex than our verdict on Hitler and Stalin. Madame de Staël's autobiography is of invaluable assistance in arriving at that verdict for she accompanies her recital of events with comments which are admirable for their lucidity and (given her personal engagement) their objectivity. Speaking of the political murder of the young Duke d'Enghien in 1804, after which Bonaparte made himself emperor, she notes that, contrary to general expectation, this single act was not followed by other acts of tyranny. "Bonaparte only wanted to teach the French one thing: that he was capable of anything, to make them grateful for the evil he did not do, as one is grateful to others for the good they do." As usual, Madame de Staël is just, and she is moderate. This kind of comment alone makes *Ten Years of Exile* important. Her analysis of the events of her time is always enlightening and exciting.

—PETER GAY

Auguste de Staël's Preface to the Edition of 1821

The work you are about to read is not a finished product, and should not be judged as such. It consists of parts of memoirs which my mother intended to finish at her leisure, and which would perhaps have undergone various changes if a longer life had permitted her to revise and complete them. This thought alone made me consider scrupulously whether I had a right to publish them. Fear of any kind of responsibility is unthinkable where our deepest affections are involved, but painful anxiety is unavoidable when one can only guess at wishes whose fulfillment is a sacred obligation. However, having seriously reflected on what duty required of me, I was convinced that in pledging not to omit any publishable writing from this edition of my mother's works I had fulfilled my mother's intentions. My fidelity to this pledge gives me the right to disavow—in advance—anything that might ever be proposed as an addition to a collection, which—I repeat—includes everything my mother would not have expressly forbidden to be published.

The title *Ten Years of Exile* was chosen by the author herself. I had to keep it, although the work, never having been completed, covers a span of only seven years. The story begins in 1800—in other words, two years before my mother's first exile—and stops in 1804, after Monsieur Necker's death. The narrative begins again in 1810, and breaks off abruptly with my mother's arrival in Sweden in the autumn of 1812. There is therefore an interval of nearly six years between the first and second parts of her

memoirs, which is clarified through a faithful examination of
the manner in which they were written.

I shall not anticipate the story of the persecutions my mother
endured under the imperial government; those persecutions, petty
as well as cruel, form the subject of this work, and I could only
weaken its interest by doing so. It is enough if I remind the
reader that after having banished her first from Paris, and then
from France; after having suppressed her work *On Germany* by
the most arbitrary caprice, making it impossible for her to publish
anything even on subjects unconnected with politics, the government went so far as to make her almost a prisoner in her own
residence, forbidding her any kind of travel and depriving her
of the pleasures of society and the consolations of friendship.
That was the situation when my mother started her memoirs,
and one can readily appreciate her frame of mind at that time.

While she was writing this work, the thought of publishing
it someday—even in the most distant future—hardly occurred
to her. Europe was still so bowed down under the yoke of Napoleon that no independent voice could make itself heard. The press
on the Continent was curbed, and the most rigorous measures excluded anything published in England. Therefore, my mother
did not think in terms of composing a book but rather of pre-
serving her recollections and thoughts. While relating the circumstances which concerned her personally she included in her
account various reflections about the state of France and the
course of events since Bonaparte's advent to power. If one takes
into account that printing such a work at that time would have
been an unheard-of act of temerity, actually writing it demanded
a great deal of courage and prudence, especially in my mother's
precarious situation. She could not help but know that she was
under police surveillance; the prefect who had replaced Monsieur
de Barante in Geneva claimed to be informed of everything that
happened in her home, and the slightest pretext would have justified seizure of her papers. She was obliged to take the greatest
precautions, and no sooner had she written several pages than
she had them transcribed by one of her most trusted friends, who
took care to replace all proper names with names of persons

taken from the history of the English revolution. She took along her manuscript in this form when, in 1812, she left, resolving to escape from ever-increasing harassments.

On her arrival in Sweden, after having crossed Russia and avoiding the armies that were advancing on Moscow by the narrowest of margins, my mother made a fresh copy of the first part of her memoirs, which, as I have already mentioned, ends in the year 1804. Before continuing them chronologically she wished to take advantage of her vivid memories of more recent events to narrate the remarkable circumstances of her flight and the persecutions that had made it—in a manner of speaking—a duty. She therefore resumed the story of her life with the year 1810, the time when her work *On Germany* was suppressed, and continued it up to her arrival in Stockholm in 1812: hence the title, *Ten Years of Exile*. This also explains why, in writing about the imperial government, my mother at times expresses herself as living under its power, and at other times as having escaped from it.

Finally, after she had conceived the format for her work *Considerations on the French Revolution*, she extracted the historical passages and general reflections that were suitable to this new setting from the first part of *Ten Years of Exile*, reserving personal details for the time when she expected to finish her memoirs, for she counted on being able—without compromising them— to thank by name all from whom she had received generous testimonies of friendship.

The manuscript entrusted to my care was thus composed of two distinct parts: the first, which naturally offered less interest, contained several passages already incorporated into *Considerations on the French Revolution;* the second formed a sort of journal, no portion of which was yet known to the public. I have followed the plan indicated by my mother by deleting from the first part of her manuscript all passages that, with a few modifications, had already found a place in her great political work. My function as editor has been limited to that alone, and I have not permitted myself any additions whatever.

As for the second part, I present it to the public with no changes, and I have hardly felt myself entitled to make even slight corrections in its style, so important did it seem to me to retain all the vividness of the original version. A perusal of her opinions about Russia's political conduct will convince everyone of my scrupulous respect for my mother's manuscript, but even without taking into account the influence that gratitude exercises on noble souls, no doubt it will be recalled that Russia's sovereign was at that time fighting for the cause of independence and liberty. Was it possible to foresee that after so short a time the enormous forces of this empire would become instruments of oppression for an unfortunate Europe?

If one compares *Ten Years of Exile* with *Considerations on the French Revolution*, it will perhaps be evident that Napoleon's reign is judged with more severity in the first of these writings than in the second, and that here he is attacked with an eloquence that is not always free from bitterness. This difference is easy to explain: one of these works was written after the despot's downfall and with the dispassion and impartiality of an historian, while the other was inspired by a courageous feeling of resistance to tyranny, and at the time my mother wrote it imperial power was at its height.

I have not chosen one time in preference to another for the publication of *Ten Years of Exile*. Chronological order has been followed in this edition, and the posthumous works naturally had to be placed at the end of the collection. Moreover, I am not afraid of the charge that it was ungenerous to publish—after Napoleon's downfall—an attack directed against his power. My mother, whose talent was always devoted to the defense of the most noble causes, whose house was frequently a sanctuary for the oppressed of all parties, would be far above such a reproach. Such a charge could, in any case, be addressed only to the editor of *Ten Years of Exile*, but I confess I would be very little affected by it. Actually it would be making a great concession to despotism if, after having imposed the silence of terror during its time of triumph, it could still ask history to spare it after its defeat.

No doubt memories of the last government have been the pretext for many persecutions. No doubt men of integrity are revolted by the cowardly invectives that are still hurled against those who, having enjoyed the favors of that government, have had enough dignity not to disavow their past conduct, and no doubt—finally—fallen grandeur can captivate the imagination. But it is not merely the personal character of Napoleon that is in question; it is not he who today can be an object of blame to persons of noble disposition, and neither is it the men who, under his reign, usefully served their country in the various branches of public administration; but what we can never criticize too severely is the system of egoism and oppression which Bonaparte founded. And does not this deplorable system still rule in Europe? Are not the powerful still enjoying the shameful inheritance of the man they have overthrown? And if we look at our country, how many of these tools of Napoleon's do we not see who, after having wearied him with their monotonous servility, come to offer the tribute of their petty Machiavellism to yet another power? Now, as then, does not their contemptible science rest on vanity and corruption and is it not from the traditions of the imperial regime that their counsels of wisdom are drawn?

Therefore, by painting this disastrous regime in the most vivid colors, it is not a vanquished enemy that is being insulted; it is a still powerful adversary that is being attacked; and if, as I hope, *Ten Years of Exile* is destined to increase people's abhorrence to arbitrary governments, I may indulge myself in the pleasant thought that by publishing this work I shall be serving the holy cause to which my mother never ceased to be faithful.

PART ONE

CHAPTER I

Causes of Bonaparte's animosity toward

Madame de Staël—Offers he made to her—

Madame de Staël's answer

It is not to attract public attention that I have decided to narrate the circumstances of my ten years of exile. The misfortunes I have experienced, however bitterly I have felt about them, are so minor in the midst of the public calamities we have all been witnessing that I would be ashamed to speak of myself if the events that concern me were not connected with the greater cause of a threatened humanity. Emperor Napoleon, whose character reveals itself completely in each phase of his life, has persecuted me with meticulous care, ever-increasing diligence, and inflexible harshness, and my relations with him taught me to understand him long before Europe had discovered the key to this enigma, and while it was still allowing itself to be devoured by the sphinx, through inability to understand it.

I shall not review the facts preceding Bonaparte's arrival on the European political scene. If I achieve my ambition of writing my father's biography, I shall relate there my impressions of the early

Note in the manuscript: Started in the summer of 1811. (This note is not in Madame de Staël's handwriting.)

days of the Revolution whose influence has changed the fate of the entire world. My object at present is only to sketch the portion of this vast tableau that concerns me personally. However, in directing attention to the whole picture from so limited a point of view, I am confident that much of the time I can remain inconspicuous while telling my own story.

Emperor Napoleon's greatest grievance against me is my unfailing respect for true liberty. This sentiment was transmitted to me as a legacy, and I made it my own as soon as I was able to appreciate the lofty ideas from which it was derived as well as the noble actions it inspires. Since the cruel scenes that have dishonored the French Revolution are only tyranny disguised as democracy, they could not, in my view, damage the cult of liberty. At most, we could become discouraged for France, but if the French were so unfortunate as to be unable to enjoy that most noble of blessings, liberty should not on that account be denied to others. When the sun disappears below the horizon of the northern countries, the inhabitants do not curse its rays because they are shining in other places more favored by heaven.

Shortly after 18 Brumaire, it was reported to Napoleon that I had warned my friends against the dawning oppression whose growth I foresaw as clearly as if the future had been revealed to me. Joseph Bonaparte, whose intelligence and conversation I enjoyed, came to see me and said, "My brother is complaining about you. Yesterday he said to me, 'Why does Madame de Staël not support my government? What does she want? Is it the restitution of her father's deposit? [1] I will order it done. The right to stay in Paris? I will grant it. In short, what does she want?' " To this I replied, "My God, it is not a question of what I want, but of what I think." I do not know whether this answer was reported back to him, but if it was I am certain that he attached no importance to it, for he does not believe in the sincerity of opinions. He views all morality as a formality with no more meaning than the ending of

---

[1] The reference is to the 2,400,000 livres advanced by Necker to the Treasury in 1778. In September, 1790, the Constituent Assembly had reimbursed 400,-000 livres. There remained two million that Madame de Staël vainly claimed from Napoleon's government and that she ended by getting from King Louis XVIII.

a letter; when you have assured someone that you are his most humble servant it does not entitle him to ask anything of you; and similarly, when someone says that he loves liberty, believes in God, and prefers his conscience to his interests, Bonaparte believes that he is a man only conforming to custom and following the accepted manner in pursuing his ambition or his selfish calculations. The only human beings he cannot comprehend are those who sincerely hold to an opinion regardless of the consequences. Bonaparte considers such men to be either simpletons, or merchants who overcharge; in other words men who wish to sell themselves too dearly. And so, as will be seen later on, he has never deluded himself except about honest people, either as individuals or, above all, as nations.

CHAPTER II

Beginning of opposition in the Tribunate—

Speech by Benjamin Constant—The First

Consul's irritation—Madame de Staël and

Fouché—Madame de Staël and Talleyrand:

portrait of Talleyrand

Some tribunes wanted to institute an opposition to their assembly similar to the one in England, and to take the constitution seriously,[1] as if the rights it appeared to guarantee had any basis in reality, and as if the pretended divisions within the state were anything more than an affair of protocol, a set of distinctions among the various antechambers of the Consul, in which magistrates with different labels could be grouped. I must confess that I looked with pleasure on those few members of the Tribunate who did not want to compete with the Councillors of State in obsequiousness. It was my strong belief that those who had previously let themselves be

---

[1] The Constitution, promulgated 24 Frimaire, year VIII (December 15, 1799), after Bonaparte's coup of 18 Brumaire. The Tribunate, one of the legislative chambers, did not have the initiative for legal proposals, but it could express wishes, receive petitions, and it alone had the power to discuss laws publicly.

carried too far in their love for the republic owed it to themselves to remain faithful to their point of view, even when it had become the weakest and most threatened.

One of these tribunes, Monsieur Benjamin Constant, a friend of liberty who was endowed with one of the most remarkable minds ever given to any man, consulted me about a speech he proposed making as a warning of the approach of tyranny. I encouraged him with all the strength of my convictions. Nevertheless, since it was known that he was one of my intimate friends, I could not help fearing what might happen to me as a result. I was vulnerable because of my liking for society. Montaigne once said, "I am a Frenchman through Paris," and if that was his view three centuries ago, what would it be now when so many persons of intellect are gathered together in one city, and are accustomed to drawing on their intelligence for the pleasures of conversation? The specter of boredom has always pursued me; because of my terror of it, I might have yielded to tyranny if the example of my father, and his blood that flows in my veins, had not enabled me to triumph over this weakness. Be that as it may, Bonaparte knew this foible of mine very well. He is quick to discern a person's weak points, for it is through their flaws that he subjugates people. To the power with which he threatens and the treasures with which he entices, he adds relief from boredom: always anathema to a Frenchman. A period of residence forty leagues from the capital—in contrast to all the advantages concentrated in the most agreeable city in the world—soon weakens the resolve of most exiles, accustomed as they are from childhood to the charms of Parisian life.

The night before Benjamin Constant was to give his speech, I had as guests Lucien, Joseph, Messieurs de Talleyrand, Roederer, Regnault de Saint-Jean d'Angély,[2] and several others whose conversation, in differing degrees, has that ever-fresh interest produced by intellectual power and grace in expression. Each one of them, with the exception of Lucien, had grown tired of being proscribed by the Directory and was preparing to serve the new

[2] Edition of 1821: all these names except Lucien Bonaparte are suppressed and replaced by asterisks.

government, asking only to be well rewarded for their support.
Benjamin Constant came up to me and whispered: "Tonight your
drawing room is filled with people whom you like. If I make a
speech that puts me with the opposition, it will be deserted tomorrow. Think about that."

"One must follow one's convictions," I said to him. Euphoria
inspired that response, and I confess, if I had foreseen what I have
suffered since that day, I would not have had the strength to
refuse Monsieur Constant's offer to renounce his project in order
not to compromise me.

Today, as far as opinion is concerned, it means nothing to incur
Bonaparte's disfavor; he can ruin you, but he cannot tarnish your
reputation. At that time, however, the nation was not aware of his
tyrannical intentions, and since everyone who had suffered from
the Revolution looked to him for help in bringing back a brother
or a friend, or for the restitution of property, anyone who dared
oppose him was branded a Jacobin, while society ostracized those
who were out of favor with the government: an unbearable situation—especially for a woman—and one so painful that it cannot
be appreciated except by those who have experienced it.

On the day when my friend's call for opposition was given in
the Tribunate I had invited several people to my house whose
company I enjoyed, even though all of them supported the new
government. By five o'clock I had received ten cancellations. I
bore the first and second rather well, but when the third and
fourth arrived, suddenly all that threatened me became very clear.
In vain, I appealed to my conscience, which had counseled me to
renounce all pleasures dependent on Bonaparte's favor. So many
good people reproached me that I did not know how to take a firm
stand in a defense of my own point of view. Bonaparte had as yet
not done anything specifically blameworthy, and many men declared that he had saved France from anarchy. In truth, if at that
moment he had given any sign that he wished a reconciliation,
I would have been overjoyed. But Bonaparte always demands
some base action in return for a reconciliation, and in order to
induce this base action he usually engages in exhibitions of feigned
rage, which cause such fear that one gives in to him completely.

By that I do not mean to imply that Bonaparte is not truly enraged, for what is not calculation in him is hatred, and hatred generally expresses itself in rage, but his calculation is so much stronger that he never goes beyond what it suits him to display, according to the circumstances and the people involved. One day a friend of mine saw him lose his temper with a war commissioner who had not done his duty. Hardly had the poor man left, trembling all over, when Bonaparte turned to one of his aides-de-camp and, laughing, said to him, "I hope I have given him a good fright"; yet the moment before anyone would have believed that he had lost his self-control.

The day after Bonaparte lashed out at me in an ill-tempered outburst, he publicly reproached his older brother, Joseph Bonaparte, for coming to visit me. Joseph felt obliged to keep away from my house for three weeks after that, and his example was followed by three-fourths of my acquaintances. Those who had been proscribed on 18 Fructidor blamed me for having recommended Monsieur de Talleyrand to Barras for the Ministry of Foreign Affairs, yet these same people spent their days with the very Monsieur de Talleyrand whom they accused me of having favored. All those who treated me badly would not admit that it was because they were afraid of displeasing the First Consul. However, each day they invented some new pretext to injure me, using the full strength of their political opinions against a persecuted, defenseless woman, and prostrating themselves at the feet of the most despicable Jacobins as soon as the First Consul had reinstated them by flooding them with his favors.

The Minister of Police, Fouché, summoned me two days later[3] to tell me that the First Consul suspected me of having incited my friend to speak in the Tribunate. I replied—and it was certainly true—that Monsieur Constant was too intelligent a man for it to be possible to blame a woman for his opinions, and besides, that

---

[3] Fouché was on very good terms with Madame de Staël, who, through the intervention of Fauriel—then secretary to Fouché—interceded often with him on behalf of certain émigrés who returned to France, in order to obtain removal of their names from the proscription lists or prolongation of their permits. It was in this context that she pressed for the request for deletion of Chateaubriand's name.

the speech in question contained only reflections on the independence which any deliberative assembly ought to possess; not
a word in it attacked the First Consul personally. The minister
admitted as much, and I added a few more remarks about the
respect due to freedom of opinions in a legislative body, but I
could see that he took no interest in these general considerations.
He already knew perfectly well that, under the man he had chosen
to serve, principles were out of the question, and he was shaping
his conduct accordingly. However, being a man of transcendental
intelligence in matters revolutionary, he had already devised a
policy of accepting unavoidable objectives and then doing as little
evil as possible beyond what was strictly necessary.

His previous conduct in no way reflected a sense of morality,
and he often referred to virtue as an old wives' tale. Nevertheless,
his remarkable sagacity made him choose the good because it was
reasonable, and his intelligence at times led him to the same result
that others would have reached by the dictates of their conscience.
He advised me to go to the country,[4] and assured me that in a few
days everything would quieten down. But upon my return this was
far from true, for I met with all the social unpleasantness that
differences of political opinions can create.

For instance, I had performed services of the greatest consequence for Monsieur de Talleyrand, and—more precious than any
services I might have been able to render—we had enjoyed the
most perfect friendship for years. He was to give a grand ball, and
I heard through Madame Bonaparte—who has always done as
much for unfortunate people as her situation permitted—that she
would persuade the First Consul to speak to me at this ball, in the
hope that our conversation would end all my anxiety about the
possibility of exile. So I waited impatiently for the ball, and it
never crossed my mind that Monsieur de Talleyrand might not
invite me. However, that is what happened, even though one of my
friends had let him know how important it could be for me to be
at that party. The man who had spent half his time at my house
over a ten-year period, who was obligated to me for his return
from America as well as for the management of his affairs during

---

[4] She retired to Saint-Ouen, to a country house belonging to her father.

his absence, the man who owed a large measure of his success to me, and from whom I had a dozen letters telling me that he owed me more than life itself; that is the man who gave the signal for my persecution and was chiefly responsible for my subsequent exile. For, faced with having to justify himself, he did me both the honor and the injury of describing me to Bonaparte and his supporters as a person of powerful intellect, endlessly repeating that I was irresistible; all this from a man over whom I had no hold other than the simple bond of friendship. I have not seen Monsieur de Talleyrand since then.

He is a man eminently well-suited to direct worldly affairs, and I am amazed that he has lost the Emperor's favor, for I have always seen in him a rare ability to judge human nature. He does not talk much, which makes it easier for him to weigh his words. Since he only learns through conversation, he does not care for discussions which might betray his lack of careful study. He does not make up for it in eloquence because eloquence requires inspiration, and he is a man of such complete self-control that he cannot give way to emotions. He has no facility in expressing himself, for in order to speak well one must write with ease, and he—so clever in other ways—is not capable of composing a single one of the pages published under his name; though when it suits him, he has inimitable charm and good taste in conversation, and when he needs ideas he is a master at making other people's wit his own. He is an excellent judge, a subtle but extraordinarily sterile critic, a man who needs power and fortune not only to satisfy his tastes but to show off his wit to good advantage, which he does by uttering a few appropriate biting or flattering words, but only when surrounded by people who will scoop up what he lets drop and serve him a new ball exactly where he wants it. He takes greater pains with persons he wishes to enthrall, but I question whether he plays this game as well as the other. I have watched him at the Directory, doing his utmost to appear cordial and to formulate firm opinions. He was not able to inspire confidence, and when he mingled with men from a plebeian background and political party, he looked like a parvenu, ill at ease in his republicanism, rather than like a great lord in disguise. He was a little more in his element at Bonaparte's court, and I am not surprised that his style captivated Bonaparte, without the latter even realizing it. He taught him the ways of old regime society, something Bonaparte knew little about, but sought to know better in order to endow his dynasty with venerability from its first day.

Moreover, where skill in dealing with the great powers was required, no one could have been more useful to Bonaparte than Monsieur de Talleyrand. He combined an imperturbable face, brazen silence when the situation warranted it, well-calculated insolence when necessary, with polite and charming manners when he wanted to smooth the ruffled feathers of people fighting their anger and anxious to appear composed, and these qualities more than sufficed to captivate all the German princes of the Confederation of the Rhine. What a miserable spectacle it was—all those great lords, attempting to retain their dignity while rivaling one another in their servility toward a man whose fine name at least mollified their pride! At present all such precautions have become useless, and force counts so much that discretion is superfluous.[5]

I have taken the time to describe Monsieur de Talleyrand at length because he had a large part in influencing Bonaparte to reestablish decorations, titles, and a treasure chest of tokens which would appeal to men's vanity. He prided himself that he could become indispensable by acquainting Bonaparte with all the subtle nuances of pride among the former nobles, but he misjudged Bonaparte if he thought this was the way to hold him. Vanity was merely one more vice, and Bonaparte was perfectly willing to make use of it, but this would not preclude his ruining —if it suited him—the person whose advice he had followed.

---

[5] Written in 1811. See Madame de Staël's portrait of Talleyrand in her novel *Delphine*, under the name of Madame de Vernon, an extremely seductive but false and dangerous person, who "in her heart loved nothing, believed in nothing and troubled herself about nothing," and whose "only thought was success, for herself and her relatives, in all the affairs of which worldly life, fortune, and status are composed." (*Delphine*, part I, letter 7.) Madame de Staël portrayed herself in the person of Delphine, which prompted Talleyrand to remark, "They say that Madame de Staël has portrayed us, herself and me, *disguised as women.*" Cf. in *Corinne* the portrait of Monsieur de Maltigues, who is very much like Talleyrand. It would be interesting to compare the portrait in *Ten Years in Exile* with Chateaubriand's superb and impassioned pages about Talleyrand in old age in *Mémoires de outre-tombe* (Ed. Biré, VI, 415ff): "He had received so much scorn," writes Chateaubriand, "that he was impregnated with it, and *he had concentrated it in the two drooping corners of his mouth.*"

CHAPTER III

System of fusion adopted by Bonaparte—
Character of his government—Publication
of the book <u>On</u> <u>Literature</u>—Pleasures of
literary reputation

While Monsieur de Talleyrand directed foreign affairs, Fouché, as head of the police, was charged with the revolutionary side of Bonaparte's government. Where Christian kings have been known to have two confessors in order to examine their consciences more carefully, Bonaparte chose two ministers—one from the old and the other from the new regime—whose business was to place the Machiavellian methods of two opposite systems at his disposal.

In all his appointments Bonaparte followed much the same rule, drawing—as it were—sometimes from the right, sometimes from the left; or, in other words, choosing his officers alternately from among the aristocrats and the Jacobins. The middle party—the partisans of liberty—pleased him less than all others because it was composed of the small number of Frenchmen who had opinions; he preferred to deal with those who had supported royalist interests or were discredited through popular excesses. He even went so far as to want to name Barère Councillor of State, but the negative response from his colleagues dissuaded him; he would have liked to use that appointment as a striking proof that he could regenerate, as well as destroy, everything. This time, however, he limited himself to commissioning the man in question to publish a newspaper, *Le Mémorial*, whose objective was to attack England as an immoral country; so that this man, who had put his writings at the service of the executioner, who had been known as the Anacreon of the guillotine, this man dared to lay his stained hands on the Ark of the Lord,[1] and Bonaparte was not even afraid that the nation itself would undertake the defense of his enemy against such an adversary.

What particularly characterizes Bonaparte's government is his profound contempt for all the intellectual riches of human nature: virtue, dignity, religion, enthusiasm; in his eyes they are "the eternal enemies of the continent," to use his favorite expression. He would like to persuade men by force and by cunning, and he considers all else to be stupidity or folly. The English especially irritate him because they have found a way to achieve success honestly, a feat which Napoleon would like people to regard as impossible. That luminous spot on the earth's surface has offended him from the first days of his reign, and being unable to get at England with his weapons, he has ceaselessly aimed his entire artillery of sophisms at her.

I do not believe that when Bonaparte became head of the government he had yet formulated the plan for a universal monarchy, but I do believe what he himself said to one of my friends, a few days after the 18 Brumaire. "It is necessary," he said, "to do something new every three months, in order to captivate the imagination of the French nation, with whom anyone who stands still is lost." His system was to encroach daily upon France's liberty and Europe's independence; but in this respect he knew how to accommodate himself to circumstances; when an obstacle was too great he went around it, and when the contrary wind was too violent he

---

[1] Madame de Staël customarily designates England in this manner: "It is the Ark which has saved the example of all that which is good in a deluge of mud." (Paul Gautier, *Madame de Staël et Napoléon*, p. 333. Letter to Lord Campbell, October 9, 1812.)

simply came to a halt. Although this man is so impatient by nature, he has the ability to remain immobile when necessary; he gets it from the Italians, who know how to control themselves in order to attain the object of their passions, as if they had been perfectly composed while selecting it. By alternating between cunning and force he has subjugated Europe, although Europe is too big a word. It consisted then of a few ministers, none of whom had as much wit as many men chosen at random from the nations they governed.

Toward spring in the year 1800 I published my work *On Literature*, and its success completely restored me to favor in society. My drawing room was filled again, and I rediscovered the pleasure of conversing, and conversing in Paris, which—I must admit— has always been for me the most delightful of all pleasures. There was not a word about Bonaparte in my book, and the most liberal sentiments were—I believe, forcefully—expressed in it. At that time Bonaparte did not yet exercise complete control over the press, as he does now; the government censored newspapers but not books, a distinction which might have been justified if that censorship had been used with moderation; for newspapers exert an influence on the populace, while books, for the most part, are read only by educated men and may enlighten opinion but not inflame it.[2] Later, a committee on freedom of the press was established in the Senate—probably as a mockery—as well as another committee on personal liberty whose membership is still renewed every three months. The bishoprics *in partibus*, and the *sinecures* of England undoubtedly have more to do than these committees, unless they are to be considered vestals, charged with burning funeral lamps in front of tombs.

Since my work *On Literature*, I have published *Delphine*,

---

[2] Madame de Staël under the Directory had been one of the most fiery partisans of the censoring of newspapers, a measure which she considered to be "a safeguard against tyranny." She claimed for the government at that time the right to supervise newspapers, to suspend them provisionally, to put seals on presses, and to take away their weapon from the "disturbers of public order." (*Des Circonstances actuelles qui peuvent terminer la Révolution*, Bibliothèque Nationale, Manuscrits, *Nouv. acquisit. franç.* 1300, fol. 121 and following, and *Revue des Deux Mondes* (November 1, 1899.) She had been very fiercely attacked by the newspapers even concerning her private life; from that came her severity with regard to the press, which she was to be sorry for later on.

Corinne, and finally my book *On Germany*, which was suppressed
at the moment it was to appear. Although this last work has
brought me cruel harassment, I am no less devoted to literature
as a source of pleasure and respect, even for a woman. I attribute
what I have suffered in life to the circumstances which have linked
me—almost from my entry into the world—with the cause of
liberty supported by both my father and my friends; but the kind
of talent which has made me talked of as a writer has always
brought me more pleasure than pain. Criticism of one's works can
be borne quite easily when one has self-respect and when noble
ideas are appreciated for their own sake rather than for the success
they may bring. Moreover, after a certain length of time, the
public seems almost always to be very equitable. We must therefore learn to dispense with immediate praise, for in due course we
get what we deserve. Finally, even when we have to suffer injustice
for a long time, I cannot conceive of a better refuge than philosophical meditation and self-expression. The exercise of these dis-
ciplines places a whole world of truths and feelings at our disposal,
where we can always breathe freely.

CHAPTER IV

Necker's conversation with Bonaparte—The victory of Marengo—Madame de Staël's regrets—Servility of the governments of Europe to the First Consul: the Emperor Paul I—Lucien Bonaparte's disgrace

In the spring of 1800, Bonaparte set out to wage the Italian campaign known especially for the battle of Marengo. He passed through Geneva and, since he had expressed a desire to see Monsieur Necker, my father visited him, more in order to help me than for any other reason. Bonaparte received him very cordially and spoke to him of his plans of the moment with the sort of confidence so characteristic of him, or rather, of his calculations, for this is the way one should always qualify a description of his character. My father did not have the same reactions as I;[1] he was

---

[1] Here is an unedited fragment, taken from another manuscript of *Ten Years in Exile*, which shows the "impression of terror" that Bonaparte caused in Madame de Staël after his return from Italy in 1797: "I was at the Minister of the Interior's ball and, as General Bonaparte was not dressed in any distinctive way I found myself at his side without recognizing him at first, when suddenly I perceived that it was he, and I experienced such a shock that I drew back to let him pass with an involuntary exclamation. I saw him again frequently at the same epoch and each time I felt more constrained in his presence."

not impressed by Bonaparte and he found nothing extraordinary in his conversation. I have tried to account for this difference in our opinions, and I believe that it arose first from the fact that the simple and sincere dignity of my father's manners assured him the respect of all who talked with him; and second, from the fact that since Bonaparte's kind of superiority consists more of ingeniousness in evil acts than of high-minded thoughts about doing good, his words may not reveal his distinguishing traits; after all, he neither could, nor would explain his own Machiavellian instinct. My father did not say a word to Bonaparte about his two million deposited in the public treasury; he only wanted to indicate his concern for me, and he told him, among other things, that as the First Consul liked to surround himself with illustrious names, he ought to take equal pleasure in encouraging persons of noted talent, as the ornaments of his power. Bonaparte answered him kindly, and the result of this interview was to ensure a residence in France for me, at least for the time being. This was the last time my father's protecting hand reached over my life; he has not witnessed the cruel persecutions that I have since endured and which would have angered him even more than they did me.

Bonaparte went to Lausanne to prepare for the Mont Saint-Bernard expedition. The old Austrian general [2] had no faith in so bold an enterprise, and did not make the necessary preparations to oppose it. It is said that a small corps of troops would have been sufficient to destroy the French army in the mountain passes through which Bonaparte was directing his men, but in this as in several other cases the following verses of Jean-Baptiste Rousseau could be applied to Bonaparte's triumph:

> The undisciplined inexperience
> On the part of Paul-Emile's companion
> Caused the success of Hannibal.

I went to spend the summer with my father—as was my custom —at about the time when the French army was crossing the Alps.

---

[2] General Mélas.

Troops were to be seen continually passing through those peaceful regions, which the majestic bulwark of the Alps ought to have shielded from turmoil and politics. During those beautiful summer evenings on the shores of Lake Geneva, face to face with such a serene sky and such pure waters, I was almost ashamed to be so concerned about worldly affairs, but I could not overcome my inner turmoil. I wanted Bonaparte to be beaten, because it seemed the only way of stopping the spread of his tyranny. However, I did not yet dare to confess this wish, so the Prefect of Léman, Monsieur d'Eymar, a former deputy to the Constituent Assembly, remembering the time when we both cherished the hope of liberty, sent couriers every hour to inform me of the French progress in Italy. It would have been difficult for me to explain to this very interesting man that France, for her own good, needed a defeat at this time, so I received the supposed good news with a degree of restraint quite uncharacteristic of me. But after all, for ten years we have had to hear continually of the triumphs of a man whose successes are bought at the expense of his subjects, and one cannot help wondering whether poor France ever benefited from any of his victories.

The battle of Marengo was virtually lost during a two-hour period; negligence on the part of General Mélas, who was overconfident, and audacity on the part of General Desaix, enabled the French to win. While the battle was going badly, Bonaparte, on horseback, rode slowly before his troops, pensive, with his head lowered, more courageous in the face of danger than in misfortune, attempting nothing, simply waiting for a change of fortune. He has reacted this way several times, and has always found it advantageous. I still believe that if he had encountered a man of firmness as well as integrity among his adversaries, Bonaparte would have been stopped short in his career. His great talent lies in terrifying the weak and making use of unprincipled men. When he encounters honesty anywhere, it is almost as though his deviousness is exorcised, as evil spirits are, by the sign of the cross.

The armistice that followed the battle of Marengo—which required the ceding of all fortified towns in northern Italy—was most disadvantageous to Austria. Bonaparte could not have gained more, even by further victories. But it might be said that the continental powers went out of their way to cede what they should never have permitted to be taken from them except in battle. In their relations with Napoleon the great powers behaved as if they were eager to sanction his injustices and legitimize his conquests, whereas even if he could not be conquered, they ought never to have accepted his behavior. This certainly was not asking too much of the old governments of Europe, but they were totally confused by such a novel situation; Bonaparte so bewildered them by his barrage of simultaneous threats and promises that they believed they would gain by conceding, and rejoiced at the word "peace" as if the word still carried its former meaning. The illuminations, the obeisances, the dinners, and the cannon booming to celebrate the peace were exactly the same as on earlier occasions, but far from healing wounds, this new peace undermined the government that signed it.

Typical of Napoleon's good luck are the sovereigns he found on the various European thrones. Paul I in particular rendered him incalculable services.[3] Paul I was as enthusiastic about Napoleon as his father had been about Frederick II, and he abandoned Austria while it was still attempting to fight on. Bonaparte persuaded him that all of Europe would enjoy peace for centuries if the two great empires of East and West were in accord, and Paul I, who was somewhat chivalrous by nature, let himself be taken in by these lies. It was a stroke of luck for Bonaparte to encounter a monarch so easily duped, in whom violence and weakness were joined in equal measure; and so he grieved for Paul I when he died, for no man had been more susceptible to his tricks.

Lucien, the Minister of the Interior, who thoroughly understood his brother's schemes, published a pamphlet entitled *Monk, Cromwell, and Bonaparte*, in which he claimed that the role of neither the first nor the second was suitable in present circum-

---

[3] Emperor of Russia from 1796 to 1801. The First Consul had won the heart of Paul I by returning to Russia—without any conditions—in July, 1800, six or seven thousand soldiers made prisoner the preceding year, with their officers, their flags, and their arms. Paul I was assassinated in Petersburg on the night of March 23 to 24, 1801, by conspirators directed by Count Pahlen and General Benningsen.

stances, and that therefore it was necessary to turn to more gran-
diose ideas, a change of dynasty, and a new Charlemagne. This
publication was premature and had a bad effect. Fouché used it to
get rid of Lucien: he convinced Bonaparte that the secret was
being revealed too soon, and told the republican faction that Bonaparte disavowed what his brother had done. As a consequence
Lucien was sent as ambassador to Spain.[4] Bonaparte's system was
to advance gradually, month by month, toward his objective of
gaining power. He was constantly spreading rumors about his
plans, in order to test public opinion. As a rule he even had the
rumors exaggerate his real intentions, so that when the event itself
occurred, it came as a relief to the apprehensive public. Lucien
had gone too far this time, and for appearance' sake Bonaparte
judged it necessary to sacrifice him for a while.

---

[4] Lucien received the official notice of his nomination as ambassador to Spain
on November 6, 1800; he left on the ninth. The brochure, out in October, entitled *Parallel between Caesar, Cromwell, Monk, and Bonaparte*, had as principal
author Fontanes, who was then official reporter for literature and fine arts at the
Ministry of the Interior and a special friend of Lucien. It showed the instability
of Bonaparte's power and the necessity for consolidating it. It ended with the
words: "Frenchmen! You are sleeping on the edge of an abyss!" The impression
produced in France was distressing, as Madame de Staël states.

CHAPTER V

Moreau's victories—Bonaparte and the

Revolution—The infernal machine—Arbitrary

deportations—The peace of Lunéville

I returned to Paris in November, 1800. Peace was not yet concluded, although Moreau, by his victories, had made it a practical
necessity for the foreign powers. How he must since have regretted
the laurels of Stockach and Hohenlinden, seeing them transformed into a crown of thorns, and France no less enslaved than
Europe over which he had made her victorious. Moreau thought
only of France when executing the First Consul's orders; but a
man of his caliber should have judged the government that employed him and decided for himself, in such circumstances, what
were the true interests of his country. However, it must be admitted that in the autumn of 1800, at the time of Moreau's most
brilliant victories, there were as yet few people who understood
Bonaparte's real intentions. What was obvious to most was the
improvement in the finances and the restoration of order in several
branches of the administration. Napoleon was obliged to pass
by way of good actions to reach the bad ones: he had to increase
France's strength before using it for his personal ambition.

He had a strange way of expressing himself concerning the

Revolution to which he owed his existence. Sometimes he said that the terrorists—that is, the partisans of Robespierre—were the only ones who had shown character in the Revolution, but he always condemned the original leaders, whose liberal principles produced much the same effect on him as water thrown on men shaking with rage.[1] One day he went to Ermenonville to visit Rousseau's tomb. "And yet this is the man," he said to the proprietor of the place, "who is responsible for our present condition!" It must be acknowledged that Bonaparte had no cause to complain about the condition he spoke of; but he enjoyed affecting a certain disdain for his situation, and he liked to express his antipathy toward those who, throughout this whole period, had hated despotism.

One evening while I was conversing with some friends we heard a loud explosion, but believing it to be cannon, fired for some military exercise, we paid no attention. A few hours later we learned that on his way to the opera the First Consul had just missed being killed by the detonation of a trail of gunpowder across his route.[2] Since he had escaped, everyone, of course, appeared greatly concerned about him. Philosophers proposed the reestablishment of cruel punishments for the perpetrators of this outrage, and at last he could see on all sides a nation offering its neck to the yoke. At home that same evening he discussed—very calmly—what would have happened if he had perished. Some people said that Moreau would have replaced him, but Bonaparte claimed that it would have been General Bernadotte. "Like Antony," he said, "he would have presented Caesar's bloody robe to the aroused populace." I do not know whether he really believed

---

[1] This recalls Madame de Staël's word for Bonaparte: *idéophobe* [idea-hater]. And Bonaparte's exclaiming, "That's very nice! Ah! She wants war . . . *idéophobe!* That is charming . . . why not *hydrophobe* [hater of water]? . . . One cannot rule with people like that." (Iung, *Lucien Bonaparte et ses Mémoires,* II, 233 ff.)

[2] This whole passage is modified in the edition of 1821. The attack of the infernal machine took place 3 Nivôse (December 24, 1800), rue Saint-Nicaise, between the Carrousel and the rue Richelieu. The chief authors of it were Carbon, Saint-Réjant and Limoëlan, agents of Georges Cadoudal. Carbon and Saint-Réjant were arrested and executed. Limoëlan was able to escape and reach America.

that France would have called upon General Bernadotte to be head
of state, but I am quite sure that he said so only to arouse envy
against the general.[3]

If the infernal machine had been planted by the Jacobins the
First Consul would have been able to double his tyranny immediately; public opinion would have backed him, but since this plot
was the work of royalists, Bonaparte was unable to derive much
advantage from it. He tried to hush it up rather than to make use
of it, for he wanted the nation to believe that his only enemies
were the enemies of order and did not include partisans of a different regime, specifically, of the former dynasty. What is extraordinary is that when confronted with a royalist plot, Bonaparte, by
means of a *senatus-consultum*, was responsible for deporting 130
Jacobins to Madagascar, or perhaps to the bottom of the sea, for
they have never been heard from since.[4] This list was made up in
the most arbitrary way possible; names were added or removed
according to suggestions from Councillors of State with the sanction of the senators. When complaints were made concerning the
way in which this list had been compiled respectable people said
that it consisted, after all, of culpable men. That may well be true;
but it is law, not fact, that establishes the legality of an action. If
we allow 130 citizens of any kind to be deported arbitrarily, there
will be nothing to prevent the same treatment from being inflicted
on very respectable persons, as indeed we have since witnessed.

It will be said that public opinion will protect them. Public
opinion! What is it, without the authority of the law? What is it,
without independent organs to express it? Public opinion was on
the side of the Duke d'Enghien, of Moreau, and of Pichegru, but

---

[3] It is certain that Bernadotte sought to supplant Bonaparte, of whom he was
jealous, and that in 1802, according to Madame de Staël, he actually entered a
conspiracy to get rid of the First Consul. (See *Dix années d'exil*, chap. IX;
Rovigo, *Mémoires*, I, 434 ff.)

[4] They were condemned to deportation out of the territory of the Republic by
a decree of the First Consul, on 14 Nivôse (January 4, 1801), approved by the
Senate in the session of January 5. The next day, the sixth, these unfortunates
were assembled and sent to Nantes to embark. The list included several deputies of the Convention, several members of the former Commune and some
septembriseurs [participants in the September massacres of 1792]. They were
deported to the Seychelles Islands.

it was not able to save them. There will be neither liberty, nor dignity, nor safety in a country which is preoccupied with proper names, when a justice is at stake. Every man is innocent until condemned by a legal tribunal; and even if a man were the greatest of criminals, if he were to be denied access to legal procedures, all honest men should tremble. But—just as, in the English House of Commons, when an Opposition deputy leaves the hall he requests that a deputy from the ministerial side leave with him in order to maintain the balance of the two parties— Bonaparte never struck the royalists or the Jacobins without allotting an equal number of blows to each. That is the only kind of distributive justice from which he almost never deviated; it was his way of making friends of those to whose hatreds he catered. As we shall demonstrate, he has always counted on hate to strengthen his government, for he knows that it is less inconstant than love. After a revolution, party spirit is so fierce that a new leader can manage it more easily by ministering to its thirst for vengeance than by supporting its interests; if necessary men will abandon those who agree with them, provided those who disagree will be punished.

The peace of Lunéville by which Austria lost only the republic of Venice—recently received in compensation for Belgium—was proclaimed;[5] and so this ancient queen of the Adriatic, once so proud and powerful, passed again from one master to another. Respect for history is unknown to this man, for he conceives of the world only in contemporary terms.

---

[5] The treaty of Lunéville was signed on February 9, 1801, by Monsieur de Cobenzl, representing Austria, and Joseph Bonaparte, representing France. It recognized French predominance on the left bank of the Rhine and in Italy.

CHAPTER VI

The diplomatic corps under the Consulate:

Messieurs de Lucchesini and de Cobenzl—

Madame de Staël at Mortfontaine—Death of

Paul I—Interview of Madame de Staël

and the First Consul

My winter in Paris passed quietly. I never visited the First Consul, and never saw Monsieur de Talleyrand. I knew that Bonaparte did not like me, but he had not yet reached the degree of despotism which he has since displayed. Foreigners treated me with great courtesy, the diplomatic set were my constant visitors, and this cosmopolitan atmosphere served as a safeguard for me.[1]

Monsieur de Lucchesini, recently arrived from Prussia, believed that a republic still existed, and aired some philosophical

---

[1] Madame de Staël lived on the rue de Grenelle-Saint-Germain, not far from the former Swedish embassy on the rue de Bac, which she had lived in for a long time. Among the regular visitors from the diplomatic world who frequented her salon were the Russian general, Sprengtporten, the chevalier de Kalitscheff, Count de Markoff, Monsieur de Lucchesini, Monsieur de Gallo, and the Count de Cobenzl.

principles he had acquired through his conversations with Frederick II. He was warned that he was mistaken about the current state of affairs, and was advised to rely only on his best knowledge in court matters. He took up the suggestion very quickly, for he is a man of great flexibility, but what a pity that such superior faculties belong to such a humble soul. He ends your sentence for you, or begins one that he thinks you will complete, and it is only by turning the conversation to facts about another century, or to classical literature, or some subject remote from current affairs, that you can discover his superior intellect.

Monsieur de Cobenzl was a totally different kind of courtier, though no less anxious to please those in power. Monsieur de Lucchesini was well-read, like a man of letters; Monsieur de Cobenzl knew nothing of literature beyond the French comedies in which he had acted the parts of Crispin and Chrysale. The story is told that when he was at Empress Catherine II's court he once received some dispatches while disguised as an old woman; it was with great reluctance that the courier could be made to recognize his ambassador in that costume. Monsieur de Cobenzl was an extraordinarily insipid man who addressed the same remarks to everyone he met in a drawing room, approaching one and all with an easy cordiality devoid of sentiments or ideas. His manners were perfect, and his conversation fairly well-formed by society; but the fact of sending such a man into negotiations with Bonaparte's forceful and ruthlessly revolutionary entourage was to produce a pitiable spectacle. Duroc complained about Monsieur de Cobenzl's lack of formality; he thought it poor taste for one of the foremost Austrian nobles to shake his hand without ceremony. These novices in politeness could not believe that being at ease was in good taste. Indeed, if they had been at their ease, they would have committed terrible mistakes, and arrogant stiffness was still their safest posture in the new role they wished to play.

Joseph Bonaparte, who had negotiated the peace of Lunéville, invited Monsieur de Cobenzl to his charming residence, Mortfontaine, and I was invited with him. Joseph was very fond of country life, and would stroll in his gardens with ease and pleasure for eight hours at a time. Monsieur de Cobenzl tried to keep up with him, more out of breath than the Duke de Mayenne, whom Henry IV—for his amusement—would make take walks, in spite of his corpulence. Of all country pleasures the poor man especially praised fishing, because it allowed him to sit down; he would speak with forced enthusiasm about the simple pleasure of catching some little fish with a line.

Paul I had shamefully mistreated Monsieur de Cobenzl when he was ambassador in Petersburg. He and I were playing backgammon in the drawing room of Mortfontaine, when one of my friends came to tell us of Paul's sudden death. Monsieur de Cobenzl began making the most formal lamentations imaginable. "Although I had reason to complain about him," he said, "I shall always acknowledge the prince's excellent qualities, and I cannot help regretting his loss." Both as a man and as an Austrian he rightly welcomed Paul's death, but his words reflected an insincere tone of court mourning which was quite exasperating. We must hope that in due course the world will be rid of courtiers' mannerisms which are utterly insipid, to say the least.

Bonaparte was rather frightened by Paul I's death and it is said that at the news he uttered the first "Oh, my God!" he was ever heard to say. He had no reason to be troubled, however, for at that time the French were more disposed to endure tyranny than the Russians.

I went to General Berthier's[2] one day when the First Consul was to be there, and as I knew how hostile he was to me, I thought that he might perhaps use some coarse expressions with which he liked to address even women who paid him court. Before going to the party I wrote out at random several dignified and biting responses that I might make, depending on what he said to me. I did not want to be taken by surprise if he insulted me, for that would have been to show myself even more lacking in character than in wit; and since no one can be certain of not being confused in his presence, I prepared myself beforehand to face him. Fortunately, the precaution was unnecessary; he asked me

---

[2] Then Minister of War.

the most ordinary question imaginable.[3] The same thing happened to all his opponents whom he thought capable of forceful
replies: whatever the contest, he never attacks except when he
believes he is very much the stronger. During supper, Bonaparte
stood behind Madame Bonaparte's chair, balancing himself first
on one foot and then on the other, in the manner of the Bourbons.
I pointed out his already evident vocation for kingship to my
neighbor. And indeed, since princes must give long audiences
without sitting down, several have adopted the disagreeable habit
of balancing themselves in this way. Bonaparte has always been
rather awkward in manner, which makes his compliments clumsy,
but does not soften his insults.

---

[3] *Cf. Considérations sur la Révolution française*, part III, chap. 26, and this
unedited passage taken from another manuscript of *Dix années d'exil:* "Before
the dinner [at Talleyrand's, on the return from the campaign in Italy], Bonaparte was approached by a woman famous in France for her beauty, her wit,
and the liveliness of her opinions [without doubt Madame de Condorcet]; and
he said to her suddenly, stopping before her: 'Madame, I do not like women
to meddle in politics.' 'General,' she answered him, 'you are right; but in a
country where one cuts off their heads, it is natural for them to want to know
why.' In the same abrupt manner he said to me at the table, 'Madame, I do not
like women to write.' 'General,' I said to him, 'if I had the honor of calling
myself Madame Bonaparte, I would not seek personal glory.' He did not appear
to appreciate either the severe response of Madame ——, or my conciliatory answer." Madame de Staël has not told all about this interview with Bonaparte at
Berthier's. We know what was "the most ordinary question imaginable." She
had confided it to the Russian Golovkin, who recorded it in his unedited
Souvenirs. Madame de Staël had spent "two days and two nights" writing out
answers to all subjects that her enemy might bring up. Well, Bonaparte, followed by his brother Lucien, stopped before Madame de Staël, perceived her
bare shoulders, and said brusquely, "You doubtless nursed your children yourself?" Madame de Staël remained mute, petrified: she had not foreseen that
question. And Bonaparte went away, saying to Lucien, "You see, she does not
even want to say yes, or no!" (Cf. L. Pingaud, *Madame de Staël et le duc de
Rovigo, Revue de Paris*, December 1, 1903.) See on the coarseness of Napoleon
in regard to women, Madame de Rémusat, *Mémoires*, II, 77, 179; Chaptal, *Mes
souvenirs sur Napoléon*, p. 321.

CHAPTER VII

Persistence of opposition in the

Tribunate—Eagerness of the French to

serve the government of the First Consul—

Bonaparte and the Institute—The King and

Queen of Etruria in Paris—Progress of

Bonaparte's tyranny

Opposition in the Tribunate persisted, with about twenty members out of eighty attempting to speak out against the various measures that were paving the way for tyranny. A crucial issue arose concerning the law by which the government acquired the fatal power to create special tribunals to try persons accused of state crimes;[1] as if delivering a man to these special tribunals were not already judging him, that is, determining whether he was

---

[1] The special tribunals were to be composed of three regular judges, three military judges, and two others chosen by the government. Their purpose was to judge acts of brigandage and assassination attempts against government officials. This law was severely attacked and was passed by the Tribunate only by a majority of forty-nine votes to forty-one. Among the more effective opponents were Daunou, Ginguené and Benjamin Constant, Madame de Staël's friend (February, 1801).

a criminal, and also a state criminal; as if, of all crimes, political offenses are not the ones which have to be examined with the greatest precaution and impartiality, since the government is nearly always the opposing party in such cases. In Robespierre's day it was said seriously, "Judiciary procedure is worthless. The innocent do not need it, and the guilty do not deserve it." As if judiciary procedure had not been established for the specific purpose of determining whether a man is innocent or guilty in the first place.

We have since seen what those military commissions for judging state crimes amounted to. The Duke d'Enghien's death dramatizes the horror that everyone must feel at the sight of hypocritical power cloaking murder in the mantle of the law.

The Tribunate's resistance, feeble as it was, displeased the First Consul. Not that it was an obstacle, but it did encourage the nation to think, something he did not want, at any price. He had an absurd argument against the opposition published in the press. Nothing is so natural, it said, as an opposition in England, where the king is the enemy of the people, but in a country where the executive power is chosen by the people, to oppose the nation's representative is to oppose the nation. How many similar phrases have Napoleon's writers not thrown out to the public during the past ten years. In England, a simple peasant would laugh at this kind of sophism, but in France, all people want is precisely some such phrase to lend credence to their pursuit of selfish interests.

Bonaparte continued to appoint men of all factions to public office. The first condition for eligibility was devotion to his power; one's former life did not count either favorably or unfavorably, and it might have been said that everyone's political birth dated from 18 Brumaire. Few men were indifferent to having positions, for a great many were impoverished, and concern for their wives and children, or their nephews if they had no children, or their cousins if they had no nephews, forced them—they said— to seek employment in the government. In France the great strength of the heads of state lies in people's prodigious desire to hold office; and vanity even more than need for money explains this desire. The French are partial to anything which distinguishes one man from another; no nation is less suited to equality; they proclaimed it in order to displace the old upper classes, wanting to change that inequality, but without subjecting themselves to the only political code worthy of admiration, one that makes all men equal before the law. Bonaparte received thousands of requests for each post, from the lowest to the highest. If he had not naturally had a deep contempt for the human race, he would have acquired it while examining these requests, signed by so many names—illustrious of ancestry or famous for revolutionary actions—a complete contrast to the new functions to which these petitioners now aspired.

The winter of 1801 in Paris was rather pleasant for me, owing to Fouché's readiness to grant my various requests for permits enabling émigrés to return. In this way he gave me—in the midst of my disfavor—the pleasure of being useful, and I am grateful to him for that.[2] There is always a bit of coquetry in everything women do, and even most of their virtues are mixed with the desire to please, and to be surrounded by friends who, because of the services they have received, are more intimately attached

---

[2] She means by the words "winter of 1801" the first months of that year. Indeed, we know that Madame de Staël, with her characteristic generosity, was an active intermediary with Fouché—through the cooperation of Fauriel, his secretary—in easing the lot of the émigrés who had returned to France. Here are three notes taken from Madame de Staël's letters to Fauriel, preserved in the library of the Institute (Mohl bequest), which confirm this part of *Dix années d'exil*. The first note, undated: "Fouché has authorized a surveillance over Madame de Cerisy [?], my dear Faurielle [sic]; it has not yet been expedited in his offices. Can't you get it and give it to me? It is of much concern to a friend of mine, a woman. Benjamin has given me the hope of seeing you this evening." Second note, dated "this 3 of Pluviôse": "The Minister of Police promised me that surveillance yesterday, because priests who have taken the oath are in a special category. Be kind enough, my dear Fauriel, to give him this note from me and bring me as soon as you can a brief word for my poor priest. Best regards. Have you used my recipe for melancholy?" The third note, undated: "I saw Fouché yesterday. He promised to attach an extension of thirty days to the bottom of the permit. So do me the pleasure, my dear Fauriel, of transmitting this permit to Eugène [Madame de Staël's business manager], and of having him speak to the minister. I am sending him a note to take to him. He said nice things about you yesterday, but I cannot console myself for having given you an unpleasant moment. See you tomorrow at dinner, won't I?" In a fourth note, she intercedes for Mathieu de Montmorency's friend, Monsieur de la Trémouille, "arrested this morning." Last, it is known that in 1801 Chateaubriand obtained his removal from the proscription list partly through Madame de Staël's influence. (See "Chateaubriand et Madame de Staël," *Revue des Deux Mondes*, October 1, 1903.)

to them. If only for this reason they must be forgiven for seeking appreciation; but we must know how to sacrifice, for the sake of dignity, even the pleasure of being obliging, for we may do everything for others except degrade our moral strength. Our own conscience is a treasure from God: we are not permitted to spend it on anyone else.

Bonaparte was still rather attached to the Institute,[3] which had been a source of pride to him when he was in Egypt; but there was—among the men of letters and scientists—a small philosophical opposition, unfortunately of a very bad sort, in that its efforts were directed mainly against the reestablishment of religion. By some distressing peculiarity, enlightened men in France wished to console themselves for their slavery in this world by seeking to destroy people's hopes of another. This singular inconsistency would not have existed under the Protestant religion; but the Catholic clergy had enemies not as yet disarmed by its courage and misfortunes, and perhaps it really is difficult to reconcile the authority of the Pope and of priests subject to the Pope with a system of political liberty. Be that as it may, the Institute did not view religion as such, quite apart from its ministers, with the profound respect that should have been forthcoming from persons of superior character and mind, and Bonaparte was able to use as a weapon against worthier men than himself opinions that were worthier than those men.[4] However, he did not even bother to be genuinely hypocritical. Faithful to his custom of deceiving openly, by providing lies for those who ask nothing more than to make use of them as pretexts, he assured the priests that the Catholic religion was the only truly orthodox one; and on the same day, speaking with Cabanis, a philosopher in the style of the eighteenth century, he said to him, "I want to reestablish

---

[3] The Institut de France was founded in 1795 to consolidate five learned or literary societies dating from the seventeenth century. Napoleon had been a member since 1797. (Trans.)

[4] Unedited passage from another manuscript of *Dix années d'exil:* "However, the philosophical party protested the reestablishment of religious forms, as if the only possible consolation for having no liberty on earth would be having no God in heaven. This miserable school of thought did not attack Napoleon on the basis of all his arbitrary acts which trampled justice and security underfoot; but these rallying words, *priests, superstition,* were still pronounced, even when they had no meaning.

religion the way you do cowpox—use it to inoculate in order to destroy it." This witticism is worthy of note. He made several others which might be included in an anthology on the principles of evil; for one would certainly never preserve an expression of his for its grace or true nobility.

In this year (1801), the First Consul ordered Spain to make war on Portugal, and the feeble king of the illustrious Spanish nation subjected his army to that base and unjust expedition. He marched against a neighbor who wished him no harm, against a power allied to England—a country that has since shown itself to be so true a friend of Spain—all for the sake of obeying a tyrant preparing to deprive him of his very existence.[5] Now that we have seen these same Spaniards so vigorously give the signal for the resurrection of the world,[6] we are learning to recognize what nations are, and the consequences of denying them a legal means of expressing their opinions and influencing their own destiny.

Toward the spring of 1801, the First Consul decided to create a king, and a king of the house of Bourbon: he gave this king Tuscany, designating it by the classical name of Etruria, thus inaugurating his great European masquerade. This poor Spanish Infante was ordered to Paris for the purpose of affording the French the spectacle of a prince of the former dynasty humbled before the First Consul, more humiliated by the gifts he received than he could ever have been by persecution. Using this royal lamb, Bonaparte experimented with making a king wait in his antechamber; he allowed himself to be applauded at the theater when this verse was recited:

> I have made kings, madam, and have not
> wished to be one . . .

resolving to be more than a king when the opportunity presented

---

[5] The king of Spain, Charles IV—dominated by the queen and the Prince of Peace [Godoy, the queen's favorite], and grateful to the First Consul for having, by the treaty of Lunéville, made sure of Tuscany for the young Infante de Parme, with the title of king—consented to make war on Portugal, to make it break with England. A French army of 25,000 men, commanded by Leclerc and Gouvion-Saint-Cyr, had to aid him in this enterprise.

[6] This is a reference to Spain's war of liberation against Napoleon. (Trans.)

itself. Every day some new blunder of the poor King of Etruria was the subject of conversation. He was taken to the Museum and the Bureau of Natural History, and some of his questions about fish or quadrupeds—which a well-taught child of twelve would no longer have asked—were quoted as proof of his intelligence. In the evening, he was taken to parties where dancers from the Opera mingled with the ladies of the new court; and the little king, in spite of his piety, preferred to dance with these professional dancers, and as a token of thanks sent them presents of handsome, good books for their edification on the following day.[7] This was a notable moment in French history, this period of transition from revolutionary manners to monarchical pretensions. Since there was neither independence in the first nor dignity in the second, they could in turn be gathered, each in its way, around the motley power which was making simultaneous use of the assets of the two regimes.

This year the anniversary of the Revolution, July 14, was celebrated for the last time, while all the benefits of that day were recalled in a pompous proclamation. There was not one of them, however, which the First Consul had not resolved to destroy. He was to increase taxes greatly, reestablish a host of Bastilles, exile and jail people as even Louis XIV with his *lettres de cachet* would never have been able to do; but one day's promises have always been the next day's lies for that man. Of all the anthologies ever made, his proclamations would be the strangest: a complete encyclopedia of contradictions; and if chaos itself were employed to instruct mankind, it would no doubt jumble together in like manner praises of peace and war, of knowledge and prejudices, of liberty and despotism, and of commendations and insults to all governments and all religions.

About this time, Bonaparte sent General Leclerc to Santo

---

[7] In the month of June, 1801, the king and queen of Etruria, under the name of Count and Countess of Livourno, arrived in Paris to spend an entire month. During this time, in honor of the young sovereigns, Paris was in fête. The most brilliant party of all was given for them on 19 Prairial by Talleyrand, in his château in Neuilly. Everyone was struck, as Madame de Staël says, by the naïveté and incapacity of the king. Not only did it enter into the plans of the First Consul to "make a king" with his own hand, but also to restore, for his own profit, by the spectacle of royal pomp, memories of the monarchy.

Domingo,[8] and called him in his decree *our brother-in-law*. This royal *we*, which associated the French with the patrimony of this family, was very distasteful to me. He made his pretty sister accompany her husband to Santo Domingo, where her health was ruined: an extraordinary act of despotism for a man who, moreover, is not accustomed to such high principles in his associates! But his only use for morality is as a commodity to throw in people's faces when he wants to thwart or dazzle them. A peace was concluded in due course, with the Negro leader Toussaint-Louverture. This man was a great criminal; nevertheless, Bonaparte had signed a peace treaty with him, in violation of which Toussaint was taken to a prison in France, where he died in the most miserable way. Perhaps Bonaparte has forgotten this crime simply because he has been reproached for it less than for his others. His conscience has no memory, for he is perhaps the only man whom one can believe to be really devoid of remorse. As far as he is concerned, good and evil are only successful or unsuccessful calculations; he does not recognize the existence of any other element in human nature.

Once when visiting a mint, I was impressed by the violence of the machines, all set in motion by a single will; those hammers and rolling mills seem like people, or rather ferocious beasts. Should anyone attempt to resist their power, he would be annihilated. Nevertheless, all this apparent fury is calculated, and a single motor sets the springs in motion. For me, Bonaparte's tyranny evokes this same image; he makes thousands of men perish, with the remorselessness of those wheels striking iron, and most of his agents are equally unfeeling; the invisible pro-

---

[8] General Leclerc, first husband of Pauline Bonaparte, left Brest for Santo Domingo at the beginning of February, 1802; he died of yellow fever on that island on November 22. Pauline was not anxious to accompany him. "The First Consul told her that whereas Leclerc had left to wage war and earn money in Santo Domingo, he did not intend that she remain in Paris to play the coquette and amuse herself with lovers. Madame Leclerc pleaded reasons of health for not going; Bonaparte had a doctor certify that she was able to make the trip. She alleged that pregnancy and the bad roads of lower Brittany could cause some accident. Bonaparte replied that that would be taken care of. In fact he had her carried on a litter for more than forty leagues and thus forced her to accompany her husband." (*Relations secrètes des agents de Louis XVIII*, p. 69.)

pulsion of these human machines comes from a will both violent and methodical, which transforms moral life into a servile instrument. Finally, to complete the analogy, if one could stop the motor everything would return to a state of peace and tranquillity.

CHAPTER VIII

Interlude at Coppet—Necker's last work—

Preliminaries of peace with England—

Progress of monarchical institutions;

adulation of Bonaparte

As I was in the pleasant habit of doing, I went to spend the summer with my father. He was extremely upset about the course events were taking; and since he had, throughout his life, loved true liberty as much as he had detested popular anarchy, he now wanted to write against one-man rule, after having fought for so long against the tyranny of the multitude. My father had a taste for fame, and even though he was prudent by nature, taking risks of any kind did not displease him when they were necessary to merit public esteem. I certainly appreciated the fact that I would be endangered by any work of my father's that displeased the First Consul, but I could not bring myself to stifle this swan song which might be heard once more over the tomb of French liberty. Therefore, I encouraged my father in his plan, but we postponed the question of whether his book should be published until the following year.[1]

---

[1] The book in question was *Dernières vues de politique et de finances*, which appeared at the beginning of August, 1802, and which aroused the anger of

The news of the signing of the peace preliminaries between England and France[2] was the crowning touch to Bonaparte's good fortune. When I learned that England had recognized him I thought I had been wrong to despise his power, but it was not long before circumstances relieved me of this concern. The most extraordinary condition of these preliminaries was the complete evacuation of Egypt; that entire expedition had therefore had no other result than to provide Bonaparte with public attention. Several accounts published in places beyond Bonaparte's reach accuse him of having had Kléber assassinated in Egypt, out of jealousy over his power,[3] and trustworthy people have told me that the duel in which General Destaing was killed by General Reynier was provoked by an argument on this subject. However, it is difficult for me to believe that Bonaparte would have been able to arm a Turk against a French general when he himself was so far away from the scene of the crime. It seems to me that nothing that has not been proved ought to be said against Bonaparte; the discovery of a single error of this kind among the most obvious truths would serve to diminish them. We must not fight that man with any of his own weapons. He must fail only because mankind has a conscience and the universe has a God.

I delayed my return to Paris so that I would not have to be present at the great peace festival. Nothing is more distressing than these public celebrations when one's heart is not in them. One feels a kind of contempt for the gaping crowds who come to honor the yoke which is being prepared for them: dull-witted victims danc-

---

the First Consul. It was Madame de Staël, he said, who had made "all those false reports" on the state of France to her father. From this day is dated the definite rupture between Bonaparte and Madame de Staël. Cf. the grievances of the First Consul against Necker and his daughter, *Madame de Staël et Napoléon*, chap. VII, and *Considérations*, part 4, chap. VII.

[2] These preliminaries were signed in London on October 1, 1801, in the midst of extraordinary enthusiasm.

[3] Kléber was assassinated in Cairo on June 14, 1800, by a fanatic Turk, Soliman, who struck him with four dagger blows. As for General Reynier, after having served with distinction under Pichegru and Moreau, he accompanied Bonaparte to Egypt, where he played a brilliant part in the battle of the Pyramids and at Heliopolis. He could not get along with General Menou and returned to France, where he published a pamphlet, *De l'Egypte après la bataille d'Héliopolis* (Paris, 1802). This book was seized by the police; it was the occasion for a duel between Reynier and Destaing; the latter, struck by a bullet, was killed instantly (1803).

ing in front of the palace of their sacrificer—this First Consul, whom they call "Father of the Country," the very country he is going to devour—the whole mixture of foolishness on one side and cunning on the other; the tasteless hypocrisy of courtiers concealing the master's arrogance; all of this evoked in me a feeling of insurmountable disgust. One had to exercise self-control, and this was more difficult than usual in the midst of such ceremonies and official rejoicing. Among the inscriptions commemorating this peace festival was one to the effect that Napoleon shared his empire with Jupiter. Some years later it was to be with Pluto.

At that time, however, Bonaparte was proclaiming that peace was the world's first need. Every day he signed some new treaty, rather in the careful manner of Polyphemus counting the sheep as he drove them into his cavern. The peace treaty with the Regency of Algiers began thus: "The First Consul and the Regency of Algiers, recognizing that war is not natural between the two states, are agreed, etc." These two governments were indeed fraternal. The United States of America, who also made peace with France, sent as their ambassador a man who did not know a word of French; they were apparently unaware of the fact that even the most perfect command of the language scarcely sufficed to pry the truth from a government so expert at concealing it. The First Consul—when Mr. Livingston was presented to him—complimented him through an interpreter on the purity of morals in America, and added, "The old world is very corrupt." Then, turning to Monsieur Talleyrand, he repeated twice: "Well, tell him the old world is very corrupt. You know something about that, don't you?" This was one of the milder remarks which he addressed publicly to this most fastidious of his courtiers, who would have liked to preserve some outward dignity even though he was sacrificing his self-respect to his ambition.

Meanwhile, monarchical institutions were springing up under the shadow of the republic. A praetorian guard was established; the crown jewels were used to ornament the First Consul's sword, and in his dress—just as in the political situation of the day—there was a mixture of old and new regimes. He had clothes all in gold, and with his straight hair, short legs, and huge head, he seemed both awkward and arrogant, disdainful and embarrassed, combining a parvenu's lack of grace with a tyrant's audacity. His smile has been described as pleasant. My own opinion is that it would certainly have been displeasing in anyone else, for this smile, which sprang suddenly from a serious expression and back, resembled a mechanical rather than a natural movement, while his eyes never reflected the expression of his mouth; but since his smile had the effect of reassuring those around him, the relief they felt was attributed to charm. I recall once being told quite seriously by a member of the Institute—a Councillor of State—that Bonaparte's fingernails were perfection; he must have meant his claws. General Sébastiani exclaimed, "The First Consul's hands are beautiful."

"Ah!" replied a young lord of the old French nobility, who at that time was not yet Chamberlain, "for heaven's sake, General, let us not talk politics." That same general, speaking affectionately of the First Consul, said, "He frequently displays a childlike gentleness." It is true that in his own home he sometimes indulged in simple games; he has been seen to dance with his generals; it is even said that one evening in Munich, in the palace of the Queen and King of Bavaria, who, I believe, were not much entertained by these high spirits, he dressed up in the Spanish costume of Charles VII, the Elector of Bavaria—who was pretender to the imperial crown of Bavaria—and began to dance an old French country dance, the *Monaco*.

CHAPTER IX

*Elimination of the Tribunate; Madame de
Staël's sarcasms—Bonaparte, President of
the Italian Republic—Conspiracy of General
Bernadotte—Departure for Coppet; Madame de
Staël's anxiety—Educational reform—The
French in uniform*

The friends of liberty in the Tribunate were still trying to struggle against the ever-increasing power of the First Consul, but
public opinion gave them no support. Most of the opposition
tribunes merited the highest esteem in every respect, but three or
four of them had been guilty of excesses during the Revolution,
and the government took great pains to blame the whole body
for the deeds of a few. However, in the long run men united in
a public assembly always tend to bring out the best in each other,
and this Tribunate, such as it was, would have prevented tyranny

had it been allowed to continue. Already, the majority had nominated as a candidate for the Senate a man of whom the First Consul disapproved, Daunou, an honest, enlightened republican, but certainly no one to be feared.[1] This was cause enough for the First Consul to decide to *eliminate* the Tribunate, by expelling—on the senators' designation—the twenty most spirited members of the assembly one by one, and having them replaced by twenty men devoted to the government.[2] A fourth of the eighty remaining members had to undergo the same process each year. In that way, the tribunes were shown what they had to do to retain their places, or rather their salaries of fifteen thousand livres; for the First Consul still wanted to preserve this mutilated assembly for a while longer to serve for two or three years as a popular mask for his acts of tyranny.

Several of my friends were among the proscribed tribunes, but my opinion in the matter was independent of my feelings. For all that, I was perhaps more sensitive to injustices suffered by people close to me, and I suppose I allowed myself to express some sarcastic remarks about this hypocritical manner of interpreting even such an unfortunate constitution as the current one, from which there had been an effort to exclude the slightest breath of liberty.

During the year 1802, every one of the First Consul's moves indicated more openly that his ambition was boundless. While peace with England was being negotiated at Amiens, he had the

---

[1] The opposition was anxious to designate Daunou as candidate in order to spite the First Consul; for the same reason it had previously chosen Abbé Grégoire. Daunou received 135 votes in the Legislative Corps and General Lamartillière, the government candidate, 122; in the Tribunate Daunou received forty-eight votes and Lamartillière thirty-nine. The next day, 12 Nivôse (January 2, 1802), the First Consul, in an audience to the senators, declaimed vehemently: "I notify you that if you elect Monsieur Daunou senator, I will take it as a personal affront, and you know that I have never tolerated that from anyone." The Senate used a subterfuge and nominated Lamartillière.

[2] Among the twenty tribunes *eliminated* by successive votes of the Senate in 1802 were Chénier, Ginguené, Chazal, Bailleul, Courtois, Ganilh, Daunou, and Benjamin Constant. It was in connection with this that Madame de Staël made a well-known witticism: Bonaparte said, "I have purified the Tribunate." "He means skimmed," she replied. (Cf. *Lucien Bonaparte et ses Mémoires* [II, 237.]) She herself acknowledges, further on, her "sarcasms," which very much irritated her enemy.

Cisalpine Assembly[3] meet at Lyon, that is, the deputies from Lombardy and adjacent states, which had been constituted as a republic under the Directory, and who now asked what new form of government they were to assume. Since people were not yet accustomed to the fact that the unity of the French Republic was now concentrated in the person of one man, no one dreamed that he would want to assume both the office of consul of France and the presidency of Italy. Therefore they expected that Count Melzi would be elected, which seemed appropriate due to his intelligence, illustrious birth, and the respect which his fellow citizens had for him. Suddenly the word was spread that Bonaparte had had himself nominated, and at this news public opinion showed a momentary vitality. It was said that the French constitution revoked the citizenship of anyone who accepted employment in a foreign country; but could this man be a Frenchman, who wanted to use that great nation only to oppress Europe, and Europe only to oppress France? Bonaparte concealed his nomination for president from all the Italians, and they did not learn that they would have to choose him until a few hours before going to vote. They were told to add the name of Monsieur de Melzi, as vice-president, to Bonaparte's nomination. They were assured that they would be governed only by the former, who would always reside among them, and that the latter only wanted an honorary title. Bonaparte himself said, in his most emphatic manner, "Cisalpines, I shall reserve for myself only the grand design of your affairs." The grand design, of course, meant all the power. The day after the election, they continued with great seriousness to draw up a constitution, as if it could function next to that iron hand. The nation was divided into three classes: the *possidenti*, the *dotti*, and the *commercianti* —the proprietors to be taxed, the men of letters to be silenced, and the merchants to have all ports closed to them. These resonant

---

[3] The Cisalpine *Consulte*, assembled in Lyon in January, 1802, comprised 452 members taken from the nobility, the clergy, the great landowners, commerce, universities, tribunals, and national guards. On January 11, 1802, the First Consul arrived in Lyon in the midst of general enthusiasm; on the twenty-fifth the *Consulte* named by acclamation Napoleon Bonaparte President of the Italian Republic.

Italian words lend themselves even better to charlatanism than their French equivalents.

Bonaparte had changed the name Cisalpine Republic to Italian Republic, thereby alerting Europe to his future conquests in the rest of Italy. Such a step was anything but conciliatory, and yet it did not prevent the signing of the treaty of Amiens, so strongly did Europe and even England desire peace! I was at the home of the English ambassador, Mr. Jackson, when he was informed of the terms of this treaty. He read them aloud to all who were dining with him, and I cannot express the astonishment I felt as I heard each article. England returned all her conquests: she returned Malta, about which, when it was captured by the French, General Desaix had said that if there had been no one in the fortress, they would never have been able to enter it. She yielded everything—without receiving any compensation—to a power she had constantly beaten at sea. How strange a result of the passion of peace! And the man who had almost miraculously obtained these advantages did not even have the patience to make use of them for a few years by strengthening the French navy so that it would be able to challenge England! Hardly had the treaty of Amiens been signed when Napoleon annexed Piedmont to France by a *senatus-consultum*. During the year the peace lasted, every day was marked by some new proclamation which implied a breach of the treaty. The motive for this behavior is easy to discern. Bonaparte wanted to dazzle the French, by unexpected treaties, or by wars that would make him indispensable to the nation. In every field of activity he believed violent agitation was favorable to usurpation. The newspapers, which were ordered to praise the advantage of peace, said in the spring of 1802, "The moment is approaching when politics will be useless." Indeed, if Bonaparte had wished to do so, he might easily at that time have given twenty years of peace to a frightened and ruined Europe.

At that time there was a group of generals and senators forming around General Bernadotte who wanted him to indicate whether measures could be taken to stop the usurpation which was so rapidly approaching. He proposed various plans, all based on legislative action, for he regarded any other method as contrary to his principles. Such procedures, however, required the cooperation of several members of the Senate, and not one of them dared to consent to such an act. During the entire time this very dangerous negotiation was proceeding, I frequently saw General Bernadotte and his friends: this was more than enough to ruin me if their schemes had been discovered. Bonaparte remarked that people always left my house less faithful to him than when they entered. In short, he was preparing to single me out as the only one guilty among the many who were so much more involved than I, but whom it was more useful to him to spare.[4]

In the midst of all this I left for Coppet. Monsieur de Staël's poor state of health obliged me to accompany him to a spa. He died of a sudden attack of apoplexy on the way,[5] and I arrived at my father's feeling terribly dejected and anxious. Letters from Paris informed me that after my departure the First Consul had spoken out strongly against my friendship with General Bernadotte. There were indications that he had decided to punish me, but he stopped short at the idea of attacking General Bernadotte, either because he had too great a need for his military talents, or because family ties restrained him, or because the general's popularity with the French army was greater than anyone else's, or, in the last analysis, because Bernadotte has a certain charm which makes it difficult—even for Bonaparte—to be altogether his enemy. They also wrote that the First Consul had launched into great harangues against me. What provoked him even more than the opinions he assumed I held, was the number of foreigners who visited me. The son of the Stadtholder, the Prince of Orange, had paid me the honor of dining at my home, and Bonaparte had reproached him for doing so. The popularity of a woman because of her literary reputation was a trifling matter; but that trifling

---

[4] Madame de Staël gives no further explanation of this plot of the year X, which is still obscure and which Bonaparte did not want divulged for political reasons. We know that at the last moment Bernadotte avoided action. But the First Consul knew about Madame de Staël's intrigues, which she acknowledges here. He was aware that she received generals in her home; he alluded to these meetings in conversations on Saint Helena. . . .

[5] The Baron de Staël died at Poligny, May 9, 1802.

matter was completely independent of him, and that was reason enough for him to want to crush it.

Napoleon's lackeys were not satisfied with the decrees that assured Bonaparte's supreme authority, nor were they satisfied with the subjugation of the press on the one hand, nor—on the other—with constant sophisms in the newspapers, which each morning spilled lies into all those people who read without actually reading: people incapable of concentrating on a book but who enjoy serialized stories. Not satisfied—I repeat—with these measures intended to confuse the public's good sense, they meddled in education, in ways of preparing the future generation for slavery, as if the example set by their fathers were not enough. The Revolution, which produced very few lasting institutions, had nevertheless founded a polytechnical school, and most of the brave and independent men on whom France can still build her hopes have been educated there. A Councillor of State, charged with investigating the school, made sure that in the future there would be only sensible men there—which, in current usage, means men who would be submissive to force and always put the requirements of personal interest first.

It was very difficult to obtain the First Consul's permission to teach Latin, but Greek was positively forbidden. Naturally, since it is hardly of use in a state whose leader wants only farmers and soldiers. Moreover, he is even annoyed that farmers are necessary to feed the soldiers whom he will send to their deaths. All public education has taken on a military character; a drum roll announces the grammar lesson, and corporals preside over literary instruction. Bonaparte has been compared to Charlemagne, but he could rather be contrasted with him, for the latter was ahead of his century, and the former is behind his. That is perhaps the meeting ground for both rulers. Bonaparte spoke more truthfully about himself in conversations with his relatives, when he deplored not having—like Tamerlane—unreasoning peoples to rule. There is no question that the poor French have rectified this lack since those days, for they have held onto their characteristic intelligence without even as much freedom of thought and speech as they enjoyed under their most despotic kings. Furthermore, even

had Bonaparte had more liberal ideas about public education, the
policy of conscription—given the degree to which he has extended
it in France—was quite enough to discourage parents from providing, and young men from receiving, any kind of instruction.
His entire despotic organization is such that, whatever happens,
its unfortunate legacy will be bequeathed to future generations.

That year, August 15, the First Consul's birthday, was celebrated for the first time, and this anniversary took precedence over
all others. Among the many congratulations which filled the columns of the *Moniteur* there is one from a prefect on the French
coast opposite England telling Bonaparte that "God had rested
after creating him." In short, each day vulgarity further undermined the foundations of human dignity. All employees, from
doormen to consuls, were given uniforms; the members of the
Institute had olive branches embroidered on their coats, and
whereas in England even officers wore uniforms only in their
regiments, the lowest government clerk in France now wore a
small piece of gold or silver thread in his lapel to distinguish
him from an ordinary citizen. All these trappings of vanity, concentrated in one man's hands, were paving the way for despotism
under the guise of monarchy; for actually the Republic no longer
existed, and enlightened men were concentrating their hopes on
a limited monarchy. But the latter prospect was more irrecon-
cilable with Bonaparte's character than even a regime dominated
by factions; for he would rather have risked being oppressed
than renounce the chance of being the oppressor.

In this year 1802 the matter of indemnities for German
princes was taken up. The whole negotiation was conducted in
Paris, to the great advantage—it is said—of the ministers who
were in charge of it.[6] Be that as it may, the diplomatic dissection
of Europe, which was to extend to all of its borders, was begun
at this time. All the great noblemen of feudal Germany appeared
in Paris, exhibiting their ceremonial etiquette with obsequious
formalities that pleased the First Consul more than the casual

---

[6] The problem was to indemnify the German princes of all ranks who, as a
result of the treaties of Campo-Formio and Lunéville, had suffered considerable
losses in territory and revenue.

manner of the French. These men asked for the return of their property with a servility which almost invited seizure of the remainder of their possessions, so completely did they seem to discount the authority of justice.

Although a nation of eminently proud people, England was not at this time entirely exempt from a degree of curiosity—almost bordering on homage—about the person of the First Consul. The party in power saw him for what he was, but the opposition party —which should have had an even greater hatred of tyranny, since it is considered to be a greater partisan of liberty—and Fox himself, whose talent and goodness cannot be recalled without admiration and deep feeling, made the mistake of showing excessive respect for Bonaparte; and they thus perpetuated the error of those who still insisted on identifying the French Revolution with the most decided enemy of its own basic principles.

CHAPTER X

*New indications of Bonaparte's malevolence
toward Madame de Staël and her father—
Affairs in Switzerland: the Act of
Mediation—The First Consul's fury at the
English papers*

At the beginning of the winter of 1802–1803, when I read in
the papers that so many illustrious Englishmen and so many
brilliant Frenchmen were assembled in Paris, I must confess
that I felt a strong desire to be there with them. I do not conceal the fact that for me Paris has always been the most pleasant
of places. I was born there, I spent my childhood and early youth
there, and only there can I again encounter people who knew my
father, the friends who endured the perils of the Revolution with
us. This love of country, which grips the strongest souls, has an
even greater hold on us when it unites intellectual inclinations
with the heart's affections and the habits of the imagination.
French conversation exists only in Paris, and conversation has been
my greatest pleasure since childhood. I was so emotionally upset by
the fear of being deprived of this visit that reason was powerless

to help me. I was overflowing with zest for life at that time; and it is precisely the need for intense pleasures which most often leads to despair, for it makes resignation—without which one cannot bear life's vicissitudes—very difficult.

No order to deny me passports for Paris had been received by the Prefect of Geneva, but I knew that the First Consul had remarked to his inner circle that I would do well not to return there. He had already made a practice of dictating his wishes about such things in conversation, so that people would make it unnecessary for him to act, by anticipating his orders. If in this way he had said that such and such an individual ought to hang himself, I believe he would find it inexcusable if the dutiful subject did not respond to the hint by buying a rope and preparing the gallows. Another indication of Bonaparte's ill will toward me was the manner in which the French press treated my novel *Delphine*, which had just appeared; they decided to denounce it as immoral, and so the work, which had received my father's approbation, was condemned by these servile critics. In this book could be found the youthful impulsiveness and appetite for happiness which ten years, and ten years of suffering, have taught me to come to terms with in other ways. But my critics were incapable of appreciating failings of that kind, and they simply obeyed the same voice that had ordered them to rip apart my father's book before attacking his daughter's. Indeed, we heard from all quarters that the real reason for the First Consul's anger was my father's latest work, in which he predicted the entire structure of Bonaparte's monarchy.

My father shared my liking for stays in Paris, and my mother, during her lifetime, had also greatly enjoyed them. I was extremely unhappy to be separated from my friends, to be unable to give my children the artistic appreciation so difficult to acquire in the country. Since there was no specific prohibition of my return in Consul Lebrun's letter, but merely unpleasant innuendos, I made a hundred plans for returning, in order to test whether the First Consul—who was then still humoring public opinion—would be willing to brave the uproar my exile would undoubtedly cause. My father, who always reproached himself for having had

any part in damaging my future, thought of going to Paris himself to speak to the First Consul on my behalf. At first I agreed
to accept this proof of my father's devotion. I imagined so vividly
the influence of his commanding presence that I thought it impossible to resist him: his age, the fine expression in his eyes, all that
nobility of soul combined with his refinement of intellect seemed
likely to captivate even Bonaparte. I did not know then how
annoyed the First Consul was with his book. But fortunately for
me, I reasoned that my father's very qualities would only provoke
the Consul to a greater desire to humiliate their possessor; and
he would surely have found a means of doing so, at least outwardly. Power, in France, has many involuntary allies, and if a
spirit of opposition has frequently been displayed in this country,
it is only because the weakness of the government has offered it
easy victories. It cannot be repeated too often that what the French
love above all is success, and in this country, power can easily
make misfortune look ridiculous. Ultimately, thank heaven, I
awoke from the illusions I had been indulging in, and I positively
refused the generous sacrifice my father wished to make for me.
When he saw I was quite determined not to accept it, I realized
how much it would have cost him.[1] Fifteen months later I lost my
father, and if he had taken that contemplated trip, I should have
attributed his illness to it, and remorse would have aggravated my
wound.

It was also during the winter of 1802–1803 that Switzerland
took up arms against the unitary constitution which was being
imposed upon her. What an extraordinary mania the French revolutionaries have for compelling all countries to adopt the same
political organization as that of France! Without doubt there are
principles common to all countries, such as those which assure the
civil and political rights of free peoples; but what matter whether
the political organization is a limited monarchy like England, or
a federal republic like the United States, or the thirteen Swiss
cantons? It is surely not necessary to limit Europe to a single

---

[1] There exist in the archives at Coppet some reflections written in Necker's
hand which show that he was well aware of the astonishment that this ghost
from another age would have produced on the Parisians.

idea—like the Roman people to a single head—in order to be able to command and change everything in one day!

The First Consul certainly attached no importance to any one form of constitution, or even to any constitution whatever; but what mattered to him was to use Switzerland for his own best advantage, and in this respect he acted with prudence.[2] He combined the various plans offered him, and formed a single constitution from them which effectively reconciled the old customs with the new demands, and, by having himself named Mediator of the Swiss Confederation, he drew more men from that country than he could have wrung from it if he had governed it directly. He summoned deputies chosen by the cantons and principal cities of Switzerland to Paris, and on January 29, 1803, he had a seven-hour discussion with ten delegates chosen from that general deputation. He stressed the necessity of reestablishing the democratic cantons in their previous forms, declaiming some high-flown truisms about how cruel it would be to deprive the shepherds, isolated as they were in the mountains, of their only amusement, namely, the popular assemblies; and also giving (and this was his real concern) his reasons for distrusting the aristocratic cantons. He laid great stress on the importance of Switzerland to France. He spoke in short clipped sentences intended to suggest oracular profundity. These were his exact words as recorded in an account of this meeting: "I declare that since I have been at the head of the government, no power has been interested in Switzerland. It was I who had the Helvetian republic recognized at Lunéville. Austria had not given it a thought. I wanted to do the same at Amiens but England refused. However, England has nothing to do with Switzerland. If she had expressed any fear that I might

---

[2] The First Consul had been obliged to intervene in order to extricate Switzerland from England's intrigues and from the counter-revolution. This country, because of its Alpine routes, was the necessary link between the Italian republic and France. Bonaparte profited from the fact that the Helvetic government, in refuge in Lausanne, had asked for France's intervention, and he directed his proclamation "to the inhabitants of Helvetia," on whom he imposed his mediation. His aide-de-camp, Rapp, went to Switzerland to remit this proclamation to all the regular and insurrectional authorities, and General Ney was ordered to support him with thirty thousand men.

make myself your *Landamman*, I would have done so. It has been said that England encouraged the last insurrection. If her cabinet had taken any official step, or if there had been a word on this subject in the London gazette, I would have assembled you."

What incredible language! Thus, the existence of a people who had secured their independence, in the middle of Europe, by heroic efforts, and maintained it for five centuries by moderation and wisdom, might have been destroyed through a burst of temper which the slightest provocation could have aroused in so capricious an individual. Bonaparte added in this same conversation that he found it disagreeable to have to establish a constitution because that exposed him to being hissed at, something he didn't want. This remark has the quality of falsely affable vulgarity, which he often likes to affect. Roederer and Desmeunier wrote the Act of Mediation[3] at his dictation, and this whole episode took place while his troops were occupying Switzerland. Since then the troops have been withdrawn, and it must be acknowledged that this country has been treated better by Napoleon than the rest of Europe, although politically and militarily it is entirely under his domination; consequently it will remain quiet in the general insurrection. The European peoples were endowed with such an enormous supply of patience that it has required a Bonaparte to exhaust it.

The London papers attacked the First Consul rather bitterly, for the English nation was too intelligent not to perceive where all of his actions were leading. Every time translations of the English papers were brought to him he made a scene before Lord Whitworth,[4] who replied, calmly and reasonably, that even the King of Great Britain was not protected from journalists' sarcasms, and that the constitution did not permit any interference

---

[3] By the Act of Mediation, February 11, 1803, Bonaparte, while leaving the local government of the cantons to the aristocracy, reserved for himself the central authority, which he entrusted to a local magistrate chosen by himself, President d'Affry. "I will not tolerate any influence but mine in Switzerland," he said.

[4] "Many times it happened that we saw the First Consul in a gloomy, trying mood, and heard him say to Madame Bonaparte that it was because he had read some article directed against him in the *Courrier* or *Sun*." (Madame de Rémusat, *Mémoires*, I, 222.) Lord Whitworth was English ambassador in Paris.

with their liberty in this respect. Bonaparte, with his short stature, revolved around the tall, fine figure of Lord Whitworth as he did around the principles of English liberty, able neither to damage nor to tolerate them. However, a lawsuit was brought against Peltier for articles in his newspaper against the First Consul.[5] Peltier had the honor of being defended by Mr. Mackintosh, who, on this occasion, delivered one of the most eloquent legal arguments of modern times: I will relate later on the circumstances whereby this speech came into my hands.

---

[5] Peltier, having taken refuge in London after the fall of the monarchy on August 10, 1792, had been publishing there, since 1800, the *Ambigu, variétés atroces et amusantes*, which appeared every ten days. Bonaparte and his family were periodically showered with insults in it. Upon the refusal of the English government to act, Peltier was subpoenaed by the French ambassador and sentenced to a small fine and expenses.

CHAPTER XI

Rupture with England: the "great farce" of

the invasion—Bonaparte and legitimacy:

ludicrous joy of Portalis—Arrival of

Madame de Staël at Mafliers—Contemptible

conduct of Madame de Genlis—Madame de

Staël at Madame Récamier's—Madame de

Staël's arrest; her exile

I was in Geneva, living partly by my own choice and partly by chance among the English residents, when news of the declaration of war reached us. Rumors immediately circulated that English travelers would be imprisoned.[1] As there had never been anything like this in European international law, I did not believe it, and my lack of apprehension almost brought harm to several of my friends. However, they managed to escape. But persons

---

[1] Previous to any signs of the diplomatic break, some English ships had seized several merchant ships of French registry. In reprisal, the First Consul issued a decree declaring all Englishmen traveling in France to be prisoners of war.

totally unconnected with politics, such as Lord Beverley—the father of eleven children, who was returning from Italy with his wife and daughters—and a hundred other people with French passports who were going to universities to study or to the southern provinces for health reasons—all of them traveling under the protection of laws recognized by all nations—were arrested. They have now been languishing in provincial towns for the past ten years, leading the saddest lives imaginable. This scandalous action served no useful purpose. Scarcely two thousand English— very few of whom were of any military importance—were among the victims of this tyrannical caprice: a few poor individuals made to suffer because of his irritation at their invincible fatherland.

During the summer of 1803, the great farce of the invasion of England began. The construction of flat-bottomed boats was ordered from one end of France to the other, in the forests, and along the edges of the main highways. The French, who have great zeal for imitation, cut plank after plank and coined phrase after phrase. In Picardy a triumphal arch was erected on which was written *Route to London;* others wrote "To Bonaparte the Great: we beg you to allow us on the vessel that will carry you to England, and with you the destiny and vengeance of the French people." The vessel Bonaparte was supposed to board has had plenty of time to rot away in port. Others took as a motto for their flags along the roads—*A good wind and three hours.* In sum, all France reverberated with boastful sayings whose significance Bonaparte alone fully understood.

In the manner of a king, Bonaparte sent a circular to all the archbishops and bishops of France, asking them to pray for the success of his mission. Woe to those who did so! The Archbishop of Aix, who had become Archbishop of Tours and no longer had anything to lose, stated in his pastoral letter that it was necessary to rally around a paternal, firm, and *legitimate* government. One of my friends went at that time to see the aged Portalis, who was then Minister of Religions. He found him in an immoderate state of joy. "Have you read the Archbishop of Tours's pastoral letter?" my friend asked him. "It seems to me that it does justice to the First Consul."

"Bah! Bah!" he answered, "who cares about his praises! But he has used the true word—*legitimate*, do you understand? Don't you see! The very man who consecrated Louis XVI calls us *legitimate*. That's just what we needed." How extraordinary that men who take it upon themselves to oppress nations should be so very anxious about not being in the line of succession to the throne! They admit their tyranny much more willingly than their usurpation.[2]

As the autumn of 1803 approached I believed that Bonaparte had forgotten about me. Friends wrote from Paris that he was completely absorbed in his expedition to England; he intended to go to the coast and embark there, in order to direct the invasion personally. I had very little faith in this project, but I deluded myself in thinking that he would not mind my living at a distance of several leagues from Paris, with the very few friends who would come such a long way to visit a person in disgrace. I also thought that I was well-enough known for my banishment to be talked about in Europe, and that the First Consul would prefer to avoid such a scandal. This was wishful thinking, but I still did not thoroughly understand the character of this man who was to dominate Europe. Far from wishing to spare anyone who distinguished himself—in whatever field of endeavor—he wanted to use all such persons as pedestals for his own statue, either by trampling them underfoot or by making them serve his purposes.

I settled in a small country house about ten leagues from Paris,[3] having planned to spend the winters there for as long as the tyr-

---

[2] See this amusing allusion to Monsieur de Boisgelin's pastoral letter on the First Consul's *legitimacy:* "Among the new cardinals is mentioned Monsieur de Boisgelin, who will be one, they say, very *legitimately.*" (*Relations secrètes*, p. 238.) Monsieur de Boisgelin, successively Bishop of Lavaur and Archbishop of Aix, famous for his sermon at the coronation of Louis XVI and member of the French Academy, had returned to France under the Consulate; he had spoken at the official ceremony at Notre Dame on Easter Sunday, 1802, and had been named Archbishop of Tours. He received a cardinal's hat. He died in 1804 at the age of seventy-two.

[3] At Mafliers, near Beaumont-sur-Oise, north of the forest of Montmorency. Madame de Staël arrived there in September, 1803. She had not dared to go directly to Paris and had chosen Mafliers because that residence was near Saint-Brice, where Madame Récamier lived, and near Luzarches, where Benjamin Constant was residing. Mafliers is in fact about *five* leagues from Paris, not ten.

anny endured. All I wanted was to receive my friends and occasionally go to a play or a museum. This was all I hoped for from a stay in Paris in view of the atmosphere of suspicion and spying beginning to be felt there, and I must say I do not see what inconveniences the First Consul could have suffered from allowing me to remain in this voluntary exile. As a matter of fact I had already spent one undisturbed month there, when a woman—the kind frequently encountered,[4] who seeks to gain favor at the expense of another woman better known than she—informed the First Consul that the roads were crowded with people going to visit me. Certainly nothing could have been less true. Exiles who received visits were those who—in the eighteenth century—had almost as much influence as the kings who had banished them; but when power can be questioned, it is not tyrannical, for power can only be tyrannical through unequivocal submission. Be that as it may, Bonaparte took advantage of this pretext to exile me, and one of my friends warned me that a gendarme would arrive within a few days with an order for me to depart. No one—in countries where the individual is routinely protected from injustice—has any idea of the terror that the sudden news of such an arbitrary act can inspire. Moreover, I am by nature very impressionable; my imagination more readily turns to pain than hope, and although I have often found that my sorrow is dissipated by a new set of circumstances, at first I am always sure that nothing can rescue me from it. It is so easy to be unhappy, especially for those who set their sights on life's finer prizes.

I immediately withdrew to the home of a truly good and intelligent woman[5] to whom I was recommended by a man who held an important post in the government.[6] I will never forget his courage in offering me a refuge: indeed he would want to do the same today, even if such an act should be his ruin. The more conces-

---

[4] Madame de Genlis, former maid of honor of the Duchess of Chartres, in charge of the education of the Orléans children; she had returned to France under the Consulate. Like Fiévée, she carried on a secret correspondence with Bonaparte. She detested Madame de Staël, especially because the fame of *Delphine* had eclipsed that of her own writings. She drew a malicious portrait of Madame de Staël in her novel *Mélanide*.

[5] Madame de la Tour. (Note of A. de Staël, edition of 1821.)

[6] Regnault de Saint-Jean d'Angély. (Note of A. de Staël, edition of 1821.)

sions one makes to tyranny, the more it expands before our gaze, like a phantom, though its grip is that of a real being. Thus I arrived at the home of a person whom I scarcely knew, in the midst of a group of people who were complete strangers, bearing a bitter sorrow in my heart, which I did not want to reveal. At night, alone with a devoted woman who had been in my service for several years, I listened at the window for the hoofbeats of a mounted gendarme. During the day I tried to be sociable so as to hide my problems. From this country house I wrote a letter to Joseph Bonaparte in which I frankly expressed all my unhappiness. A retreat ten leagues from Paris was my sole ambition, and, despairingly, I felt that if I were once exiled it would be for a long time, perhaps forever. Joseph and his brother Lucien generously made every effort to save me, and they were not the only ones, as will presently be seen.

Madame Récamier, so celebrated for her beauty, and whose character is manifest in her very appearance, invited me to live at her country place at Saint-Brice, two leagues from Paris. I accepted, for at that time I had no idea that my behavior could injure a person so uninvolved in politics. I fancied her to be immune to all dangers, notwithstanding the generosity of her character. The most delightful company was gathered at her house, and there, for the last time, I enjoyed the social and intellectual pleasures I was soon to leave behind. It was during these stormy days that I received a copy of Mr. Mackintosh's speech and read those fine pages in which he portrays a Jacobin who had terrorized children, old men, and women during the Revolution, and now bows under the cudgel of the Corsican, who is robbing him of even the last scraps of liberty for which he once professed to fight. This eloquent passage moved me to the depths of my being: superior writers sometimes unknowingly bring comfort to the unfortunate in any country and at any time. France was so profoundly silent around me that this voice, which suddenly spoke to my condition, seemed to come directly from heaven: it came from a free country. After having spent several days with Madame Récamier without hearing any mention of my exile, I convinced myself that Bonaparte had abandoned the idea. Nothing is more normal than to reassure oneself about a danger when there are no immediate indications of its approach. Knowing myself to be so totally devoid of hostile schemes or devices, even against that man, I could not imagine his being unwilling to leave me in peace; and so, after a few days I went back to my house in the country, convinced that he had deferred any action against me and was satisfied with having given me a fright. And he had indeed frightened me, though not enough to make me change or disavow my opinions, but enough to stifle the remains of the republican habit in me that had led me to speak with too much candor the year before.

At the end of September, I was at dinner with three friends in a room from which the highway and the entry gate could be seen. At four o'clock, a man on horseback wearing a gray riding coat stopped at the iron gate and rang. I was certain of my fate. He asked for me, and I went to receive him in the garden. As I walked toward him, I was struck by the perfume of the flowers and the slanting rays of the sun. The sensations we owe to nature are so different from those of society. This man told me that he was chief of gendarmes at Versailles, but that he had been ordered not to wear his uniform for fear of alarming me. He showed me a letter signed by Bonaparte which ordered my removal to a distance of forty leagues from Paris within twenty-four hours, treating me—however—with all the respect due a woman of distinction. He added that as a foreigner I was under police jurisdiction: this regard for individual liberty did not last long, and soon after my case other French men and women were exiled without any formal proceedings. I told the gendarmerie officer that an order to move at twenty-four hours' notice was perhaps suitable for recruits, but not for a woman with two children, and consequently I proposed he accompany me to Paris, where I needed three days to make the necessary arrangements for my trip. I entered my carriage with my children and this officer, who had been selected to be my escort because he was the most well-read of the gendarmes. Indeed, he began complimenting me on my writings. "You see, Monsieur," I said to him, "the consequences of being a woman of intellect. I would recommend that you dissuade any females of your family from attempting it, if you have occasion to do so." I was trying to keep up my spirits by a show of pride, but I felt something like a claw in my heart.

I stopped for a few minutes at Madame Récamier's. There I found General Junot,[7] who, because of his devotion to her, promised to go and speak to the First Consul on my behalf next morning. He certainly did so with the greatest warmth. One would think that a man whose military ardor made him so useful to Bonaparte would have had enough influence to persuade him to spare a woman, but Bonaparte's generals, although they succeed in obtaining numerous favors for themselves, have no influence over him. When they ask for money or positions, Bonaparte thinks that proper; they are contributing to his power by becoming dependent upon him; but if, as seldom happens, they should want to defend some unfortunate person or oppose some injustice, they would very quickly be made to understand that they are merely tools employed to maintain slavery, while submitting to it themselves.

In Paris I went to a house I had recently rented, but which I had not yet lived in. I had chosen it with great care in a neighborhood I liked, facing my favorite exposure;[8] and in my imagination I already saw myself seated in the drawing room with a few friends and pleasant conversation—in my opinion, the greatest delight the human spirit can enjoy. I entered this house knowing I would have to leave it, and I spent the nights wandering through the rooms and mourning the loss of even more happiness than I could have hoped for there. My gendarme returned each morning —like the man in the story of Bluebeard—to urge me to leave the next day, and each time I was weak enough to ask for one more day. My friends came to dine with me, and sometimes we were gay, as if to empty the cup of sadness by being as nice to each other as possible just before parting for so long a time. This man who came every day to summon me to leave reminded them, they said, of the era of the Terror, when gendarmes came to claim their victims.

---

[7] Bonaparte's aide-de-camp during the first Italian campaign. (Trans.)
[8] Number 540, rue de Lille.

Some may be astonished, perhaps, by my comparing exile to death, but there have been great men in ancient and modern times who have succumbed to this punishment. One finds more people who are brave at the prospect of the scaffold than at the loss of country. In all legal codes perpetual banishment is considered one of the severest penalties; yet one man, in France, inflicts casually and at a whim what conscientious judges impose on criminals only with regret. Unusual circumstances made it possible for me to find a refuge and some financial ease in my parents' country, Switzerland; in this respect I was less to be pitied than others, but nevertheless I have suffered cruelly. Therefore, I will be rendering a service to the world by drawing attention to the reasons why no sovereign should ever be allowed to have the arbitrary power of banishment. No deputy, no writer will ever express his thoughts freely if he can be banished when his frankness has displeased someone; no man will dare to speak sincerely if it can cost him his entire family's happiness. Women especially—whose destiny it is to encourage and reward enthusiasm—will try to stifle their generous sentiments if expressing them leads either to their being torn away from the people they love, or to ruining their own lives by following their loved ones into exile.

On my next to last day in Paris, Joseph Bonaparte made yet another attempt on my behalf, and his wife, a person of the most perfect sweetness and simplicity, had the kindness to call on me and propose that I spend several days at her country estate, Mortfontaine. I accepted the invitation gratefully, for I could not help being touched at Joseph's kindness in receiving me in his home at the very time when his brother was persecuting me. I spent three days at Mortfontaine, but in spite of the perfect courtesy of the master and mistress of the house, my situation was very painful. I saw only men connected with the government, I breathed only the air of that authority which had declared itself my enemy, and yet the most basic rules of politeness and gratitude forbade my showing what I felt. I had only my elder son with me,[9] who was

---

[9] Auguste de Staël.

still too young for me to be able to converse with him on such subjects. I spent hours examining the Mortfontaine gardens, which are
among the most beautiful in France; its owner, still untroubled at
that time, seemed to me very deserving of envy. He has since been
exiled to thrones from which I am sure he has mourned the loss of
his beautiful sanctuary.

CHAPTER XII

Departure for Germany; Madame de Staël's

anguish–Metz; meeting with Charles de

Villers–Frankfort; illness of Albertine

de Staël–Arrival at Weimar

I hesitated over the choice to make in going away. Should I return to my father, or should I go to Germany? My father would have welcomed his poor bird, beaten by the storm, with indescribable goodness, but I dreaded the prospect of returning, under duress, to a country that I was accused of finding rather monotonous. I also wanted to experience the good reception that had been promised me in Germany, and in this way to recover from the outrage I had received from the First Consul. I wanted to contrast the benevolent welcome of the ancient dynasties with the impertinence of the new one that was preparing to subjugate France. It was unfortunate that this impulse of pride prevailed, for I should have seen my father again had I returned to Geneva.

I asked Joseph to find out if I might go to Prussia; for at least I had to be certain that the French ambassador would not lay claim to me as a French woman traveling abroad, even though I was proscribed within France as a foreigner. Joseph left for

Saint-Cloud. I was obliged to wait for his answer at an inn, two leagues from Paris, not daring to return to my house in the city. A day passed without my receiving an answer. Not wanting to attract attention by remaining any longer at that inn, I went all the way around the walls of Paris to find another inn, also two leagues away, but on a different road.[1] This wandering existence, no more than a few steps away from my friends and my own home, caused me such grief that I cannot recall it without shuddering. Even now, I can still see the room and the window where I spent the whole day watching for the messenger; a thousand painful details of the kind that misfortune always draws in its wake, the extreme generosity of some friends, and the veiled calculation of others, all this put me in a cruel state of agitation such as I could not even wish for an enemy. At last came the message on which my remaining hopes were based. Joseph sent me some excellent letters of recommendation for Berlin and bade me goodbye in a noble and touching manner, and so it was necessary to leave. The same very intelligent friend who had been excluded from the Tribunate[2] was kind enough to accompany me, but as he too enjoyed living in Paris, I suffered to think of what he was sacrificing for me. Each hoofbeat of the horses made me ill, and when the coachmen boasted of having driven rapidly I could not help sighing at the unhappy service they were rendering me. In this state of mind I traveled forty leagues without being able to regain my self-control. Finally we stopped at Châlons, and for at least a few minutes Benjamin Constant, rallying his spirits, managed to lift, with his extraordinary conversation, the weight that was oppressing me. The next day we continued our journey as far as Metz, where I wished to await news of my father. There I spent two weeks, and met one of the most amiable and witty men whom France and Germany combined could produce, Monsieur Charles Villers. His company delighted me, but it revived my regrets over losing that supreme pleasure: conversation in which there is perfect harmony in all that is felt and expressed.

---

[1] At Bondy. She left Paris on October 19.
[2] Edition of 1821: Benjamin Constant.

My father was indignant at the treatment I had received in Paris; he pictured his family proscribed in this manner, driven, like criminals, from the country he had served so well. He himself advised me to spend the winter in Germany and not to return to him until the spring. I wish I had not listened! I counted on bringing back to him the harvest of new ideas I was planning to gather on this trip. For several years he had been telling me frequently that he remained in touch with the world only through my conversations and letters. His mind was so lively and keen that the pleasure of talking with him stimulated thought. I observed, in order to recount to him; I listened, in order to repeat to him. Ever since I have lost him, I see and feel only half of what I did when my objective was to please him by describing my impressions.

At Frankfort, my five-year-old daughter fell dangerously ill. I knew no one in the city; the language was foreign to me, and even my child's doctor spoke only a little French. Oh, how deeply my father shared my distress! What letters he wrote me! He sent me innumerable doctors' opinions from Geneva, all copied in his own hand! Never has the harmony of sensibility and reason been as exquisite as in him. There has never been anyone like him, so strongly moved by the troubles of his friends, always active in helping them, and always careful to choose the best way; in short, a man admirable in every respect. My heart requires me to make this declaration, for what does even the voice of posterity matter to him now?

I proceeded to Weimar, where my courage was revived on encountering—in spite of language difficulties—the immense intellectual riches that existed outside of France. I learned to read German; I listened to Goethe and Wieland, who, fortunately for me, spoke French very well. I understood the soul and genius of Schiller, in spite of his difficulty in expressing himself in a foreign language. I found the society of the Duke and Duchess of Weimar extremely pleasant, and I spent three months there, during which time my study of German literature provided my mind with the intense mental activity I always require if I am to remain healthy.

CHAPTER XIII

Berlin; the absence of public spirit—

German partisans of the French

Revolution—Prince Louis-Ferdinand

I left Weimar for Berlin on March 1 [1804], and there I met that charming queen who has had so many misfortunes since then.[1] The king received me with great kindness, and I may say that during the six weeks I remained in that city[2] I never heard a single person express dissatisfaction with the fairness of the government. This does not prevent me from believing that it is always desirable for a country to have constitutional forms which guarantee it— through the permanent cooperation of the nation—the advantages to be derived from the virtues of a good king. Prussia, under the reign of its present monarch, no doubt possessed most of these advantages; but the public spirit that has since been developed in response to misfortune did not yet exist at that time; the military regime had prevented public opinion from acquiring strength, and the absence of a constitution under which every individual could achieve recognition by his merit had deprived the state of talented

---

[1] Queen Louise, wife of Frederick William III of Prussia, whom she influenced to resist Napoleon. (Trans.)
[2] She left on April 18, 1804.

men capable of defending it. The king's favor, being necessarily arbitrary, is not enough to develop talent through competition; circumstances having to do with life at court may keep a man of merit from the helm of state or place a very mediocre man there. Routine is also singularly powerful in countries where the royal power has no opposition; the very sense of justice of a king leads him to provide some barriers to his own will by allowing everyone to keep his office. In Prussia there was hardly an example of a man's being removed from his civil or military position for incompetence. What an advantage the French army must have had, being composed almost entirely of men born of the Revolution, like the soldiers of Cadmus from the teeth of the dragon! What an advantage it must have had over those old commanders of Prussian fortresses or armies, to whom everything new was completely unfamiliar! A conscientious king who has not the *good fortune*— and I use that expression intentionally—to have a parliament like the one in England—prefers to rely on precedence in every area, for fear of using his own will too much; whereas in these times, old customs must be disregarded and we must look for strength of character and intellect wherever they can be found. Be that as it may, Berlin was one of the happiest and most enlightened places on earth.

No doubt the writers of the eighteenth century performed a great service to Europe through the spirit of moderation and taste for literature that their works inspired in most sovereigns; nevertheless, the respect that friends of knowledge accorded the French intellect was partly responsible for errors that have been the ruin of Germany for so long.[3] Many people regarded the French armies as propagators of the ideas of Montesquieu, Rousseau, or Voltaire, whereas, in fact, if there remained any traces of the opinions of these great men in the instruments of Bonaparte's power, they served only to liberate him from what they called prejudices, rather than to establish a single reforming principle. However, in the spring of 1804 in Berlin and northern Germany there were many former partisans of the French Revolution who had not yet per-

---

[3] It is well-known that the book *De l'Allemagne* was written in great part to invite the Germans to react against this admiration for the French mind.

ceived that Bonaparte was a much fiercer enemy of the first principles of that revolution than the old European aristocracy.

I had the honor of making the acquaintance of Prince Louis-
Ferdinand,[4] whose warlike ardor was so overpowering that his
death in battle was almost to anticipate the first of his country's
setbacks. He was a man overflowing with warmth and enthusiasm,
yet who, for lack of glory, sought excitement with too much intensity. What especially irritated him in Bonaparte was his way
of slandering all those whom he feared, and even of damaging the
reputation of those who served him to make doubly sure that
they would remain dependent on him. More than once he said to
me, "I can tolerate his killing, but his moral assassinations I find
disgusting." And indeed, anyone can imagine the state in which
we found ourselves when that great libeler became master of all
the newspapers of the European continent and could, as he has
frequently done, write that the bravest men were cowards, and the
purest women contemptible, without there being any way to con-
tradict or to punish such assertions.

---

[4] Prince Louis-Ferdinand, cousin of King Frederick William, died in the
battle of Saalfeld, October 10, 1806, killed by Gaindé cavalry sergeant of the
Tenth Hussars.

CHAPTER XIV

Conspiracy of Moreau and Pichegru—Méhée's

mission—Arrest of Moreau, Pichegru, and

Georges—Messages to the First Consul

A rumor about the great conspiracy of Moreau, Pichegru, and Georges Cadoudal began to circulate in Berlin. Of course there was a strong desire among the principal leaders of the republican and royalist parties to overthrow the authority of the First Consul and block the even more tyrannical power that he would assume upon having himself declared emperor. But this conspiracy—so useful to the enforcement of Bonaparte's tyranny—was originally encouraged by Bonaparte himself in order to use it for his own purposes, with a diabolical skill and with intricacies worthy of careful examination. First, he sent an exiled Jacobin to England, whose only hope of returning to France was to perform services for the First Consul. This man, Méhée,[1] presented himself like Sinon in the city of Troy, when he claimed to be persecuted by the

---

[1] Méhée de la Touche, former assistant clerk of the Paris city government in 1792; in this capacity he had played a role in the September massacres. Editor of the *Journal des hommes libres* after 18 Brumaire, he was arrested as a *septembriseur*, exiled first to Dijon and then to Oléron, from which he escaped to England. He presented himself to the English government and to Count d'Artois as the agent of a party working for Bonaparte's overthrow. On his return to France he published a *Mémoire*, to which Madame de Staël alludes.

Greeks. After visiting several émigrés who were neither immoral nor clever enough to recognize his particular kind of trickery, he found it very easy to entrap an old bishop, a former officer, and various other fragments of a potential government in exile whose backing was extremely obscure. He later wrote a pamphlet ridiculing with considerable wit all those who had believed him, who should really have been able to make up for their lack of perspicacity by the firmness of their principles; in other words, by never trusting a man guilty of evil deeds. We all have our own ways of looking at things, but when someone has shown himself to be treacherous or cruel, God alone can pardon him; for He alone can read deeply enough into the human heart to know if it has changed. Mortal man must remain permanently aloof from those he has ceased to respect. This disguised agent of Bonaparte's claimed that there were great potentialities for revolt in France. He went to Munich to meet an English agent, Mr. Drake, whom he also succeeded in deceiving. A citizen of Great Britain should have had nothing to do with this web of deception woven from threads of Jacobinism and tyranny.

Georges and Pichegru, who were entirely devoted to the Bourbons, came into France secretly and plotted with Moreau, who wished to deliver France from the First Consul without depriving the French nation of its right to decide what form of government it preferred. Pichegru wanted to arrange an interview with General Bernadotte, who refused—not liking the way the enterprise was being conducted—for he desired above all a guarantee of France's constitutional liberties. Moreau, a man of indisputably moral integrity and military talent, whose mind is precise and well-informed, let himself go too far in criticizing the First Consul in conversations before being sure of being able to overthrow him. Expressing one's opinion, even in an imprudent manner, is a very natural failing of a noble soul, but General Moreau was too close to Bonaparte for such conduct not to be the cause of his downfall. Some pretext was needed to justify the arrest of a man who had won so many battles, and this pretext was found in his words since it could not be found in his actions.

Republican manners were still in vogue; people called each

other "citizen," as if the most terrible inequality of all—exempting some from the power of the law while treating others arbitrarily —did not prevail throughout France. The days of the week were still reckoned according to the Republican calendar; boasts were made about being at peace with all of continental Europe; reports were issued—as they still are—on the building of roads and canals, and the construction of bridges and fountains; the government's accomplishments were praised to the skies; in short, there was no apparent reason for changing a system with which people professed to be so perfectly satisfied. A plot involving the English and the Bourbons was therefore needed to reawaken the nation's revolutionary elements and direct them toward the establishment of an ultramonarchist power, with the pretext of preventing a return of the old regime. This scheme, which seems very complicated, is in reality extremely simple: it was necessary to give the revolutionaries a good fright concerning their private interests, after which they would be offered relief and security in return for a final abandonment of their principles—and this is what was done.

Pichegru had become a royalist, just as completely as he had formerly been a republican; his opinions had been reversed: he had a stronger character than intellect, though neither the one nor the other enabled him to attract followers. Georges had more drive but was not suited either by education or nature to be a leader. When the authorities learned they were in Paris, Moreau was arrested and the gates of the city were closed. It was announced that whoever gave asylum to Pichegru or to Georges would be executed, and all the old Jacobin measures were reactivated to protect the life of one man. Not only is this man too important in his own eyes to take any personal risk, but in addition he planned to frighten people, by recalling the days of the Terror, so as to make them feel—if possible—the need to rush into his arms to escape the troubles he himself was stirring up. Pichegru's hiding place was discovered, and Georges was arrested in a cabriolet;[2] for, since he no longer dared live in a house, he

---

[2] Georges Cadoudal was arrested on March 9, 1804, at the Carrefour de Bussy, when he was attempting to flee in a cabriolet. He was executed on July 25 on

roamed the city night and day in this manner in order to escape pursuit. The police agent who seized Georges was rewarded with the Legion of Honor. The French military, it seems to me, should have wanted him to have an entirely different reward.

Le Moniteur was filled with written discourses to the First Consul congratulating him on his escape from danger; the constant repetition of the same stock phrases, coming from all corners of France, shows a generalized state of servility perhaps without precedent in any other nation. In leafing through back copies of the *Moniteur*, one can find essays on liberty, on despotism, on philosophy, and on religion, according to the period, in which the good citizens and departments of France strive to say the same thing in different terms. It is amazing that men as clever as the French should be content only with stylistic success and never once experience the desire to have ideas of their own; it could be said that verbal competition is sufficient for them. These dictated hymns, with their paeans of admiration announced, however, that all was peaceful in France, and that the few agents of perfidious Albion had been seized. It is true that one general, although he was perfectly sane, saw fit to announce that the English had thrown bales of Levantine cotton on the coasts of Normandy in an effort to infect France with the plague, but these solemnly ridiculous tales were merely regarded as flatteries addressed to the First Consul; and since the leaders of the conspiracy, as well as their agents, were in the government's hands, there was good reason for believing that calm had been restored in France; but this did not suit the purposes of the First Consul.

---

the Place de Grève with eleven accomplices. Of the two police inspectors who aided in the arrest, one, Rebuffet, was killed by a pistol shot; the other, Cayolle, was seriously wounded. The First Consul had their children brought up at state expense.

CHAPTER XV

The Duke d'Enghien's execution; Prince Louis-Ferdinand's indignation—State of public opinion in France—Bonaparte and State policy—Reasons for the execution

In Berlin I lived on the quay of the Sprée, and my apartment was on the ground floor. One morning at eight o'clock I was awakened and informed that Prince Louis-Ferdinand was on horseback under my windows, and wanted to speak with me. Very surprised at this early visit, I arose quickly in order to go to him. He was a singularly graceful horseman, and his emotion heightened the nobility of his features. "Do you know," he said, "that the Duke d'Enghien was kidnaped on Baden territory, turned over to a military commission, and shot twenty-four hours after his arrival in Paris?"

"What nonsense!" I answered. "Don't you see that this can only be a rumor spread by France's enemies?" Indeed, I must admit that, strong as my hatred of Bonaparte was, it did not allow me to consider the possibility of such an atrocity.

"Since you doubt what I am saying," Prince Louis replied, "I will send you the *Moniteur*, in which you can read the decree."

With these words he left, and the expression on his face could only mean revenge or death. A quarter of an hour later, I had the *Moniteur* of March 21 (30 Ventôse) in my hands. It contained the death sentence handed down by the military commission in session at Vincennes, headed by General Hulin, a man of the very lowest origins, like all the other individuals on the commission. They began by stating—as if in mockery—that none of them needed to disqualify himself since none of them was a relative of the accused. Yes, certainly, the men who behaved with such despicable cowardice were not relatives of the Condé, but what insolent irony that there should be such a declaration concerning someone they called "the person named Louis d'Enghien"! This was the way in which Frenchmen referred to the descendant of heroes who brought glory to their country! Even while renouncing all prejudices in favor of illustrious birth—which a return to monarchical forms would necessarily revive—how could anyone insult the memory of the battles of Lens and Rocroi like that? Bonaparte, who has himself won battles, does not even know how to show respect for them. There is neither past nor future for him; his overbearing and contemptuous soul does not wish to recognize anything as sacred by virtue of public esteem; he acknowledges only respect for existing force. Prince Louis wrote a note to me, opening with these words: "The person named Louis of Prussia begs to know of Madame de Staël . . ." He felt deeply the insult to the royal blood from which he was descended, and to the memory of the heroes among whom he was eager to take his place. How, after that horrifying act, could any king in Europe ally himself with such a man? Necessity, someone will say! There is a sanctuary of the soul where the empire of necessity should never enter, for if this were not so, what would virtue be on earth? A generous pastime suitable only to the untroubled leisure of men in private life.[1]

---

[1] There is at this point in the manuscript a long passage crossed off by Madame de Staël (?), about the role of Savary in the affair of the Duke d'Enghien and about Bonaparte's attitude. To recall the remarks of the First Consul about the Duke d'Enghien: "He was playing checkers with a lady of the court and said, 'He is a little weasel-faced person, smaller than I am.' Who was this lady of the court? Was it Madame de Rémusat? She played checkers the

An acquaintance of mine told me that a few days after the Duke d'Enghien's death she took a walk around the dungeon of Vincennes: the ground, still fresh, marked the place where he had been buried. Some children were playing quoits on this mound of grass, the only memorial permitted for such remains. An old white-haired soldier, seated not far from there, had remained motionless for some time watching the children; finally he arose, and taking them by the hand, weeping a little, he said to them, "Do not play there, children, I beg of you." These tears were the only honors paid to a descendant of the great Condé, and the earth did not retain their impression for long.

For a short time at least, French public opinion seemed to be aroused, and there was a general feeling of indignation. But when these noble sentiments died down, despotism was established all the more firmly for having overcome efforts to resist it. For several days the First Consul was rather anxious about the prevailing mood. Fouché himself disapproved of the act. He had made this remark, so characteristic of the present regime: "It is worse than a crime; it is a mistake." There are many ideas implied in this sentence, but happily it can be turned around, and made to express a truth, that the greatest of errors is crime. Bonaparte asked an honest senator, "What do people think about the Duke d'Enghien's death?"

"General," he replied, "they are very upset."

"That does not surprise me," said Bonaparte. "A family that has ruled in a country for a long time is always the focus of interest."

In that way he could relate the most natural feeling the human heart can experience to his own situation. On another occasion he asked the same question of a tribune, who, being anxious to please him, answered, "Well, General, if our enemies take atrocious measures against us, we are right to do the same," not perceiving that this was tantamount to saying that the measure was atrocious.

---

evening of March 20 at Malmaison, with the First Consul, but she does not report these remarks of Bonaparte's. It is known that Madame de Rémusat burned her *Mémoires* during the Hundred Days. The ones we have, according to the word of Chateaubriand are no more 'than memories reproduced from memories.' " (Cf. Madame de Rémusat, *Mémoires*, I, 314 ff.)

The First Consul pretended that the act was dictated by reasons of state. One day, about this time, when he was discussing the plays of Corneille with an intelligent man, he said, "You see, public safety, or—to be more exact—state policy, has assumed for the moderns the meaning that fatality had for the ancients. There are men who by nature would be incapable of crime, but political circumstances force it on them, as if it were a law. In his tragedies Corneille has shown that he understood state policy, and so, if he had lived in my time I would have made him my first minister." All this seeming good humor in the discussion was intended to prove that no passion was involved in the Duke d'Enghien's death, and that circumstances—meaning a situation where the head of state is the only judge—motivated and justified everything. It is perfectly true that there had been no passion in his decision about the Duke d'Enghien, and while there are those who believe that rage inspired this heinous crime, it had nothing to do with it. For what could possibly have provoked this rage? The Duke d'Enghien had not offended the First Consul in any way; as a matter of fact Bonaparte was at first hoping to capture the Duke de Berry,[2] who —the rumor ran—was to have landed in Normandy, if Pichegru had notified him that it was the right moment. This prince is closer to the throne than the Duke d'Enghien, and moreover, he would have broken the law by entering France. Therefore it suited Bonaparte better in every way to kill the Duke de Berry rather than the Duke d'Enghien. However, after coldly weighing the matter, he chose the second, since he could not get the first. Between the order to kidnap him and the order to kill him more than a week had elapsed, which means that Bonaparte ordered the Duke d'Enghien's martyrdom a long time in advance, as unconcernedly as he has since sacrificed millions of men to his ambitious whims.

Looking back, one is bound to wonder what were the motives for this horrible act, and I believe it is easy to unravel them. First,

---

[2] Colonel Savary was sent to the cliff of Biville with fifty men to wait for the prince and arrest him. For a long time he watched a suspicious brig which, at night, tacked in sight of the coast; but since no one disembarked, he returned without having been able to accomplish his mission.

Bonaparte wanted to reassure the revolutionary faction by contracting an alliance of blood with it. Hearing the news, an old Jacobin exclaimed, "So much the better! General Bonaparte has now become a member of the Convention." The Jacobins had long maintained that only a man who had voted for the death of the king could be chief magistrate of the Republic; that was what they called giving a pledge to the Revolution. Bonaparte fulfilled this criminal qualification, which was substituted for the property qualification required in other countries; he provided a guarantee that he would never serve the Bourbons; thus persons of that party who transferred their loyalty to him had to burn their ships, *never to return*.

On the eve of his coronation by those same men who had placed a ban on royalty, and of his reestablishment of a nobility with the support of the partisans of equality, he felt it necessary to reassure them with a monstrous guarantee: the assassination of a Bourbon. In the Pichegru-Moreau conspiracy, Bonaparte knew that the republicans and the royalists had united against him, and this strange coalition, whose sole bond was hatred of him, had astonished him. Several men who owed their positions to him had been chosen to work for the revolution that was to break his power, and so it was important to him that henceforth all his agents should believe themselves irretrievably ruined if their master should be overthrown. Finally, what he wanted above all—at the moment of seizing the crown—was to inspire such terror that no one would know how to resist him. He violated everything by a single act: the international law of European nations, the constitution as it then existed, public decency, humanity, and religion. Nothing could have been worse than this action; therefore everything was to be feared from the man who had committed it.

In France, it was believed for some time that the Duke d'Enghien's murder was the sign of a new revolutionary system and the scaffolds were about to be erected again. But Bonaparte wanted to teach the French only one thing: that he was capable of anything, to make them grateful for the evil he did not do, as one is grateful to others for the good they do. He was now considered merciful when he allowed a man to live, for it had been clearly

demonstrated how easily he could cause one to die! Russia,[3] Sweden—and especially England—complained of the violation of the
Germanic empire, but the German princes themselves were silent,
and the weakling sovereign on whose territory the atrocity had
been committed requested—in a diplomatic note—that nothing
more be said about *the event that had occurred*. The use of that
innocuous, veiled terminology for designating such an act certainly characterizes the baseness of those princes, who equated
their sovereignty with their revenues, and treated a state as a
capital asset on which interest must be collected as quietly as
possible.

---

[3] When Emperor Alexander imprudently complained of the violation of
German territory, the First Consul ordered our envoy, General Hédouville, to
leave Petersburg within forty-eight hours, and replied to the Russian government by a note in which he alluded to Paul I's assassination, which his son had
left unpunished.

CHAPTER XVI

Illness and death of Necker; Madame de

Staël's grief—Return to Coppet

My father lived long enough to hear of the Duke d'Enghien's assassination, and his last letters, written in his own hand, express his indignation at this atrocity.

Unexpectedly, at a time when I felt completely free from apprehension, I found two letters on my table, telling me that my father was dangerously ill.[1] I was not informed that the courier who had brought them had also brought the news of his death. I set out with hope, which I retained in spite of all the circumstances that should have extinguished it. At Weimar, when the truth was revealed to me, I was seized by a feeling of inexpressible terror and despair. I saw myself with no support in the world, compelled to face misfortune all by myself. There was still much in life to interest me, but the loving admiration I had felt for my father exercised an influence over me that nothing else could equal. Grief —the truest of prophets—made me realize that henceforth I should never be as completely happy as I had been as long as this exceedingly compassionate man watched over my fate, and not a single day has passed—since the month of April, 1804—in which

---

[1] Necker died on April 10, 1804. Madame de Staël learned on the morning of the eighteenth, while in Berlin, that he was "dangerously ill."

I have not connected all my sorrows with his loss. While my father
lived I suffered only through my imagination, for with real problems he always found a way to help me. After losing him, I had
to deal directly with destiny. However, I owe what strength I
still have to the hope that he is praying for me in heaven. It is not
filial love, but intimate knowledge of his character which makes
me affirm that I have never seen human nature closer to perfection
than in him; if I were not convinced of a future life, I would go
mad at the idea that such a being could have ceased to exist. There
was such a sense of immortality about his feelings and thoughts
that very often when I experience unusually exalted emotions I
can believe that I am hearing him still.

During my sad journey from Weimar to Coppet I felt envious
of all the life that was stirring in nature, even the birds and insects
flying around me. I prayed for a day, a single day to be able to
speak to him again, to arouse his pity. I envied those trees in the
forest that live longer than centuries. There is something about the
inexorable silence of the tomb which overwhelms the human spirit,
and although it is a well-known truth the profound impression it
produces can never be effaced. As I approached my father's house,
one of my friends pointed out some clouds on the mountain, resembling an immense human figure, which disappeared toward
evening. It seemed to me that the heavens were offering me a symbol of the loss I had just sustained. He was indeed great, this man
who never in his lifetime allowed the most important of his own
interests to take precedence over the least of his duties. His virtues
were so inspired by his goodness that he could have dispensed
with principles, and his principles were so sound that he could
have dispensed with goodness.

When I arrived at Coppet I learned that my father, during the
nine days of illness that had taken him from me, had continually
and anxiously thought about my future. He reproached himself
for his last book, as being the cause of my exile, and during his
fever, he wrote a letter in a trembling hand to the First Consul
assuring him that I had had nothing to do with the publication of
his last book, and that, on the contrary, I had not wanted it to be
printed. This dying man's voice had so much solemnity, this last

request from a man who had played so major a role in France, asking the return of his children to the place of their birth as an only favor and seeking pardon for imprudences that a daughter— who was still young at that time—might have committed, all this seemed irresistible to me. And although I knew the man's character, something happened to me which I believe is natural in those who wish ardently for the end of a great affliction: I hoped against all hope. The First Consul received this letter and no doubt thought me unusually simple-minded for deluding myself into believing that he would be touched by it. In this respect I share his opinion.

CHAPTER XVII

Moreau's trial–Pichegru's death–Moreau

before his judges

Moreau's trial was still going on,[1] and although the newspapers were completely silent on the subject, the public nature of the proceedings was enough to attract attention. In Paris, public opinion had never been so strongly anti-Bonaparte as it was then. The French have a greater need than any other people for a certain degree of freedom of the press; they need to think and feel in common. They need the spark of their neighbors' emotions if they are to experience something themselves, and their enthusiasm never develops in isolation. Therefore, anyone who wishes to become their tyrant would be wise to deny public opinion any form of expression. To this idea—common to all despots—Bonaparte adds a trick peculiar to this period: the art of spreading factitious opinions in newspapers which appear to be free, when in fact they are written under orders. It is undoubtedly only our French writers who can improvise in this way on the same sophisms each morning, and who revel in superfluity, even of servitude.

In the middle of the legal preliminaries of this famous affair, the newspapers informed Europe that Pichegru had strangled him-

---

[1] Moreau had been arrested on February 15 and taken to the Temple.

self in the Temple prison. The press printed a most outrageously ridiculous surgical report; they did not even know how to make the lie appear plausible. It would seem that a crime, in certain circumstances, can even upset those who boast of committing it with the utmost indifference. What appears certain is that one of the Emperor's mamelukes was ordered to suffocate Pichegru, and that General Savary supervised the deed. The state of mind of a brave general overcome by brutes in the depths of his dungeon, condemned for the past several days, defenseless, to that prison isolation which drain's one's courage, where he does not even know whether his friends will ever learn how he died, whether his death will be avenged, or whether his memory will be desecrated, is not hard to imagine. In his first interrogation Pichegru had shown a great deal of courage, and threatened, it is said, to give proof of the promises made by Bonaparte to the Vendéens concerning a Bourbon restoration. Some people claim that he had been tortured, as had two of the other conspirators, one of whom —named Picot—showed his mutilated hands to the Tribunal; and they say that the court did not dare show the French people one of their former defenders subjected, like a slave, to such torture. I do not agree with this conjecture. Bonaparte's acts should always be scrutinized to discover the calculation that caused them, and a close scrutiny yields no support for such a hypothesis, whereas the appearance of Moreau and Pichegru at the bar of a tribunal might perhaps have had the effect of arousing public opinion. Even so, there was an immense crowd in the tribunes, and several officers, headed by a loyal man, General Lecourbe, showed the deepest and most courageous concern for General Moreau. When he went before the Tribunal, the gendarmes who were guarding him respectfully presented arms. There was already a feeling that honor was on the side of the persecuted, but Bonaparte, by having himself suddenly proclaimed Emperor at the height of this ferment, diverted attention to other perspectives and concealed his course better in the midst of the storm surrounding him than he would have been able to do in a period of calm.

In court, General Moreau gave one of the finest speeches in the annals of history. He recalled, modestly, the battles he had won since Bonaparte had been governing France. He apologized for having frequently expressed himself with too great candor, and in an indirect way he compared the character of a Breton with that of a Corsican; in sum, he exhibited both a great deal of wit and the most perfect presence of mind at a very critical moment. At that time the Ministries of Police and Justice were combined under Régnier, in the absence of Fouché, who was out of favor. After leaving the tribunal, Régnier went to Saint-Cloud, where the Emperor asked him about Moreau's speech: "Pitiful," he answered. "In that case," said the Emperor, "have it printed and distributed throughout Paris." Afterward, when Bonaparte found out how mistaken his minister had been, he turned again to Fouché, the only man who could really support him and yet maintain—unfortunately for everyone—a kind of clever moderation in the service of a system that had none.

A former Jacobin—one of Bonaparte's tools—was commissioned to speak to the judges and persuade them to sentence Moreau to death. "It is necessary," he told them, "out of consideration for the Emperor, who had him arrested. But you need have no scruples about consenting to it, for the Emperor has resolved to pardon him."

"And, who will pardon us, if we involve ourselves in such an infamous decision?" asked one of the judges, whose name cannot be revealed, for fear of exposing him. General Moreau was sentenced to two years' imprisonment; Georges—and several others of his friends—to death; one of the Messieurs de Polignac to two years, the other to four years in prison, and both are still there, as well as several others whom the police seized after the sentence ordered by the court had been served. Moreau wanted his prison term changed to perpetual banishment; perpetual in this case means for life, and all the misery of the world is borne by a man in this situation. Bonaparte consented to this banishment, which suited him in every respect. The town mayors along Moreau's route responsible for stamping his passport often showed him the most respectful consideration. "Gentlemen," said one of them to those around him, "make way for General Moreau," and he bowed before him as he would have done before the Emperor. France still lived in these men's hearts, although people had ceased acting according to their convictions to the extent that nowadays one wonders whether people still have anything resembling convictions, after stifling them for so long. When he arrived at Cadiz, those same Spaniards who a few years later were to set such a splendid example rendered every possible homage to this victim of tyranny. When Moreau passed before the English fleet, the vessels saluted him as if he had been the commander of an allied army. Thus, France's so-called enemies undertook to pay off her own debt to one of her most illustrious defenders.

When Bonaparte had Moreau arrested, he said, "I could have made him come to me and I could have told him, 'Listen, you and I cannot remain on the same territory. Go away, since I am the stronger,' and I believe he would have left. But chivalrous manners are infantile when applied to affairs of state." Bonaparte believes, and has persuaded several Machiavellian apprentices of the new generation that any generous sentiment is childish. It is about time for him to be taught that virtue has something manly in it, more manly than crime in spite of all its audacity.

CHAPTER XVIII

Beginning of the Empire: Bonaparte

proclaimed Emperor—Creation of a new

nobility; servility of the old—The

"universal monarchy"

The motion to ask Bonaparte to assume the imperial crown was made in the Tribunate by a former Jacobin and member of the Convention, supported by Jaubert—a lawyer and commercial representative from Bordeaux—and seconded by Siméon, a man of wit and good sense, who had been proscribed as a royalist under the Republic. Bonaparte wanted the partisans of the old regime—and those with substantial interests in the nation—to unite in choosing him. It was agreed to open all the voting registrars in France so that everyone could express his wish regarding Bonaparte's coronation. However, without waiting for the result—foreordained though it was—he took the title of Emperor by means of a *senatus-consultum;* and the hapless Senate did not even have the strength to insist that the new monarchy be a constitutional one. A tribune—whose name I wish I could mention[1]—had the honor

---

[1] M. Gallois. (Note of A. de Staël, 1821 ed.)

of making a special motion for that purpose, but Bonaparte, in a clever move to forestall such a plan, summoned a few senators and said to them, "It distresses me greatly to put myself in such a prominent position. I really prefer my present situation. Still, the continuation of the republic is no longer possible, for everyone is sick of that regime. I believe the French want royalty. I had at first thought of recalling the old Bourbons, but that would only have ruined them, and myself with them. I am convinced, after due consideration, that there must be one man at the head of the nation, but perhaps it would be better to wait a while longer. . . . I have made France a century older in the last four years. Liberty means a good civil code, and the only thing modern nations care for is property. However, if you have confidence in me, name a committee, organize the constitution. And I tell you this in plain language," he added, smiling, "take precautions against my tyranny. Take them, believe me."

This conspicuous joviality seduced the senators, who, to tell the truth, wanted nothing more than to be seduced. One, a rather distinguished man of letters—but the kind of philosopher who always finds philanthropic reasons for being satisfied with the powers that be—said to a friend of mine, "It is so admirable—the simplicity with which the Emperor allows anything to be said to him! The other day I spent a whole hour proving to him the absolute necessity of basing the new dynasty on a charter which would assure the nation's rights."

"And what did he reply?" he was asked.

"He clapped me on the shoulder with perfect good humor, and told me, 'You are quite right, my dear Senator, but trust me, this is not the moment for it.'" And this senator, like many others, was quite satisfied with himself for having spoken out, even though his opinion was totally ignored. To the French, the requirements of self-esteem are more important by far than those of character.

A peculiarity of the French that Bonaparte has analyzed with extraordinary shrewdness is that they, so clever at ridiculing others, ask nothing better than to be ridiculous themselves the moment their vanity can profit by it. Indeed, nothing invites greater ridicule than the creation of an entirely new nobility such as the one which Bonaparte established to support his new throne. The princesses and queens, yesterday's citizennesses, could not even keep from laughing upon hearing themselves called "Your Highness." Others, more serious, delighted in having their title "Your Lordship" repeated from morning to night, like *Le Bourgeois Gentilhomme*. Old archives were searched for the best documents on etiquette; worthy men set about gravely composing coats of arms for the new families; in short, no day passed without some situation worthy of Molière arising. But the terror lurked in the background of this scene, and it prevented the grotesque in the foreground from being mocked as it deserved to be. Besides, the victories of the French generals redeemed everything, and obsequious courtiers glided to and fro in the shadow of the military men, who undoubtedly merited the austere honors of a free state, but not the empty decorations of such a court. Valor and genius are gifts from heaven, and those who are endowed with them need no other ancestry. In republics or limited monarchies honors are necessary to reward services rendered to the *patrie*, and all may aspire to them equally; but there is no greater mark of despotism than a whole host of honors emanating from the caprice of a single man.

Endless puns were made about this freshly minted nobility; a thousand remarks from the new ladies were quoted, all revealing them to be novices at the art of good manners. And certainly nothing is harder to learn than a form of politeness which is neither pompous nor too familiar; it may seem easy, but it has to be almost instinctive, for no one acquires it except from childhood training or nobility of character. Bonaparte himself is disconcerted in matters of deportment, and frequently, at home—and even with strangers—he reverts happily to vulgar expressions and habits which remind him of his revolutionary youth. Bonaparte was very much aware that the Parisians made jokes about his new nobles, but he also knew that their opinions would be expressed only in the form of mockery and not in violence. They did not venture beyond the ambiguity of puns; and just as in the Orient one is reduced to allegory, in France people had sunk even lower, limiting themselves to the rattling of syllables. One play on words does, however, deserve more than the fleeting attention usually afforded this genre. One day as the princesses of the blood were announced, someone cried out, "*Of the blood of Enghien!*" And indeed, the baptism of this new dynasty was just that.

Surrounding himself with his own nobility was not enough for Bonaparte; he wanted to mix the aristocracy of the new regime with that of the old. Several nobles who had been ruined by the Revolution consented to accept positions at court.[2] Bonaparte thanked them for their compliance with a gross insult, which is well-known. "I proposed to give them commissions in my army, and they declined," he said. "I offered them posts in the administration, and they refused. But when I opened my antechambers, they rushed forward in droves." During this period a few noblemen set an example by their courageous resistance, but untold numbers pretended to be threatened before they had anything to fear, and many solicited offices for themselves or their families, which all of them should have refused! Only in military or administrative careers can one feel confident of being useful to one's country, whoever the head of the government may be; positions at court, however, make one dependent on the man and not on the state.

Registers similar to those which had been opened for the Consulate for life were prepared for voting on the Empire. Similarly, all unsigned ballots were counted as "yes" votes; the few individuals who dared write "no" were dismissed from their positions. Monsieur de La Fayette—faithful advocate of liberty—again exhibited his invariable resistance,[3] which was all the more admirable since, in this land of bravery, courage was no longer

---

[2] Among Empress Josephine's ladies-in-waiting were noted, in addition to the former ladies-in-waiting (Mesdames de Rémusat, de Talhouët, de Lauriston, de Luçay), Mesdames de Chevreuse, de Mortemart, de Montmorency, de Bouillé, de Turenne, de Colbert, Octave de Ségur, etc. A Rohan was first chaplain of the Empress, Messieurs de Courtomer, d'Aubusson de la Feuillade her chamberlains, and the Count de Ségur, grand master of ceremonies. But what was most painful to Madame de Staël was the rumor that Monsieur de Narbonne, her former friend, agreed to serve Bonaparte.

[3] Here it seems that Madame de Staël confuses the facts. La Fayette had stated his vote against the Consulate-for-life thus: "I cannot vote for such a magistracy until public liberty is sufficiently guaranteed; then I will give my vote to Napoleon Bonaparte." But he did not take part in the vote on the Empire.

appreciated. This distinction must certainly be made, considering that in France fear reigns like a divinity over the most intrepid soldiers. Bonaparte would not even subject himself to the law of a hereditary monarch, but reserved the right to adopt or choose a successor, as they do in the Orient.[4] Since he had no children at that time, he did not want to give his family any rights whatever; and while elevating them to ranks to which they certainly had no claim he subjected them to his will through intricately contrived decrees which entwined their new thrones with chains.

The Fourteenth of July was celebrated again this year (1804), because—it was said—the Empire consecrated all the benefits of the Revolution. Bonaparte said that turmoil had strengthened the roots of government; he claimed that the throne would guarantee liberty; he stressed that Europe would be reassured by the reestablishment of a monarchy in France. All of Europe, in fact, except for England the illustrious, recognized his new dignity: he was called "my brother" by the former potentates of venerable royal chivalry. We have seen how he has rewarded them for their disastrous compliance. If he had sincerely wanted peace, old King George himself—that upright man who has had the finest reign in the history of England—would have been obliged to recognize him as his equal. But a few days after his coronation he said something which revealed his true designs: "People are joking," he said, "about my new dynasty. In five years' time it will be the oldest in Europe." And from that moment on, he has not ceased working toward that end.

He needed a pretext for continued aggressions, and this pretext was the freedom of the seas. It is quite astonishing how easy it is to make the cleverest people on earth accept something stupid for their rallying cry. Here is another of those contrasts which would be entirely inexplicable if unhappy France had not been stripped of religion and morality by a fatal sequence of ill-judged principles and unfortunate events. No man is capable of sacrifice without religion, and without morality no one speaks the truth, so public

---

[4] The *senatus-consultum* gave Napoleon the powers of *adoption;* in default of adoptive progeny, the imperial crown passed to the collateral line represented by Joseph and Louis, to the exclusion of Lucien.

opinion is forever being led astray. The result, as we have said, is that people do not have courage based on conscience, even though courage based on honor may remain; and that while outstanding intelligence goes into contriving the means, no one takes account of the end.

The sovereigns of Europe—at the moment when Bonaparte resolved to overthrow them—were all honorable men. The political and military genius of the world was extinct, but the people were happy; and although the principles of free institutions were not accepted in most countries, the philosophical ideas so widespread in Europe for fifty years had at least the effect of fending off intolerance and mollifying despotism. Catherine II and Frederick II sought the esteem of French writers, and these two monarchs, whose genius could not subjucate everything, lived in a circle of enlightened opinion and sought to captivate it. Men's natural tendency was toward the enjoyment and application of liberal ideas, and there was hardly an individual whose person or property was insecure. Advocates of freedom were certainly correct in thinking that people's faculties should be encouraged to develop; that it was unjust for a whole nation to depend on one man, and that a national representation was the only means of guaranteeing citizens the benefits that a virtuous sovereign might accord. But what did Bonaparte have to offer? Did he in fact bring foreign nations more liberty? There was not a monarch in Europe who would have committed—in an entire year—the arbitrary insolences which marked his every day. He came to offer them—in exchange for their peace of mind, their independence, their language, their laws, their wealth, their blood, and their children— shame, and the misfortune of being destroyed as nations and despised as men. In other words, he was implementing a plan for universal monarchy, the greatest scourge with which mankind can be threatened and the certain cause of perpetual war.

None of the arts of peace suits Bonaparte; he takes pleasure only in violent crises produced by battle. He has known how to make truces, but he has never sincerely said, *"Enough."* His character, at war with the rest of creation, is like the Greek flame, which no force of nature could extinguish.

A note by Auguste de Staël, Madame de Staël's son

There is a gap in the manuscript here, which I have already explained and which I could not try to fill. To enable the reader to follow my mother's story, I shall summarize the principal events in her life during the five years that separate the first part of her memoirs from the second.

On her return to Switzerland after the death of Monsieur Necker, his daughter first sought relief from her sorrow by composing an essay about her father and by collecting his last writing. In the autumn of 1804, she published her father's manuscripts, together with an essay on his character and private life.[1]

My mother's health, impaired by grief, necessitated her going to the south, and she departed for Italy.[2] The beautiful sky of Naples, the remains of antiquity, the masterpieces of art, all offered hitherto unknown sources of enjoyment. Her spirits, overwhelmed with sadness, seemed to revive at these new impressions, and she once more found strength to think and to write.

During this trip, my mother was treated without favor, but not unjustly by French diplomatic agents. She was forbidden a resi-

---

[1] *Du caractère de Monsieur Necker et de sa vie privée.* (*Oeuvres complètes,* t. XVII.) According to Benjamin Constant and Madame Necker de Saussure, this is the work which most exactly reveals Madame de Staël's character.

[2] In the spring of 1805.

dence in Paris, she was separated from her friends and her customary ways, but at least, during that time, tyranny did not pursue her beyond the Alps; persecution had not as yet been established as a system, as it was to be later on. I am even pleased to recall that some letters of introduction sent to my mother by Joseph Bonaparte helped to make her stay in Rome more agreeable.

She returned from Italy in the summer of 1805 and spent a year partly at Coppet and partly in Geneva, where several of her friends had gathered. During this period she began to write *Corinne*.

The following year her intense love for France prompted her to leave Geneva and draw nearer to Paris—forty leagues away—which was still permitted. I was then studying to enter the Polytechnical School, and because of her great concern for her children she wanted to supervise their education from a point as close as her exile would allow. She therefore settled in Auxerre, a small town where she knew no one, but whose prefect, Monsieur de la Bergerie, showed her great kindness.

From Auxerre she went to Rouen, drawing nearer by several leagues to the center which held the magnet of all her memories and childhood attachments. There, at least, she could receive daily letters from Paris; she had entered without hindrance into the circle that had been forbidden her, so she could hope that this fateful circle might gradually be narrowed. Only those who have suffered exile will understand her feelings. Monsieur de Savoie-Rollin was then the Prefect of Seine-Inférieure; the flagrant injustice of his removal from office several years later is well-known, and I have reason to believe that his friendship with my mother and the consideration he showed her during her residence at Rouen were not unconnected with the severe treatment he received later on.

Fouché was then Minister of Police. His system, as my mother reports, was to do as little evil as possible, beyond what was strictly necessary. The Prussian monarchy had just fallen; on the Continent there was no longer any enemy left to struggle against Napoleon's government; and no internal resistance thwarted his program or could serve as a pretext for arbitrary measures. There seemed to be no reason for prolonging that most unwarranted persecution of my mother. Fouché therefore permitted her to take up residence at a distance of twelve leagues from Paris, on an estate belonging to Monsieur de Castellane.[3] There she finished *Corinne* and supervised its printing. Moreover, the secluded life she led there, the extreme prudence of her conduct, and the very small number of people who braved official disfavor to visit her should have sufficed to reassure even the most suspicious despot. However, that did not satisfy Bonaparte. He wanted my mother to entirely renounce any use of her talent and to refrain from writing, even on subjects unconnected with politics. It will be seen later that even this sacrifice was not enough to protect her from an ever-increasing persecution.

Hardly had *Corinne* appeared than a new exile began for my mother, and all the hopes that had consoled her for several months vanished. By a sad coincidence which made her grief even more bitter, it was on April 9, the very anniversary of her father's death, that she received the order exiling her from her country and friends. She returned to Coppet, her heart broken, and the enormous success of *Corinne* provided very little distraction from her sorrow.

However, friendship succeeded in accomplishing what literary fame had been unable to do, and thanks to the expressions of affection she received on her return to Switzerland, the summer was even more pleasant than she had dared hope. Several friends came from Paris to visit her, and Prince Augustus of Prussia, who had gained his freedom with the coming of peace, did us the honor of spending several months at Coppet before returning home.[4]

Ever since her trip to Berlin, which had been so cruelly interrupted by her father's death, my mother had continued to study German literature and philosophy; but she needed an additional stay in Germany to complete the picture of that country which she wanted to present to France. In the autumn of 1807, she left for

---

[3] The Château of Acosta, near Aubergenville.
[4] It was in 1807 that the relationship took place which almost terminated in marriage between Prince Augustus and Madame Récamier. (See *Madame de Staël et Napoléon*, chap. 14.)

Vienna,[5] where she rediscovered—in the company of Prince de Ligne, Princess Lubomirski, and others—that urbanity of manners and facility of conversation which so delighted her. The Austrian government, exhausted by the war, did not have the strength to be an oppressor itself, and yet maintained an attitude toward France which was not without independence and dignity. Those who felt Napoleon's hatred could still find asylum in Vienna; consequently, the year my mother spent there was the most tranquil she had enjoyed since her exile.

On her return to Switzerland, where she spent two years writing her reflections on Germany, it did not take her long to perceive that the imperial tyranny was making progress each day, and that the passion for positions and the fear of disfavor were spreading with contagious rapidity. There were, to be sure, friends in Geneva and in France who maintained a courageous and constant fidelity to her in her misfortune, but anyone who had any connection with the government, or aspired to a government post, began to avoid her house and dissuade timid people from going there. My mother suffered from these evidences of servility, which she shrewdly discerned. The more unhappy she was, however, the greater was her need to overcome the difficulties of her situation and to partake of the life and intellectual activity which solitude threatened to exclude.

Her talent for elocution was her favorite means of distraction and in addition served to vary the pleasures of her guests. During this period, while continuing to write her great work *On Germany*, she also composed and played—in the theater of Coppet—most of the small pieces that I collected in her posthumous works under the title *Dramatic Compositions*.

Finally, at the beginning of the summer of 1810, having finished the three volumes of *On Germany*, she wanted to supervise its printing at forty leagues distance from Paris—a distance still permitted to her—where she might hope to see again those friends whose affections had not wavered in the face of the Emperor's disfavor.

---

[5] She arrived in Vienna early in January, 1808. (*Journal de l'Empire*, January 14, 1808.)

She therefore took up residence near Blois in the old Château Chaumont-sur-Loire, in which the Cardinal of Amboise, Diane de Poitiers, Catherine de Medicis, and Nostradamus had once lived. The present owner of this romantic castle, Monsieur Le Ray, with whom my parents had business ties and who was also a friend, was then in America. However, while we were occupying his château he returned from the United States with his family; and although he was kind enough to invite us to remain with him, the more he politely urged us to do so, the more tormented we were by the fear of inconveniencing him. Monsieur de Salaberry rescued us from this embarrassing situation with the greatest kindness by placing his property of Fossé at our disposal. Here my mother's story recommences.

PART TWO

CHAPTER I

Madame de Staël's stay at Fossé–Suppression

of her work On Germany–Exile from France:

letter from the Duke of Rovigo to Madame de

Staël–Return to Coppet

Since the owner of the Château of Chaumont had returned from America, I was no longer able to stay there, so I settled on the estate called Fossé, which a generous friend lent me. The estate was the home of a Vendéen soldier who was somewhat careless of its upkeep, but his good nature and ready wit made me feel at ease. We hardly had arrived when the Italian musician who was with us to give lessons to my daughter began to play the guitar, and my daughter, her harp, to accompany the sweet voice of my beautiful friend Madame Récamier, while peasants gathered at the windows, astonished to see this group of troubadours who had come to enliven their master's solitude. I spent my last days in France there, with a few friends of whom I still have fond memories.

Certainly this intimate group in this solitary residence, and our agreeable preoccupation with the fine arts did no harm to anyone. We often sang a charming tune composed by the Queen of Hol-

land, with the refrain "Do what you ought, come what may."
After dinner, we thought up the idea of seating ourselves around
a green table and writing notes to each other instead of conversing. These many and varied tête-à-têtes amused us so much that
we were impatient to leave the dinner table—where we spoke to
each other normally—to go and write to each other. When chance
strangers arrived, we could not bear to interrupt our diversion and
our "little post office" (which is what we called it) kept on going
all the same. The inhabitants of the neighboring town were somewhat astonished at our ways, and considered them pedantry,
whereas this game was only an expedient against the monotony
of solitude. One day a gentleman of the vicinity who had never
thought of anything but hunting all his life came to take my sons
on an outing to his woods. He remained seated for a while at our
active, silent table; in her pretty handwriting Madame Récamier
composed a little note to this rough hunter, so that he would not
feel too much of a stranger in our circle. He declined with apolo-
gies, assuring us that he could not read the writing in the lamp-
light. We laughed a little at this blow to our beautiful friend's
benevolent coquetry and we thought that a note from her hand
would not always have had the same fate. Our days were spent in
this way, and if I may judge from my own experience, no one felt
the time to be a burden.

The opera *Cinderella* was creating a sensation in Paris; I wanted
to go and see the production in a third-rate provincial theater in
Blois. When I emerged on foot, the townspeople followed me out
of curiosity, more eager to see me because I was an exile than for
any other reason. This kind of celebrity, which I owed to misfortune even more than to talent, irritated the Minister of Police,
who later wrote to the Prefect of Loir-et-Cher telling him that I
was surrounded by a court. "You may be sure at least," I told the
Prefect, "if I have a court, I do not owe it to power."

I was still determined to go to England by way of America, but
first I wanted to supervise the printing of my book *On Germany*.
The season was advancing; it was already September 15, and I
foresaw that the difficulty of embarking with my daughter would
detain me for another winter in some town or other, forty leagues

from Paris. At that time I had Vendôme in mind, where I knew several cultured people, and from which communication with the capital was easy. I, who had formerly had one of the most brilliant establishments in Paris now viewed with pleasure the prospect of living in Vendôme: fate, however, deprived me of even this modest happiness.

On September 23, I corrected the last proofs of *On Germany;* after six years' work and three volumes it was a real joy for me to write the words *the end.* I made up a list of one hundred persons in different parts of France and Europe to whom I wished to send copies; I set great store by this book, which I thought might bring some new ideas to France: it seemed to me to have been inspired by a sentiment which was uplifting without being hostile, and that people would find in it a language no longer spoken.

Provided with a letter from my publisher,[1] who assured me that the censor had authorized my book's publication, I thought I had nothing to fear, and my friends and I set out for Monsieur Mathieu de Montmorency's estate five leagues from Blois.[2] The house on this estate is in the middle of a forest. There I took walks with the man whom I respect most in the world, since losing my father. The beautiful weather, the magnificent forest, and the historical recollections associated with this spot—the scene of the battle of Fréteval between Philip Augustus and Richard the Lion-Hearted —all contributed to the calmest and most peaceful of moods. My worthy friend, whose only earthly preoccupation is to merit heaven, in this conversation as in all others we had had together, did not concern himself with current affairs but attempted only to do my soul good.

We resumed our journey the next day, and in those plains of Vendôme, where not a single habitation is to be seen and which,

---

[1] The publisher Nicolle, editor of *De l'Allemagne.* Actually Nicolle had printed the work before obtaining the censor's endorsement. Two of the three volumes had been examined, but it was not until September 26 that the inspection of the third was completed. In the view of the censors, Messieurs Pellenc and de la Salle, the work could be passed if the author would consent to some modifications (Archives nationales, F^{18}, 149^3) but on September 25 the Minister of Police had put the plates and pages under seal. The first two volumes had been printed at that time and work was about to begin on the third.

[2] The property of La Forest, or La Godinière. Madame de Staël left Fossé September 25.

like the sea, seem to present the same aspect everywhere, we lost
our way. It was midnight, and we did not know what road to take
in a countryside which looked the same from every view, and
whose fertility is as monotonous as a barren landscape is elsewhere, when a young man on horseback, guessing our difficulty,
invited us to spend the night at his parents' château.[3] We accepted
so opportune an invitation and suddenly found ourselves trans-
planted into the luxury of Asia mixed with the elegance of France.
Our hosts, who had spent many years in India, had brought back
a vast collection of Indian art. My curiosity was stirred and I felt
wonderfully contented there.[4] The next day, Monsieur de Montmorency gave me a note from my son, who urged me to return
home without delay because my book was meeting new difficulties
with the censors. My friends with me in the château advised me
to go; I did not suspect they were hiding something from me, and,
assuming there was nothing more than what Auguste had written,
I whiled away the time examining the rare Indian objects without
any idea of what awaited me. Finally, I climbed into the carriage
and my good, intelligent Vendéen, whose own perils had never
upset him, clasped my hand with tears in his eyes. Then I understood that they were keeping some new harassments a secret from
me, and Monsieur de Montmorency, in reply to my questions, told
me that General Savary, known as the Duke of Rovigo, had sent
his military police to destroy the ten thousand printed copies[5] of
my book, and that I had received an order to leave France within
three days. My children and my friends had not wanted me to hear
this news while I was among strangers, but they had taken every
possible precaution to prevent the seizure of my manuscript, and

---

[3] The Château de Conan, belonging to Monsieur Chevalier, today Prefect of
Var. (Note of A. de Staël, ed. of 1821.)

[4] (Note of A. de Staël, her son, edition of 1821.) Uneasy at not seeing my
mother arrive, I had mounted my horse to go to meet her, in order to soften—
as much as I could—the news that she must learn on her return; but I lost my
way as she had in the uniform plains of Vendôme, and it was only in the middle
of the night that a lucky chance led me to the door of the château that had
given her hospitality. I had Monsieur de Montmorency awakened and, after
having informed him of the increased amount of persecution that the imperial
police were directing against my mother, I left to finish putting her papers in
a safe place, leaving Monsieur de Montmorency the task of preparing her for
the new blow which threatened her.

[5] Five thousand of each of two volumes.

they succeeded in saving it a few hours before the police came to ask me for it.

This new setback was a great blow. I had anticipated some success with my book's publication. If the censors had initially refused to approve it, I would have understood my position. However, after having submitted to all their examinations, after having made the required changes, to learn that my book was destroyed and that I had to leave the friends who had been sustaining my courage, this made me weep. However, I tried once again to control myself in order to reflect on what must be done in a situation where my decision could have so much influence on my family's fate. Upon approaching my residence I gave my portable writing desk, which still contained some of my notes, to my youngest son; he jumped over the wall to approach the house by the garden. An English lady,[6] my very good friend, came to tell me about what had happened; from a distance I saw gendarmes prowling around my house, but they did not appear to be looking for me; they were no doubt in pursuit of other unfortunates—conscripts, exiles, people under surveillance—in short, groups of oppressed persons created by the present regime in France.

The Prefect of Loir-et-Cher came and asked for my manuscript. To gain time, I gave him a rough copy, and he seemed satisfied. I have since learned he was very harshly treated a few months afterward, to punish him for having shown me any consideration; and after having incurred the Emperor's disfavor he went into a depression which, they say, caused the illness that killed him in the prime of life. It is indeed an unfortunate country, where circumstances are such that a man of his intellect and talent succumbs to the chagrin of disfavor!

I read in the papers that some American ships had arrived in the English Channel ports, and I decided to use my passport for America, hoping it would be possible to land in England. However, I needed several days to prepare for the voyage, and I was obliged to write to the Minister of Police to request those few days.

---

[6] Mademoiselle Randall, an Englishwoman "cold, stiff, and plump," says Chamisso; she was Albertine de Staël's tutor. It was Mademoiselle Randall who copied, in her own hand, the manuscript of *Dix années d'exil.*

The French government's custom of ordering women—like recruits—to leave the country at twenty-four hours' notice has already been mentioned. Here is the Duke of Rovigo's reply; it is
interesting to observe its style.

General Police Administration
Office of the Minister
Paris, 3 October, 1810.

I have received, Madame, the letter with which you have
honored me. Your son must have informed you that I see no
objection to your delaying your departure by a week or so.
I hope this will be enough for you to make all your arrangements, for this is all I can grant.

You must not suppose that the order I sent you was motivated by your failure to mention the Emperor in your last
book. You would be very much mistaken: he could find no
place in it that would be worthy of him. Your exile is the
natural consequence of the course you have constantly pursued for the past several years. It seemed to me that the air
of this country did not agree with you and we have not yet
reached the point where we have to model ourselves on the
nations you admire.

Your last work is un-French; I am the one who stopped
its printing. I regret the losses to your publisher but I cannot allow its publication.

You are aware, Madame, that you were permitted to
leave Coppet only because you expressed the desire to go to
America. If my predecessor allowed you to reside in the
department of Loir-et-Cher, this was no reason for you to
regard that act of tolerance as a revocation of the measures
taken with regard to you. You now force me to see to their
strict execution; and you have only yourself to blame.

I am instructing Monsieur Corbigny[7] by letter to carry
out the order I have given him, as soon as the delay I have
granted you expires.

---

[7] Prefect of Loir-et-Cher.

I regret, Madame, that you have obliged me to begin my correspondence with you by a severe measure; I should have preferred to offer you only the assurances of my high esteem. I have the honor, Madame, to be

Your most humble and obedient servant,

Signed: the Duke of Rovigo.

P.S. I have good reasons, Madame, to indicate the following ports of embarkation to you: Lorient, la Rochelle, Bordeaux, and Rochefort are the only ports where you can board ship. I request you to let me know which one you choose.[8]

The sugar-coated hypocrisy with which he told me the air of this country did not agree with me, and the denial of the real reason for suppressing my book, should be noted. In fact, Savary had been more truthful in his conversation with my son; he had asked him why I never mentioned either the Emperor or the army in my work on Germany. "But," my son replied, "since the work is purely literary, I do not see how such subjects could have been introduced."

"Do you think, Monsieur," Savary replied, "that we have waged war in Germany for eighteen years so that a person as well-known as your mother may publish a book without saying a word about us? This book shall be burned, and the author deserves to be imprisoned in Vincennes."

On receiving the Minister of Police's letter, I paid attention to only one sentence, the one forbidding me to embark from the channel ports. I had already learned that they suspected me of intending to go to England, and meant to prevent that. This new chagrin was too much for me to bear; on leaving my native country, I needed to go to a country of my own choice; on parting from my lifelong friends, I at least had to be among friends of all that is good and noble, the kind of people with whom one is always in sympathy, even when not knowing them personally. All at once I saw everything which was sustaining me crumble. For a short

---

[8] This postscript is easy to understand; its objective was to keep me from going to England. (Edition of 1821.)

while, I wanted to embark on a ship for America, hoping it would
be captured en route, but I was too shaken to make such a drastic
decision; and since I was given alternatives of either America or
Coppet, I settled on the latter course, for deep feelings still drew
me to Coppet in spite of the troubles I was always subjected to
there.

My two sons tried to see the Emperor at Fontainebleau, where
he was at that time; they were told they would be arrested if they
remained there; all the more reason why I myself was prohibited
from going. I had to return to Switzerland from Blois, where I
was staying, without going nearer to Paris than forty leagues. The
Minister of Police had said—in privateering jargon—that at
thirty-eight leagues "I was a lawful prize"; that was his piratical-
minister expression. Thus, when the Emperor exercises the arbitrary right of banishment, neither the exiled person, nor his
friends, nor even his children, can reach him to plead the cause
of the unfortunate who is being torn from the objects of his affections and his habits; and these banishments, which now are
irrevocable—especially in the case of women—these banishments,
which the Emperor has rightly termed "proscriptions," are de-
creed without the victim's being allowed to present any defense,
assuming that the crime of having displeased the Emperor even
allows for any.

Although I had been restricted to forty leagues, I had to pass
through Orléans, a rather dull city but the residence of some very
pious women who have taken refuge there. While strolling
through the town I stopped in front of the monument to Joan of
Arc. "Certainly," I thought, "when she delivered France from the
English, even then, France was freer by far, and more truly
France than she is at the present time." Wandering through a
town where you are neither known nor recognized by anyone is
an odd sensation. I felt a kind of bitter pleasure in contemplating
my own isolation, and in looking once more at the France I was
about to leave—perhaps forever—without speaking to anyone,
without anything to distract me from observing the country itself.
Passers-by occasionally stopped to look at me, because I think that
in spite of myself I had a woeful expression; but they quickly

went on their way, for people have long since grown accustomed to seeing suffering.

Fifty leagues from the Swiss border the French frontier begins to bristle with fortifications, prisons, and with towns serving as prisons, and one sees nothing but individuals restrained by the will of one man, conscripts of misfortune, detained far from where they would wish to live. At Dijon some Spanish prisoners who had refused to take the oath of allegiance came to the town square to bask in the midday sun, because they considered the noon sun their compatriot. They wrapped themselves in tattered cloaks, wearing them with dignity, and they were proud of their poverty, which was a result of their pride; they took pleasure in their sufferings, which associated them with the misfortunes of their intrepid homeland. Sometimes they were seen going into a café only to read the newspaper, in order to guess the fate of their friends through the lies of their enemies; their faces were immobile but not without expression; their strength was held in check by will power. Farther along, at Auxonne, was the residence of some English prisoners who had recently saved a house from burning in the town to which they were restricted. At Besançon there were more Spaniards. Among the many French exiles throughout the French provinces, there was one—an angelic person, living in the citadel of Besançon in order not to abandon her father, and who had long shared all kinds of danger with the one to whom she owed her life.[9] This was Mademoiselle de Saint-Simon.

Entering Switzerland, one can see on the mountaintops separating it from France the fortress of Joux, where prisoners are kept; their whereabouts are frequently unknown, even to their relatives. Toussaint-Louverture died in this prison from the cold. Although

---

[9] Claude-Anne, Marquis de Saint-Simon, born in France in the Château of la Faye in 1743, belonged to the same family as the author of the *Mémoires*. He had been elected in April, 1789, by the nobility of Angoumois as deputy to the Estates-General. An émigré, a general in the service of Spain, he defended Madrid in 1808 when the French attacked that city. Made prisoner and condemned to death as a French émigré, he obtained a stay of execution, then a commutation of punishment at the entreaty of his daughter, who threw herself at the knees of Napoleon. Taken to France, he was imprisoned in the citadel of Besançon, where he remained until 1814.

he deserved his fate, because of his cruelty, the last man to have
the right to inflict it on him was the Emperor, who had guaranteed him his liberty and his life. I walked past this fortress one day
when the weather was dreadful. I thought about this Negro
suddenly transported to the Alps, for whom this residence was
an icy Hell. I thought about the more noble human beings who
had been shut up there, about those who were still suffering there,
and I also realized that if I were imprisoned there, I would never
leave it alive. Nothing can convey to the few free nations left on
this earth the total lack of security which has become the normal condition of all human creatures under Napoleon's Empire.
Other despotic governments have customs, laws, and a religion
which the ruler never violates, no matter how absolute his power.
But since in France, and in French-held Europe, everything is
new, no past traditions remain to serve as a guarantee, and there
is everything to be hoped for, or to be feared, depending on
whether or not one serves the interests of the man who dares to
make himself—and himself alone—the object of the entire human race.

CHAPTER II

More harassment–Monsieur Capelle, Prefect

of Léman–Doubling of surveillance–Removal

of Schlegel–Plan of departure for Sweden

On returning to Coppet[1] with my wings clipped—like La Fontaine's pigeon—I saw a rainbow appear over my father's house;
I dared to interpret it as a good omen; for nothing in my sorrow-
ful journey had eliminated hope. I had almost resigned myself to
living in this château and publishing nothing more on any subject.
However, in sacrificing the talents that I felt I possessed, I needed
at least to find happiness through my affections, and here is how
my private life was arranged for me, after I had been robbed of
my literary existence.

The first order received by the Prefect of Geneva was to inform my two sons that they were forbidden to enter France without a new police authorization.[2] This was to punish them for
having wished to speak to Bonaparte on their mother's behalf.
The morality of the present government thus consists in breaking
family ties so that the Emperor's will may be all-powerful. Sev-

---

[1] At the end of October, 1810.

[2] The same prohibition was made for Madame de Staël. (Letter from the
Prefect of Léman to the Minister of Police, October 27, 1810. Archives nationales F7 6331.)

eral generals are said to have declared that if Napoleon should order them to throw their wives and children into the river they would not hesitate to obey him. What this really means is that they prefer the money given them by the Emperor to the family given them by Nature. There are many instances of this kind of thinking, but few people are brazen enough to express it. Seeing my situation for the first time weigh heavily on my young sons gave me great pain. No matter how resolute we are about our own conduct when it is based on sincere convictions, when others begin to suffer because of us, it is almost impossible not to reproach ourselves. My two sons, however, generously helped me to dismiss this thought from my mind, and we found mutual support in the memory of my father.

Some days later, the Prefect of Geneva wrote me a second letter, asking, in the name of the Minister of Police, for whatever proofs of my book I still had. The Minister knew exactly how many I had handed over and how many I had retained; his spies had certainly served him well. In my reply I gave him the satisfaction of acknowledging that his information had been correct, but at the same time I told him that the proofs were no longer in Switzerland and that I neither could nor would return them. I added, however, my promise not to have an edition published on the Continent. It took no great merit to promise this, for in those days no continental government would have dared to publish a book banned by the Emperor.

Not long afterward, the Prefect of Geneva was dismissed from office and it was generally believed that I was the cause. He was one of my friends, but for all that, he had not disobeyed his orders, and although he was one of the most honest and enlightened men in France, his own principles made him scrupulously obey the government he served. Neither ambition nor selfish motives inspired this zeal. Still, I was greatly chagrined to be—or seem to be—the cause of such a man's dismissal. Generally speaking, Geneva regretted his departure, and no sooner was it believed that I had had some part in it than all aspirants to government positions kept away from my house as from a deadly epidemic. However, I still had more friends in Geneva than in any other provincial city in France; for that city's heritage of liberty has kept alive many noble sentiments. And yet, what anxiety one suffers at the thought that one's visitors will be compromised! I took to making precise inquiries about every person's relationships before extending him an invitation; for even if he merely had a cousin who wanted a position, or already had one, it was like asking for an act of Roman heroism simply to propose that he dine with me.

At last, in March, 1811, a new prefect arrived from Paris.[3] He was a man exceptionally well-suited for the present regime; in other words, he had an extensive knowledge of facts and a complete absence of principles in matters of government, calling every fixed rule vague, and placing his conscience in the service of those in power. The first time I saw him he immediately told me that my kind of talent was well-suited for glorifying the Emperor: a worthy subject for the kind of enthusiasm I had shown in *Corinne*. I answered that since I was persecuted by the Emperor all my praises would have the air of a petition, and in such circumstances I was convinced that the Emperor himself would find them ridiculous. He vigorously opposed this opinion; several times he returned to my house to beg me, in my own interest—he said —to write something in favor of the Emperor; a four-page article, he assured me, would be enough to end all my troubles. What he said to me he repeated to all my acquaintances. Finally, one day he suggested that I celebrate the King of Rome's birth in verse; laughing, I replied that I had no ideas on the subject, and that my only wish would be that he have a good wet nurse. This pleasantry put an end to the Prefect's negotiations with me about my writing in favor of the present government.

A short time afterward the doctors prescribed mineral waters for my younger son. There were spas at Aix in Savoy, a dozen leagues from Coppet. I chose early May for going, the time of year when almost no one is ever there. I informed the Prefect of this little trip, and secluded myself in a village where I had no acquaintances. Barely ten days later a courier arrived from the

---

[3] Monsieur Capelle, future minister to Charles X. He came from the Préfecture de la Meditérranée, whose capital was Livourne.

Prefect of Geneva, ordering me to return. He said that he and the
Prefect of Mont-Blanc, where I was, feared that I might leave Aix
and go to England to write in opposition to the Emperor; and although London was not exactly close to Aix in Savoy, his gendarmes were sent out to make sure that no one would give me
post horses along the way.[4] I am tempted to laugh now at all
this "prefectoral" activity against a poor and feeble creature like
myself, but at that time I was frightened to death at the very
sight of a gendarme. After so rigorous an exile I was afraid the
next step might be imprisonment, which would have been more
terrible for me than death itself. I knew that if I were once arrested, if the Emperor once braved the scandal he would not permit any further mention of me—assuming anyone would have the
courage to try—hardly likely at that court, where terror prevails
every minute of the day and in every aspect of life.

On my return to Geneva, the Prefect notified me that not only
was I forbidden to set foot anywhere on French territory but that
I was also advised not to travel in Switzerland and never to go
farther than two leagues from Coppet in any direction. I objected
that since I was domiciled in Switzerland I did not understand by
what right a French authority could keep me from traveling in a
foreign country. He undoubtedly thought me a bit stupid to discuss a question of rights at this time, and repeated his advice,
which was singularly like an order. I held to my protest, but the
next day I learned that one of the most distinguished German
men of letters, Monsieur Schlegel, who for eight years had
taken charge of my sons' education, had just been ordered to leave
not only Geneva but also Coppet. I wanted to object again that
in Switzerland the Prefect of Geneva had no right to give orders;
but I was told that, if I preferred, the orders could be conveyed
by the French ambassador: the ambassador would simply apply

----

[4] True. Capelle's letter to the Duke of Rovigo, May 22, 1811. Here is Madame
de Staël's reply to the letter which Capelle wrote her: "Aix, May 24, 1811.
Monsieur, I am in receipt of the letter that you honored me by writing to indicate that I am not to remain in Aix. As a result of this, I must say, rather
extraordinary order, I shall leave my son alone here to continue the baths, and
as soon as my carriage is ready, tomorrow or the day after at the latest, I will
return to Geneva. I have the honor . . ."

to the *Landammann*, and the *Landammann* to the canton of Vaud, which would send Monsieur Schlegel from my home. By making despotism take this detour, I managed to gain ten days, but nothing more. I asked why I was being deprived of the companionship of Monsieur Schlegel, my friend, and my children's friend. The Prefect, like most of the Emperor's agents, habitually used honeyed phrases with very harsh acts; he told me that the government was sending Monsieur Schlegel away for my own good, since he was making me anti-French. Truly touched by the government's paternal attention, I asked what Monsieur Schlegel had ever done against France. The Prefect cited his literary opinions, giving as an example a pamphlet in which—in comparing the *Phèdre* of Euripides with that of Racine—he had given preference to the former. It was indeed exquisite taste for a Corsican monarch to take sides in this way, concerning nuances of meaning in French literature. Of course, in truth, Monsieur Schlegel was exiled because he was my friend, because his conversation cheered me in my solitude, and because they were beginning to put into operation the system that would make a prison of my soul by depriving me of all the pleasures of intellect and friendship.

Once more I resolved to go away, a resolution I had renounced so often because of the thought of leaving my friends and the ashes of my parents. But a tremendous problem remained: the means of departure. The French government created so many difficulties about a passport for America that I no longer dared to take this course. Besides, I had reason to fear that when I tried to embark they would claim that I was going to England,[5] and would use against me the decree that condemned to prison all those who tried to go there without the government's authorization. Therefore, it seemed infinitely preferable to go to Sweden,

---

[5] Capelle wrote to the Duke of Rovigo (January, 1812): "Most of her fortune is in investments. She has capital in London; recently she had some of it transferred to America, where she is thinking of going. But I think I can assure you that *she has not thought of going directly to England*. However, it is possible that she has had the ulterior motive of going there, once in America."

to that reputable country whose new ruler already showed signs of the glorious conduct he has since sustained.[6] But what route to take was also a problem. The Prefect had made it perfectly clear that I would be arrested wherever France ruled; and how was I to go where she did not rule? I would have to go by way of Russia, since the Confederation of the Rhine and Denmark—those disguised French provinces—blocked every other route. However, to get to Russia I would have to cross Bavaria and Austria. I felt I would be safe in Tyrol, even though it was united to a confederated state, because of the courage its unfortunate inhabitants had shown. As for Austria, in spite of the humiliation to which it had been subjected, I had enough confidence in its monarch to believe that he would not hand me over; although I also knew that he could not defend me. After having sacrificed the ancient honor of his house, what kind of strength did he have left? So I spent my days studying the map of Europe in order to flee, just as Napoleon studied it in order to make himself its master, and my campaign—like his—always had Russia as its objective. That country was the last refuge for oppressed people; which was why it had to be the country the conqueror of Europe wanted to destroy.

------

[6] The reference is to Bernadotte, Crown Prince of Sweden. This part of *Dix années d'exil* was written in Stockholm in 1812–1813.

CHAPTER III

Application for a Russian passport—
Travel in Switzerland with Monsieur de
Montmorency—The Trappists of Val-Sainte—
Excursion on French territory; reprimand
from the Prefect

Having resolved to go by way of Russia, I now needed a passport to enter it. Another difficulty arose here: one had to write to Petersburg for this passport, a formal procedure made necessary by political circumstances, and although I was confident of not meeting with a refusal from a person as generous as Emperor Alexander, I was afraid that my request might be discussed in the offices of his ministers and that if the news reached the French ambassador I would be arrested in order to keep me from carrying out my plan. So I had to go first to Vienna, write from there for my passport, and wait for it there. The six weeks from the sending of my letter to the receipt of an answer had to be spent under the protection of a ministry which had given the Archduchess of Austria to Bonaparte; could I entrust myself to it? Still, if I remained a hostage in Napoleon's hands, not only would

I be renouncing all exercise of my own talents but I would also be preventing my sons from having careers; they could neither serve under Bonaparte, nor against him, and no education could be arranged for my daughter without either sending her away from me or cloistering her at Coppet. On the other hand, if I should be arrested while fleeing, all would be lost for my children, for they would never have consented to separate their fate from mine.

In the middle of these anxieties Monsieur Mathieu de Montmorency, a friend of twenty years' standing, proposed to visit me, as he had already done several times since my exile. It is true that other friends wrote me from Paris that the Emperor had expressed his disapproval of anyone's visiting Coppet, and in particular Monsieur de Montmorency. But I must confess I tried to forget these remarks of the Emperor's—which I dismissed as the kind he sometimes uses to frighten people—and I did not put up much resistance to Monsieur de Montmorency, who generously tried to reassure me in his letters. No doubt I was wrong; but who could believe that it would be thought criminal for an exiled woman's old friend to come and spend several days with her? Monsieur de Montmorency's life, entirely devoted to pious works and to family attachments, was so far removed from politics that unless one wished to exile saints it seemed to me impossible to attack such a man. I also wondered what could be gained by such an attack, a question I always asked myself where Napoleon's conduct was concerned. I know that he will not hesitate to do anything evil which can be the least bit useful to him; but I cannot always gauge the extent of his immense egoism and its concern with the infinitely little as well as the infinitely great.

Although advised by the Prefect not to travel in Switzerland, I did not heed a counsel that could not be made by a formal order. I met Monsieur de Montmorency at Orbe, and proposed—as an excursion in Switzerland—that we return by way of Fribourg, in order to visit the female Trappist convent not far from the men's monastery in the Val-Sainte.

We arrived at the convent in a downpour, after having had to go a quarter of a league on foot. Just as we were about to enter, the Trappist superior who directs the nunnery told us no one could be received there. Nevertheless, I tried ringing the bell at the entrance to the cloister; a nun appeared behind the grilled opening through which the sister on duty can speak to strangers. "What do you want?" she asked me in a ghostlike voice without any inflection. "I should like to visit your convent," I said to her.

"That is impossible," she replied.

"But I am very wet," I said, "and I need to dry myself." She then touched some spring, which opened the door to an outer room, in which I was allowed to rest; but no living being appeared. After a moment, impatient at not being able to enter the interior of the house, I rang again. The same sister came back. I again asked her if no females were ever received in the convent. She answered that only those could enter who intended to become nuns. "But," I said to her, "how can I know if I wish to enter your order if I am not permitted to become acquainted with it?"

"Oh," she replied, "that would be useless. I am quite sure that you have no vocation for our calling."

And having said this, she closed her window. I do not know how that nun had perceived my worldly inclinations; perhaps a lively manner of speaking, so different from theirs, is enough for them to recognize travelers who are merely curious. Since the hour of vespers was approaching, I was allowed into the church to hear the nuns sing; they were seated behind a dense black grille completely shielded from view. The only noise was the clatter of their wooden shoes and the wooden benches that they pulled forward to sit on. Their singing displayed little feeling, and I had the impression, either from their manner of praying or from the conversation I had afterward with the Trappist father who directed them, that their way of life was made bearable not by religious enthusiasm such as we conceive it, but by strict, sober self-discipline. For even the emotion of piety could drain one's strength; a certain toughness of soul is necessary for so rugged an existence.

The new Father Abbot of the Trappists in the valleys of Fribourg canton has further increased the austerities of the order.

The world has no idea of the endurance demanded of the monks: when they have to stand immobile for several hours, they are even forbidden to lean against the wall or dry the perspiration from their foreheads; their days are filled with suffering, just as worldly people fill theirs with pleasure. They seldom reach old age, and the monks who do grow old consider this fate a punishment from heaven. Such an establishment would be barbarous if one were forced to enter it, or if its hardships were concealed. But a printed statement is freely distributed in which the order's rigors are exaggerated rather than softened; and yet novices are willing to take the vows, and those admitted do not run away, although they could do so very easily. As I see it, everything is based on the powerful idea of death. The institutions and amusements of worldly society turn our thoughts toward enjoying life; but when man is obsessed with the contemplation of death, and when he also believes in the immortality of the soul, he is bound to be disgusted with worldly things; and as sufferings seem to mark the route to the future life, one is eager for them, like a traveler who willingly tires himself in order to reach his destination more quickly. What astonished and saddened me, however, was to see children brought up under this severe regime—their poor shaven heads, their young faces prematurely lined, their funereal garments before they had become acquainted with life or had voluntarily renounced it. All this made me very angry with the parents who had put them there. Horror as well as respect is inspired when anyone is made to become a novice without having any choice in the matter. The monk with whom I talked spoke only of death; all his ideas originated or related to it: death is the sovereign monarch of this place. Since we were talking about worldly temptations I told the Trappist father how much I admired him for having sacrificed everything in order to escape from them. "We are cowards," he said, "who have retired into a fortress because we feel we do not have enough courage to meet our enemy on the battlefield." This reply was as witty as it was modest.[1] A few days later the French government ordered the

---

[1] (Note of A. de Staël, Madame de Staël's son.) I accompanied my mother on the excursion here described. Struck by the wild beauty of the place and

Father Abbot, Monsieur de l'Estrange, to be seized, the property of the order confiscated, and the fathers expelled from Switzerland. I do not know what Monsieur de l'Estrange was accused of, but it is hardly likely that such a man would have meddled in worldly affairs, still less the monks, who never left their solitude. The Swiss government searched everywhere for Monsieur de l'Estrange, and I hope, for the sake of its honor, that it took care not to find him. But the unfortunate magistrates of France's so-called allies are often made to arrest designated persons without knowing whether they are delivering innocent or guilty victims to the great Leviathan who sees fit to swallow them. The Trappists' property was seized—or rather, their tomb, for they possessed nothing else—and the order was dispersed. It is said that a Trappist of Genoa had mounted the pulpit to retract his oath of allegiance to the Emperor, declaring that since the Pope had been imprisoned, ecclesiastics were no longer bound by this oath. It is also said that at the end of this act of repentance, he was judged guilty by a military commission and shot. It seems to me that they could have considered his punishment sufficient and

---

interested by the intelligent conversation of the Trappist who had received us, I requested his hospitality until the next day, when I intended to cross the mountain on foot, in order to visit the great convent of Val-Sainte and to rejoin my mother and Monsieur de Montmorency at Fribourg. This monk, with whom I continued to converse, had no difficulty in perceiving that I hated the imperial government, and I guessed that he shared my sentiment. However, after having thanked him for his kindness, I completely lost sight of him, and I did not think he had kept the slightest recollection of me.

Five years afterward, in the first months of the Restoration, I was surprised to receive a letter from this same Trappist. He said that he did not doubt that, with the legitimate king restored to the throne, I had a great many more friends at court, and he asked me to use their influence to have the property that his religious order owned in France returned. The letter was signed Father A——, priest and bursar of la Trappe; and he added as a postscript: "If twenty-three years of emigration and four campaigns in a regiment of horse troops in Condé's army give me any rights to royal favor, I beg you to make use of them." I could not keep from laughing both at the influence that this good religious man assumed I had and at the use of it that he asked of a Protestant. I sent his letter to Monsieur de Montmorency, whose influence was greater than mine, and I believe that the petition was granted.

However, these Trappists, withdrawn into the high valleys of the canton of Fribourg, were not as foreign to politics as their residence and their dress might make one believe. I have learned since that they served as intermediaries in the correspondence between the clergy of France and the Pope, then prisoner at Savona. To be sure, that does not excuse the rigor with which these religious men were treated by Bonaparte, but it explains it.

not have made the whole order responsible for his conduct.

We reached Vevey by going through the mountains, and planned to proceed as far as the entrance to the Valais, which I had never seen. We stopped at Bex, the last Swiss village, for the Valais was already annexed to France. A Portuguese brigade had come from Geneva to occupy the Valais: what a bizarre destiny for Europe, to have Portuguese soldiers, garrisoned in Geneva, taking possession of a part of Switzerland in the name of France!

People had often spoken about the Cretins in the Valais, and I was curious to see them. This sad degradation of man is a good subject for reflection; but it is extremely painful to look at the human face when it has become so repugnant and horrifying. However, some of these imbeciles had a kind of vivacity which results from their perpetual astonishment at exterior objects. Since they never recognize what they have already seen, they are always surprised, and life's spectacle is new to them each day in all its many details. Perhaps this is the compensation for their unfortunate condition, for surely there must be one. A few years ago a Cretin was condemned to death for committing a murder; as he was led to his execution, finding himself in a crowd of people he thought that they were there to honor him, and holding himself erect, he smiled and straightened his clothes so as to be more worthy of the festivity. Was it right to punish such a creature for the crime that his hands had committed?

Three leagues from Bex there is a famous waterfall where the water tumbles down from a very high mountain. I suggested to my friends that we go to see it, and we returned before dinner. It is true that this waterfall was under Valais jurisdiction, and consequently on French territory, but I forgot that I was permitted to enter only the area between Coppet and Geneva. When I returned home, the Prefect not only reprimanded me for having dared to travel in Switzerland but also wanted me to consider his silence concerning my crime of setting foot on French territory as proof of his great indulgence. I might have quoted La Fontaine's fable:

> I graze in this meadow to the extent my tongue
> will allow . . .

but I simply admitted that I was wrong to have visited the Swiss
waterfall without thinking that it was in France.

CHAPTER IV

*The exiling of Monsieur de Montmorency
and of Madame Récamier—New harassments—
Causes of Bonaparte's animosity; Coppet
prohibited—Exile of Monsieur de Saint-
Priest—Why Madame de Staël hesitates to flee*

This continual wrangling about my every move made life odious to me, and I could not distract myself by working; for I was depressed by the fate of my book and by the fact that I could no longer hope to publish anything, for I need competition as an incentive to work. However, I still could not make up my mind to leave the borders of France forever, as well as my father's residence, and my faithful friends. Every day I thought about leaving, and every day I found some pretext for remaining, but finally the ultimate blow was dealt me: God knows how I have suffered from it!

Monsieur de Montmorency came to spend a few days with me

Madame de Staël (*After a portrait by François Gérard.*)

Auguste de Staël, Madame de Staël's
(*From a portrait by Anne Louis Giro*
de Roucy Trioson. Reproduced by k
permission of the Château de Coppet.)

Napoleon Bonaparte

The Morning of the 18th Brumaire, Napoleon becomes First Consul of France. Included are Josephine and Napoleon Bonaparte (center), Joseph Bonaparte, Lucien Bonaparte, Talleyrand, and Generals Bernadotte, Leclerc, and Moreau. (*Engraving from a painting by Schopin.*)

Benjamin Constant

Joseph Fouché (*Engraving after a painting by Claude-Marie Dubufe.*)

Charles Maurice de Talleyrand (*Engraving after a portrait by François Gérard.*)

Jacques Necker, Madame de Staël's father (*From a contemporary lithograph.*)

Madame Juliette Récamier (*From a painting by David.*)

Lucien Bonaparte (*From a contemporary lithograph.*)

Church square in St. Petersburg

Harbor of St. Petersburg, bridge over the Neva River

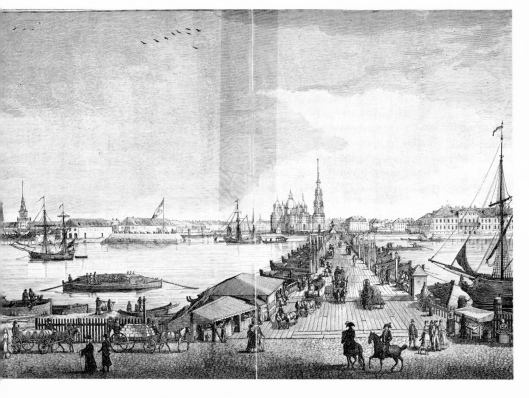

Merchants of St. Petersburg

Alexander I, Emperor of Russia

at Coppet, and the master of the great French empire so well calculated his mean, petty details that when the courier announced Monsieur de Montmorency's arrival at my house he also delivered his letter of exile. The Emperor would have been unhappy if this order had not reached him at my home, and if there had not been an indication in the minister's letter that I was the cause of his exile. Monsieur de Montmorency tried his best to soften this news for me; but—and I say this to Bonaparte so that he may congratulate himself for having attained his objective—I cried in anguish on hearing of the trouble I had caused my noble friend; and never was my heart, afflicted as it had been for so many years, closer to despair. I did not know how to dispel the agonizing thoughts that haunted me, and so I turned to opium to numb my anguish for a few hours. Monsieur de Montmorency, who remained calm and spiritual, set a good example for me; but he was sustained by his awareness of the devotion he had deigned to show me, whereas I, for my part, reproached myself for the cruel consequences of this devotion which was to separate him from his family and his friends. I prayed to God ceaselessly, but grief left me no respite, and my life was unbearably painful to me.

In the midst of all this, I had a letter from Madame Récamier, that lovely lady who has received compliments from all of Europe and has never abandoned an unhappy friend. She wrote that on her way to the spas at Aix in Savoy she intended to visit me, and that she would arrive in two days. I trembled in case she should suffer the fate of Monsieur de Montmorency. Unreasonable though it was, I feared the worst from such a barbarous and meticulous hatred and I sent a courier to meet Madame Récamier, to beg her not to come to Coppet. It was painful to know that she was only a few leagues away, she who had constantly consoled me with her kindness; to know that she was there, so near to my home, and that I was forbidden to see her again, and that this was perhaps the last chance! I implored her not to stop at Coppet; she would not listen: she could not pass under my windows without spending some hours with me, and, tearfully, I saw her enter this château where her arrival had always been such a happy event. She left the next day, and went at once to a relative's home, some fifty leagues from Switzerland. It was in vain; cruel exile was imposed upon her: she intended to visit me, and that was enough; generosity and pity had inspired her, so she had to be punished. The misfortunes she had experienced made the loss of her natural setting extremely painful for her. Separated from all her friends, she has spent entire months in a small provincial town, a victim of the saddest and dreariest solitude. Such is the fate I procured for the most brilliant woman of her time; and the leader of the French—a people renowned for their gallantry —showed no consideration for the prettiest woman in Paris. In a single day he struck at birth and virtue in the person of Monsieur de Montmorency, at beauty in the person of Madame Récamier, and—though I dare say it myself—at a certain reputation for talent in my case. Perhaps he imagined he could attack my father's memory through his daughter, so that one might truly say that in this land neither the dead nor the living, neither pity nor charm, neither intelligence nor fame counted for anything under his reign. Anyone who failed in the delicate nuances of flattery, or who did not abandon someone in disgrace, was culpable. He recognizes only two classes of men, those who serve him, and those who dare, without even harming him, simply to live their own lives. From petty housekeeping details to the direction of empires, he does not want a single will to be exercised independently of his anywhere in the world.

"Madame de Staël," the Prefect of Geneva liked to say, "has arranged a pleasant existence for herself; her friends and even foreigners come to visit her at Coppet. The Emperor will not stand for that." And why was he tormenting me in this way? To make me publish praises of him;[1] and what good would these praises do him, among the thousands constantly offered him out of fear and hope? Bonaparte once said, "If I had the choice of doing a

---

[1] It seems indeed to be true that the proposal was made to Madame de Staël that her book *De l'Allemagne* would be allowed to appear on condition that she insert in it praise of the Emperor. She wrote to Meister, October 5, 1811, "They have again offered to restore the *burnt object*, to delete something, *especially to add something*, to change the title and to publish it."

good deed myself or inducing my adversary to commit a base act, I would not hesitate to choose the debasement of my enemy." That is the complete explanation of the meticulous care he devoted to ruining my life. He knew that I was attached to my friends, to France, to my writings, to my tastes, to society; and by depriving me of everything that made for my happiness, he wanted to trouble me enough so that I would write some piece of insipid flattery in the hope that it would be worth my recall. By refusing to do so, I must say, I cannot be given credit for making a sacrifice: the Emperor wanted something ignoble from me, but something ignoble and also useless; for at a time of such idolatry of success my ridiculous situation would not have been allowed to terminate even if I had succeeded in going to Paris. In order to satisfy our master—clever as he was in the art of depriving people of their remaining self-respect—it was necessary that I should dishonor myself in the hope of obtaining my return to France, and that he should mock my zeal to praise him (he who had never ceased persecuting me) and that this zeal should be of no use to me at all. I have denied him this truly subtle satisfaction; it is the only merit I have had in the long struggle he has kept up between his omnipotence and my weakness.

Monsieur de Montmorency's family, in despair about his exile, quite properly wished him to take leave of the unhappy cause of his misfortune, and I saw this friend depart without knowing whether I would ever see him again. It was on August 31, 1811, that I broke the first and last of my ties with my country; I broke them, at least, as regards the human relationships that can no longer exist between us; but I never raise my eyes to heaven without thinking of my worthy friend, and I venture to believe that in his prayers he answers me. Fate has denied me any other communication with him.

When the exile of my two friends became known, I was assailed by a host of problems, but a great misfortune renders one numb to all new afflictions. It was rumored that the Minister of Police had declared his intention to place a guard at the foot of the Avenue of Coppet, to arrest whoever came to see me. The

Prefect of Geneva, who was instructed, by order of the Emperor, he said, to "annul" me (that was his expression), never missed an opportunity to insinuate, or even declare publicly, that no one having anything to fear or to desire from the government should approach my house.

Monsieur de Saint-Priest, a former minister of the king's and my father's colleague, honored me with his friendship; his daughters feared, with good reason, that he would be expelled from Geneva, and they joined me in begging him not to visit me. Nevertheless, in the middle of winter, at the age of seventy-eight, he was exiled not only from Geneva, but from Switzerland; for it is generally acknowledged, as had been seen in my own case, that the Emperor exiles people from Switzerland as well as from France; and when you object to French agents about this being a foreign country whose independence is recognized, they shrug their shoulders as if you were bothering them with metaphysical subtleties. Indeed, it is a real subtlety to want to distinguish anything in Europe other than prefect-kings and prefects, receiving orders directly from the French Emperor. If there is any difference between the so-called allied countries and the French provinces, it is that the former are treated rather worse. France still retains the memory of once having been called "the great nation." This sometimes compels the Emperor to be prudent; at least that used to be the case, but it becomes less necessary every day. The reason given for Monsieur de Saint-Priest's exile was that he had not persuaded his sons to resign from service in Russia. His sons had found a generous welcome in Russia during the emigration; they had been promoted, and their intrepid bravery had been properly rewarded; they had been wounded, and were high on the list of those recognized for military talents; the elder son was now more than thirty years old. How could a father have demanded that his sons sacrifice established careers for the doubtful honor of placing themselves under surveillance on French territory? For that was the enviable fate reserved for them. It was a source of melancholy satisfaction to me that I had not seen Monsieur de Saint-Priest for four months prior to his exile; had it not been for that, no one would have doubted that it was I who had infected him with the contagion of my disgrace.[2]

Not only French citizens but even foreigners were warned to shun my house. The Prefect remained on guard to prevent even old friends from seeing me again. One day, for instance, his official exertions deprived me of the company of a German gentleman whose conversation I found extremely agreeable, and on this occasion I told him that he might well have spared himself this search for ways to persecute me. "What!" he replied. "I did that to help you. I made your friend understand that he would compromise you by coming to your house." I could not help laughing at this ingenious argument. "Yes," he continued with the utmost seriousness, "the Emperor, seeing loyalty to you placed above loyalty to him, would be annoyed with you."

"So," I replied, "the Emperor expects my personal friends—and soon perhaps even my children—to abandon me in order to gratify him. That seems rather too much. Besides," I added, "I do not quite see how a person in my situation can be compromised. What you say reminds me of a revolutionary at the time of the Terror, to whom a plea was made that he try to save one of his friends from the scaffold. 'I would be afraid of harming him,' he answered, 'by speaking in his favor.'" The Prefect smiled at my quotation, but continued the arguments which, backed as they were by four hundred thousand bayonets, invariably seem completely sound. A man in Geneva said to me, "Don't you think that the Prefect states his opinions very frankly?"

"Yes," I replied, "he says with sincerity that he is devoted to the man in power, and he says with courage that he is on the side of the strongest. I do not see much merit in such an avowal."

---

[2] François Emmanuel de Saint-Priest had been a colleague of Necker's and a minister without portfolio. He had two sons, Emmanuel and Louis, in the service of Russia. At the end of the year 1811, rupture with Russia was approaching. Thanks to the Emperor Alexander's protection, Monsieur de Saint-Priest had up to that time been able to stay in Geneva. No longer having to be prudent with the Emperor of Russia, Napoleon ordered Monsieur de Saint-Priest to leave Geneva, a French city. Saint-Priest, though ill, left in the middle of January, 1812. His son Emmanuel, chief of staff of Bagration in 1812, entered France with the allies in 1814; he occupied Reims, but Napoleon retook the city and Emmanuel de Saint-Priest died a few days later from a battle wound.

Several independent-minded people in Geneva continued to show their goodwill toward me, for which I will always be grateful. But even the clerks in the Customs House considered that they had to exercise diplomacy where I was concerned, and from prefects to subprefects, to cousins of one or the other, they all would have lived in real fear if I had not spared them—as much as I could—the anxiety of keeping track of me. Every courier brought reports that more of my friends had been exiled from Paris for having kept up connections with me. It became a moral obligation on my part to avoid seeing a single prominent Frenchman, and very often I was even afraid of harming the courageous, friendly people of the region where I was living. I experienced two conflicting emotions, both, I believe, equally natural: sadness at being abandoned, and cruel anxiety for those who showed me affection. It is difficult to imagine a more distressing situation. During nearly two years of this, I did not see a day dawn without grieving for having to bear the existence it prolonged.

"But why didn't you leave?" people will ask, and did ask constantly. A man whom I cannot name[3] but who knows, I hope, how highly I regard his character and conduct told me, "If you stay he will treat you like Mary Stuart. You will have nineteen years of misery, and catastrophe at the end." Another—a witty man but not very discreet—wrote, telling me it was ignominious to remain after so much ill treatment. I did not need his advice to want passionately to leave. Since I could no longer see my friends and was only a hindrance to my children, it seemed the only sensible thing to do, except that the Prefect kept repeating that I would be arrested anyway, if I left. He said that they would demand my return from Vienna or Berlin, and that I could not even make travel preparations without his being informed of them; for he knew—he said—about everything that went on in my house. In that respect he was boasting, as events have proved. He was merely conceited about the efficiency of his espionage. Yet anyone would have been impressed at that tone of assurance with which he told all my friends that I could not take a step without being seized by the police.

[3] Le Comte Elzéar de Sabran. (Note: edition of 1821.)

CHAPTER V

Madame de Staël's anxieties—Napoleon as a

journalist—Madame de Staël decides to leave

Coppet—Her flight (May 23, 1812)

I spent eight months in an indescribable state, trying out my courage each day, but each day weakening at the idea of a prison cell. Of course, everyone is afraid of imprisonment; but I have such a dread of solitude and find my friends so necessary to sustain me, enliven my existence, and give me new perspectives when I cannot shake off painful emotions, that death has never seemed as cruel to me as prison or solitary confinement, where one can remain for years without ever hearing a friendly voice. They say that one of the Spaniards who defended Saragossa with the most incredible bravery nonetheless screams in the confinement of the Vincennes dungeon, a living example of how tragically that ghastly solitude affects the most spirited men! Besides, I had to admit that I was not a courageous person; I have a bold imagination, but am timid by nature, and all possible dangers lurk in my mind like phantoms. My kind of talent makes images so vivid that, while it enables me to see the beauties of nature more brilliantly, its dangers loom more formidable as well. At times I feared prison, at times brigands—if I should have to go by way of

Turkey because—by some political combination—Russia might be closed to me. At times, too, the prospect of crossing the immense sea between Constantinople and London filled me with terror for my daughter's and my own safety. Nevertheless, I had to set out; a deep emotion of pride was involved, and I could say, like a well-known Frenchman, "I tremble at the dangers to which my courage is about to expose me." Indeed, the persecution of women is all the more barbaric because their natures are both sensitive and weak; they suffer more keenly from punishments and are less capable of mustering the strength needed to escape them.

Another kind of terror also assailed me. I was afraid that when the Emperor heard of my departure he would publish one of those articles he dictates so well when he wants to commit a moral assassination. A senator once told me that Napoleon was the best journalist he knew. Certainly, if journalism is the art of slandering individuals and nations, he possesses it to a supreme degree. Nations can survive such treatment; but he has acquired—in the revolutionary times through which he has lived—a certain flair for defamatory statements calculated to appeal to vulgar minds and to circulate among those whose wit consists entirely of repeating phrases published by the government for their express use. If the *Moniteur* accused someone of having committed highway robbery, no newspaper—French, German, or Italian—would dare print that person's vindication. Words cannot describe what a man who heads an army of a million soldiers and has a billion in revenues is like; who has all the prisons of Europe at his disposal, with kings as his jailers; and uses the press as his mouthpiece, while his victims are scarcely permitted to make a reply even in an intimate circle of friends; in short, a man who can make even misfortune look ridiculous. How execrable is that power, and the ironic enjoyment of it which is the final insult satanic genius can inflict on the human race!

Whatever one's independence of character, I do not believe it possible not to tremble at the prospect of arousing the hostility of such a power. At least I admit to having experienced this feeling myself. In spite of my unfortunate situation, I frequently told myself that a roof for shelter, food for nourishment, and a garden to walk in were a fate with which one should be contented. Yet even this fate—such as it was—was by no means assured, for it hung on an idle word spoken and repeated, which might provoke that man—whose power is always increasing—to unimaginable outbursts of irritation. When the sun shone brightly, my courage returned; but when the sky was swathed in fog, the thought of traveling terrified me, and I discovered a sudden housekeeping fervor in myself, born of fear, but alien to my nature. Physical well-being seemed all at once of primary importance, and any thought of exertion frightened me. My health—cruelly impaired by so many troubles—also enfeebled my energetic disposition,[1] so that I sorely tried the patience of my friends during this period by constantly reconsidering my plans and overwhelming them with my uncertainties.

I tried a second time to obtain a passport for America, but was made to wait until mid-winter, only to be refused in the end. I offered to give my word not to publish anything, not even a *Bouquet to Iris*, provided I be allowed to live in Rome. In asking permission to go to Italy, I was vain enough to mention *Corinne*. No doubt the Minister of Police found no precedent for such a request in his files, and this southern climate, so necessary to my health, was mercilessly refused me.

Again and again I was told that my whole life must be restricted to the two leagues that separated Coppet from Geneva, but if I remained, I would have to relinquish my sons—who were of an age to seek careers—while in making my daughter share my fate, I was dimming her prospects. Although the city of Geneva

---

[1] "My health is in a miserable state; and if you could see me grown thin, puffed up, and pale, you could not conceive how so strong a person as I could have been laid so low." (To Meister, April 3, 1812). At this time Madame de Staël—a fact which she has so well kept to herself in her *Mémoires*—found herself in a very delicate situation, as a consequence of her secret marriage with Rocca, the young hussar officer returned from Spain. Several days after this letter to Meister, on April 17, 1812, she gave birth to a child, who was named Louis-Alphonse and was sent to a nurse at Longirod, in the Jura. However, the news was divulged; the Baron de Melun had written about the affair to the Duke of Rovigo; Madame de Staël saw herself disgraced. Therefore, when scarcely recovered, she hastened to flee from Coppet. (Cf. *Madame de Staël et Napoléon*, chap. XIX [by Paul Gautier].)

retained its liberal traditions, it was nevertheless gradually being won over by the interests which connected it to the sources of patronage in France. Each day the number of persons with whom I could communicate was diminishing, and my emotional responses were becoming more a handicap than a source of vitality. All was lost as far as my talents, my happiness, and my existence were concerned, for it is frightful to be of no use to one's children, and harmful to one's friends. Also news from all sides indicated that the Emperor was making formidable military preparations. It was evident that he first wanted to master the Baltic ports by destroying Russia, and that he then planned to use the remains of that nation against Constantinople, whence he could spearhead the conquest of Africa and Asia. Shortly before leaving Paris he had said, "This venerable Europe bores me." And there is no doubt that Europe's confines can no longer contain her conqueror's ambition. The last exits from the Continent might be closed at any moment, and I would find myself in a Europe that was like any wartime city whose gates are guarded by soldiers.

So I made up my mind to leave while there was still a means of getting to England, and that meant a detour around the whole of Europe. I set May 15 as a date for my departure, the details of which I had prepared in absolute secrecy a long time before. On the last evening, my strength completely abandoned me and I almost persuaded myself that such terror as I was experiencing could only be a presentiment that I was making a mistake. I wavered between foolishly consulting all kinds of portents, and —somewhat more wisely—discussing with my friends, and questioning myself about the morality of my decision. Resignation in all things, it seems, is the most religious policy, and I can understand how pious men should have come to distrust spontaneous decisions. Necessity seems to originate in divinity, while man's resolves may result from his pride. However, none of our faculties has been given us in vain, and that of deciding for oneself has its use too. Moreover, ordinary people are forever being astonished that persons with talent have needs different from theirs. When talent is successful, then success is within everyone's reach; however, when it causes grief, when it prompts one to depart from convention, these same people only think of it as a disease, and almost a crime. All around me I heard the hum of inevitable commonplaces: "Doesn't she have plenty of money? Can't she live and sleep well enough in a fine château?" A few rather more sensitive people realized that even my present sad situation was not secure and that it could get worse without ever getting better. But the atmosphere around me counseled inaction, because no new persecutions had occurred for six months, and because men always believe that what is, is what will be. In the midst of these depressing circumstances, I had to make one of the hardest decisions a woman can face in her personal life. My servants, with the exception of two very trustworthy persons, did not know my secret. Most of the people who visited me suspected nothing, and yet, by a single action I was going to change my life and my family's life completely.

I wandered all over the grounds of Coppet, torn by indecision. I sat in all the places where my father used to rest to contemplate nature, and I saw again that same beauty in lake and landscape that we had so often admired together. I said good-bye to them while steeping myself in their soothing atmosphere. The monument containing my parents' ashes—where, God willing, mine will also be placed—was one of my principal causes of sorrow at leaving home; and yet, on approaching it, I almost always found a kind of strength that seemed to come from heaven. I prayed for an hour before that iron gate, which sheltered the remains of the noblest of humans, and there my soul became convinced of the necessity to leave. I recalled the famous verses of a Latin poet, Claudius, in which he expresses the doubt that can arise in the most religious minds, when they see the earth abandoned to the wicked, and the fate of mortals seemingly floating at the mercy of chance. I felt I no longer had the strength to maintain the enthusiasm which I needed to bring out my potentials for good. I needed to be where I could listen to people who thought as I did if I was to remain loyal to my own beliefs and preserve the faith that my father had instilled in me. In my state of anxiety I often invoked the memory of my father, of that Fénelon of politics, whose genius was the opposite of Bonaparte's in every way; and genius he certainly had, for it takes at least as much genius to put oneself in harmony with heaven as it does to use in one's own interest any means at hand, even the violation of both divine and human laws. I went again to see my father's study, where his arm-chair, his table, and his papers still remained in their places; I embraced each cherished relic, took his cloak, which until then had been left on his chair by my order, and carried it away with me to wrap myself in, if the messenger of death approached me. Having finished these good-byes, I avoided others as much as possible, for they were too painful; I wrote to the friends I was leaving, taking care that my letters should not reach them until several days after my departure.

The next day, Saturday, May 23, 1812, at two o'clock in the afternoon, I entered my carriage saying that I would return for dinner. I had nothing with me other than the fan in my hand, my daughter had hers, and only my son and Monsieur Rocca carried in their pockets what we needed for several days of traveling. I was close to fainting as we descended the avenue of Coppet, leaving this château which had become such an old and good friend to me. My son took my hand and said, "Mother, you are setting out for England. Think of that." My spirits revived at his words. However, I was almost two thousand leagues from my objective, to which the normal route would have conducted me so speedily; but each step, at least, brought me a bit nearer to it. After I had gone some distance I sent back one of my servants to tell my household that I would not return until the next day, and I traveled day and night until I reached a farm beyond Berne, where I had arranged to meet another friend,[2] who very much wanted to accompany me. There too I had to part from my older son,[3] who, till he was fourteen, had been brought up with my father as model, and who looks like him.

All my courage abandoned me a second time at the sight of Switzerland, still so calm, and always so beautiful, whose inhabitants know how to be free through their virtues even after losing political independence. Everything in this country held

---

[2] Edition of 1821: "Monsieur Schlegel."
[3] Auguste de Staël.

me back and seemed to be telling me not to leave. There was still time to return; for I had not yet taken an irreparable step. Although the Prefect had seen fit to restrict my movements in Switzerland, I knew very well that it was for fear that I would go farther. After all, I had not yet passed the barrier that left me no possibility of returning, a train of thought that was almost unbearable. On the other hand, there was also something irreparable in the resolution to remain; for I felt—and events have certainly vindicated my instinct—that if I let this moment pass, I would no longer be able to escape. Besides, there is something rather shameful in repeating such solemn good-byes, and one can hardly be revived from the dead for one's friends more than once. I do not know what would have become of me if this uncertainty— at the very moment of action—had lasted much longer, for my judgment was disturbed by it. My children were what decided me, and especially my daughter, then scarcely fourteen years old.[4] In a manner of speaking, I relied on her, as if the voice of God must make itself heard through the mouth of a child. My son left, and when he was out of sight I could say with Lord Russell, "The anguish of death is past." I climbed into my carriage with my daughter. Once I had mastered my uncertainty, I was able to rally all my strength and spirit, and recover the capacity for action I had lacked while deliberating.

---

[4] Albertine de Staël, future Duchess de Broglie.

CHAPTER VI

Madame de Staël travels through the Tyrol;

description of the country; Innsbruck—

Alarm; arrival of Rocca—Salzburg—Entry

into Austria; demoralization of the

Austrian people—The Abbey of Melk

So it was that after ten years of ever-increasing persecutions—sent away first from Paris, then banished to Switzerland, then confined to my château, and then at last condemned to the horrible grief of no longer seeing my friends and of having been the cause of their exile—I was obliged to leave two homelands as a fugitive, Switzerland and France, by order of a man less French than I. For I was born on the banks of the Seine, where his only claim to citizenship is his tyranny. He saw the light of day on the island of Corsica, practically within Africa's savage sway. His father did not, like mine, devote his fortune and his sleepless nights to defending France from bankruptcy and famine; the air of this beautiful country is not his native air; how can he understand the pain of being exiled from it, when he considers this fertile land only as the instrument of his victories. Where is his *patrie?* It is any country that accepts his domination. His fellow-citizens? They are whatever slaves obey his orders. He once complained of not having had under his command—like Tamburlaine—nations unacquainted with reasoning. I imagine that by now he is satisfied with the Europeans; their moral standards, like their armies, have begun to resemble those of the Tartars.

I had nothing to fear in Switzerland, since I could always prove that I had a right to be there, but to leave it I had only a foreign passport. I had to cross one of France's allied states, and if some French agent had told the Bavarian government not to let me pass, it would no doubt have executed these orders, regretfully but obediently. I entered the Tyrol filled with respect for a country which had fought the French out of loyalty to its former masters,[1] but equally filled with contempt for the Austrian ministers, who had been capable of abandoning men compromised by their loyalty to their sovereign. They say that a minor diplomat, head of Austria's espionage department, saw fit during the war to assert once at the Austrian Emperor's dinner table that the Tyroleans should be abandoned. Monsieur de Hormayr, a Tyrolean nobleman—Councillor of State at Vienna, who in his actions and writings has shown a warrior's courage and the talent of a historian —scornfully refuted those shameful remarks. The Emperor supported Monsieur de Hormayr, and in so doing showed that his private feelings at least were opposed to the political behavior forced upon him by Bonaparte. Similarly, most European sovereigns, at the time when Bonaparte made himself master of France, were personally very upright men, but they no longer functioned as kings, having abandoned all government business to circumstances, and to their ministers.

The Tyrol resembles Switzerland in appearance, although its landscape does not have as much vigor or originality, and its villages do not have the same appearance of prosperity. It is, in short, a country which has been wisely governed but has never been free, and it resisted tyranny with the obduracy of the moun-

---

[1] The reference is to an uprising in the Tyrol in April, 1809, against the Bavarians and French. The head of the insurrection was the innkeeper Andreas Hofer. He was captured and shot in Mantua, February 20, 1810.

taineers on its slopes. Few Tyroleans have been considered remarkable. In the first place, the Austrian government is little
suited for developing genius, and furthermore, the Tyrol, by its
customs and geographical position, should have been a part of
the Swiss confederation; its incorporation into the Austrian monarchy was unnatural, and in such a union all it could develop
were the noble qualities of mountaineers: courage and fidelity.

The postilion who was our guide showed us a rock on which
the Emperor Maximilian, Charles V's grandfather, had almost
perished. He had been so carried away by the excitement of hunting that he had followed a chamois to heights from which he
could not descend. This legend is still popular among the Tyroleans, showing how necessary the cult of the past is to a nation.
The memory of the last war was still vivid in people's minds, and
the peasants showed us the mountaintops on which they had been
entrenched, and described their beautiful martial music as it
echoed from the heights into the valleys. While showing us the
Crown Prince of Bavaria's palace, at Innsbruck, they related how
Hofer, the courageous peasant leader of the insurrection, had
lived there; they also praised the bravery displayed by a woman
whose château the French had entered. In sum, their need to be
a nation was even more evident than their undoubted affection
for the House of Austria.

Maximilian's famous tomb is in a church at Innsbruck, which
I visited, confident that I would not be recognized in a place so
remote from the capitals where French agents reside. The bronze
figure of Maximilian kneels on a sarcophagus in the middle of
the church, and thirty statues, also in bronze, ranged on each
side of the sanctuary, represent the emperor's relatives and ancestors. So many past grandeurs, so many once formidable ambitions gathered in a family group around a tomb, inspired profound reflection. There, Philip the Good, Charles the Bold, and
Mary of Burgundy could be seen; and in the midst of these
historic personages was a legendary hero, Dietrich of Berne.
Lowered visors concealed the knights' faces, but when the visor
was lifted, a brazen countenance appeared under the brass hel-
met, and the warrior's features were of bronze, like his armor.

Historic monuments like these are restful to the soul. Someday, if future generations grant Bonaparte a tomb, people will pass peacefully in front of his ashes, whereas during his lifetime no human being could enjoy either tranquillity or independence.

From Innsbruck I had to go through Salzburg to reach the Austrian frontier. I thought all my anxieties would be over once I had entered the territory of that monarchy, which I had known to be trustworthy and good. But the moment I dreaded most was the passage from Bavaria to Austria, for a courier might be waiting to intercept me there. I had not been making good time, in spite of this fear, for the state of my health, impaired by my sufferings, did not allow me to travel at night. During this trip I often found that the worst terrors could not overcome a certain physical exhaustion that made me dread fatigue more than death. Even so, I counted on arriving without hindrance, and my fears were already vanishing as I drew closer to what seemed an assured destination. When we entered the inn at Salzburg, however, a man approached my traveling companion[2] and told him in German that a French courier had been there asking about a carriage arriving from Innsbruck with a woman and a young girl in it, and the courier had said he would return to get information about them. I did not miss a word of what the innkeeper reported, and I became pale with terror. My companion was also alarmed on my account; he asked more questions and confirmed the fact that this courier was French, that he came from Munich, that he had been as far as the Austrian frontier to wait for me, and that, not finding me, he had come back to meet me. Nothing could have seemed clearer: this was exactly what I had dreaded before my departure and during the journey. I could no longer escape, since this courier—who they said was already at the post-stop—must inevitably catch up with me. I resolved at once to leave my carriage, my companion, and my daughter at the inn, and go alone on foot into the streets of the town and take the risk of entering the first house whose master or mistress had a kind face. I would ask them for a refuge for

---

[2] Edition of 1821: "Monsieur Schlegel, who accompanied me . . ."

a few days. During this time, my daughter and my companion would have said that they were going to meet me in Austria, and I would have set out afterward, disguised as a peasant. Utterly risky as this expedient was, I had no other choice and I was getting ready for the undertaking—trembling all the while—when who should enter my room but this dreaded courier, who was none other than [Monsieur Rocca. After having accompanied me the first day of my trip, he had returned to Geneva to terminate some business, and now he was coming to rejoin me, disguised][3] as a French courier, in order to take advantage of the terror which that name inspires—especially in France's allies—and to requisition horses more quickly. He had taken the Munich road and had hurried to the Austrian frontier to make sure that no one had preceded me or reported me. He had returned to meet me and quiet my fears, and was going to cross the frontier in my carriage and share what seemed the most formidable—but also the last—of my dangers. And so my intense anxiety gave way to a very pleasant feeling of security and gratitude.

We proceeded through Salzburg, which contains many beautiful buildings, but, like most of the ecclesiastical principalities of Germany, now has a very forsaken aspect. The days of tranquil affluence are gone, along with the independence of these little governments. Their monasteries were like museums, and one is struck by the numerous institutions and buildings established by their celibate rulers during their residency; all these peaceful sovereigns benefited their people. In the last century, an archbishop of Salzburg cut a road that extends for several hundred paces under a mountain, like the grotto of Posillipo in Naples. On the front of the entrance gate there is a bust of the archbishop and below, the inscription: TE SAXA LOQUUNTUR (The Stones Speak of Thee), which has a certain grandeur.

At last I entered the Austria that I had found in such a state

---

[3] The whole passage in brackets is the Baron Auguste de Staël's, who had scratched out the original text in the manuscript in such a way as to make it illegible. Madame de Staël was full of anxiety for Rocca, who was an officer in the service of France (he had served in the war with Spain as a lieutenant in the second regiment of Hussars) and whom the French government, through its foreign agents, could search for and arrest. See Paul Gautier, *Madame de Staël et Napoléon*, pp. 295 ff.

of well-being four years before.[4] I was immediately impressed by
the visible change brought about by depreciation of the paper
money and the fluctuations in its value caused by the unsettled
state of financial operations. Nothing demoralizes a people as
much as continual oscillations which turn everyone into a specu-
lator, and set the entire working class an example of how to
obtain easy money by the use of cunning. I no longer found the
same honesty in the people that had struck me four years earlier;
paper money stimulates the imagination with hopes of rapid and
easy gain, and the hazards of chance upset the steady, even flow
of existence, the basis for honesty in the common people. During
my stay in Austria a man was hanged for forging counterfeit
money just after the old notes had been replaced; on his way to
the gallows he cried out that it was not he who had stolen, but the
state. And of course it is impossible to make the common people
understand the justice of punishing them for having speculated
in their private affairs when the government does the same things
with impunity. Moreover, this government was doubly allied to
the French state, since its sovereign was the very patient father-
in-law of a terrible son-in-law.[5] What other recourse had he? His
daughter's marriage had saved him at most two million in repara-
tions to the French; the rest had been exacted by the kind of
justice—so easily exercised—which consists in treating friends
and enemies alike; and this was the cause of the penury in the
Austrian treasury.

Another misfortune had resulted from the last war, and especially from the last peace. The ineffectiveness and seeming waste
of the generous effort that had distinguished the Austrian armies
in the battles of Essling and Wagram[6] had cooled the nation
toward its sovereign, whom it had formerly revered. The same

---

[4] During the second trip into Germany, which she took between December,
1807, and July, 1808.

[5] Napoleon had married Marie Louise, daughter of Emperor Francis I of
Austria, on March 11, 1810, by proxy, and on April 1 in person. (Trans.)

[6] The battle of Essling took place on May 21 and 22, 1809; in it, the French
army was in serious danger, and for a while seemed certain of defeat. The
battle of Wagram, which Napoleon won over Archduke Charles and which
decided the outcome of the campaign, took place on July 6, 1809.

thing has happened to all of the rulers who have had dealings with Emperor Napoleon. He has used them as tax collectors; he has forced them to put pressure on their subjects in order to meet his demands; and when it has suited him to dethrone these sovereigns, their countrymen—alienated from them by the wrongs they have committed by order of the Emperor—have not supported them against him. Emperor Napoleon has a way of reducing countries technically at peace to so miserable a condition that any change is agreeable to them, and having already been forced to give men and money to France, they hardly feel the inconvenience of being annexed to it. They are wrong, however, for anything is better than ceasing to be considered a nation; and as Europe's misfortunes are caused by one man, care should be taken to preserve what may be restored when he is no longer on the scene.

Before arriving in Vienna, while I was waiting for my second son,[7] who was to join me with my servants and baggage, I stopped for a day at the Abbey of Melk, situated on a height from which the Emperor Napoleon had contemplated the Danube and its various windings and praised the landscape upon which he was going to swoop with his armies. He frequently amuses himself by composing snatches of poetry on the beauties of nature which he is about to ravage, and on the effects of war with which he is planning to overwhelm mankind. After all, why shouldn't he amuse himself at the expense of the human race, which tolerates him. Man is checked in his career of evil only by an obstacle or by remorse. No one has blocked Napoleon with the former, and he has very easily rid himself of the latter. All alone, retracing his footsteps on the terrace from which one could see the country to a great distance, I admired its richness, and marveled at how quickly the bounty of nature repairs the disasters caused by men. Only moral riches disappear, or at the very least are lost for centuries.

---

[7] Albert de Staël, who unfortunately was to be killed in a duel in 1813 in the Tettenborn corps where he was serving.

CHAPTER VII

Visit to Vienna–Napoleon at Dresden;

Empress Marie Louise in Prague–Napoleon

and the Polish people–Monsieur de

Hudelist and Madame de Staël: Austrian

spies–Madame de Staël's perplexities

Fortunately I arrived in Vienna on June 6, just two hours before the Russian ambassador, Monsieur le comte de Stackelberg, sent a courier to the Emperor Alexander at Vilna. Monsieur de Stackelberg, treating me with his usual tactful consideration, wrote by way of this courier to request a passport for me, and assured me of a response within three weeks. When the question arose of where to spend those three weeks, my Austrian friends, who had welcomed me in the most amiable way, assured me that I could remain in Vienna without fear.

At that time the court was in Dresden, where all the German princes were assembled to pay their respects to the Emperor of France.[1] Napoleon had stopped at Dresden on the pretext of re-

---

[1] This statement is not entirely correct. Napoleon had left Paris on May 9, 1812, accompanied by the Empress and the whole court; he arrived in Dresden

opening negotiations to try to avoid war with Russia, or—in other words—to obtain through diplomacy what he would otherwise have to win on the battlefield. At first he did not wish to receive the King of Prussia at his Dresden banquet, knowing only too well how much that unhappy monarch hated to do anything he felt compelled to do. Monsieur de Metternich, it is said, obtained this humiliating invitation for the king. Monsieur de Hardenberg, who was with him, observed to the Emperor Napoleon that Prussia had paid a third more than the promised contributions. "An apothecary's bill," the Emperor replied, turning his back on him; for he takes secret pleasure in using vulgar expressions to humiliate his victims. He used a certain amount of coquetry in his relations with the Emperor and Empress of Austria because he wanted the Austrian government to take an active part in his war with Russia. "You surely see," he said to Monsieur de Metternich, according to reliable sources, "I can never have the slightest interest in diminishing Austria's present power, first because it's proper that my father-in-law should be a highly esteemed prince, and further, because I have more faith in the old dynasties than in the new ones. Hasn't General Bernadotte already chosen to make peace with England?" It was true that the Crown Prince of Sweden, as will be seen, had courageously come out in support of the interests of the country he was governing.

After the Emperor of France had left Dresden to review his troops, the Empress went to stay with her family in Prague for a time. Upon his departure, Napoleon regulated the etiquette that was to exist between father and daughter, and one can imagine that the arrangements were strict, for he loves etiquette almost as much from suspicion as from vanity, using it as a means of isolating individuals from one another under the pretense of distinguishing their ranks. The Empress, while traveling, wears a dress of gold brocade, and her ladies-in-waiting are obliged to do

---

on May 16. The Emperor and Empress of Austria joined them the following day; the King of Prussia arrived on May 26. Actually, when Madame de Staël arrived in Vienna, Napoleon had already left Dresden (May 29), and the Empress Marie Louise had gone to Prague with her relatives.

the same. She usually has a crown on her head, and as nature has not endowed her with the ability to say anything significant, she looks like a doll-queen, upon whom all the crown jewels are displayed.

My first ten days in Vienna were completely untroubled, and I was delighted to find myself in such a pleasant society, and one whose way of thinking corresponded to my own; for public opinion did not favor the alliance with Napoleon, which the government had arranged without popular support. How, indeed, could a war whose ostensible aim was the restoration of Poland be waged by one of Poland's partitioners, a power which still retained, more tenaciously than ever, a third of that same Poland?

The Austrian government had sent thirty thousand men to reestablish the Polish confederation at Warsaw, and almost as many spies to watch the movements of the Poles in Galicia, who wished to have deputies at this confederation. The Austrian government was therefore obliged to speak against the Poles while at the same time supporting their cause, and to say to its Galician subjects, "I forbid you to have the opinions that I support." [2] What metaphysics! It would all be very confusing if fear did not explain everything.

Of all the nations in Bonaparte's wake, only the Poles merit any interest. I believe they know as well as we do that they are only the pretext for the war, and that the Emperor does not care about their independence. On several occasions he has been unable to refrain from expressing his disdain for Poland and for Polish freedom to Emperor Alexander, but it suits his purposes to set Poland against Russia, and the Poles are hoping to take advantage of this to restore their national independence. I do not know if they will succeed, for despotism does not readily grant liberty, and what they gain for themselves they will lose as part of a conquered Europe. They will be Poles, but Poles as much enslaved as the

---

[2] On the eve of Napoleon's invasion of Russia the Austrian government was forced to support his policies, which included a revived Polish state, the Grand Duchy of Warsaw. Austria still ruled over the Poles of Galicia, obtained in the partitions (by Austria, Prussia, and Russia) which had formerly removed Poland from the map. (Trans.)

three former partitioner nations from whom they will have been freed. Nonetheless, Poles are the only Europeans who can serve without shame under Bonaparte's colors. The princes of the Confederation of the Rhine regard their service to Napoleon as advantageous, even if dishonorable, but Austria, by a truly remarkable coincidence, is sacrificing her honor as well as her interest. Emperor Napoleon wanted Archduke Charles to command these thirty thousand men, but fortunately the archduke refused this insulting offer, and when I saw him, wearing a simple gray suit, walking alone along the paths of the Prater, I recovered all my old respect for him.

That same Monsieur de Hudelist who had so shamefully advised abandoning the Tyroleans was in Vienna, and in Monsieur de Metternich's absence, he was in charge of keeping foreigners under surveillance. How he performed his duties is yet to be described. He left me alone at first, for I had already spent a winter in Vienna and had been very well received by the Emperor, the Empress, and the whole court. It was therefore difficult to tell me that I was unwelcome this time because I was in disgrace with Emperor Napoleon, particularly since this disgrace was partly caused by the praises of German morality and literary genius expressed in my book. What was even more difficult was the risk of incurring the slightest displeasure of a power to which—there is no denying—they could very well sacrifice me, in view of all they had already done for it. I suppose, therefore, that after I had spent several days in Vienna Monsieur de Hudelist received more specific warnings about the Emperor's attitude toward me, and felt obliged to keep an eye on me. Well, here is his method: he stationed spies at my door who followed me on foot when my carriage moved slowly and took cabriolets in order not to lose sight of me on my country drives. Their surveillance system appeared to me to combine French Machiavellism with German clumsiness. The Austrians are convinced that they were defeated for not being as clever as the French, and that French cleverness lies in their police methods. Consequently, they have begun to practice a methodical type of espionage, openly organizing what should in any

case be concealed; and, while they themselves are a virtuous people by nature, they have made it a kind of duty to imitate a state
which is thoroughly Jacobin and despotic.

I did, however, have to worry about this espionage, for anyone
with the slightest common sense could see that I was planning an
escape. I was alarmed upon hearing that my Russian passport
might take several months to arrive, for by then the war would
prevent me from traveling. It was also obvious that I would not
be able to remain in Vienna after the French ambassador returned.[3] What would become of me then? I begged Monsieur de
Stackelberg to give me some means of traveling to Constantinople
by way of Odessa. But since Odessa was in Russia, a passport
from Petersburg was equally necessary, so that nothing remained
except the direct route to Turkey through Hungary, and this
route, close to the Serbian border, was extremely dangerous. One
could indeed reach the port of Salonika by way of Greece—as
Archduke Francis had done on his way to Sardinia—but Archduke Francis is a good horseman, and I was hardly capable of
that; still less could I expose a young girl like my daughter to
such a journey. Therefore, whatever it cost me, I had to part from
her and send her separately, by way of Denmark and Sweden,
accompanied by reliable people. On the off chance, I contracted
with an Armenian to guide me to Constantinople. From there I
proposed to go by way of Greece, Sicily, Cadiz, and Lisbon, and
however risky it turned out to be, this voyage did appeal to my
imagination. At the Office of Foreign Affairs, directed by Monsieur de Hudelist in Monsieur de Metternich's absence, the Swedish envoy, under whose protection I was, requested an exit visa
which would allow me to leave Austria, either by way of Hungary
or Galicia, depending on whether I went to Petersburg or Constantinople. I was told that I had to choose; they could not issue
an exit visa for two alternative routes, and even to go to Press-
burg—which is the first city inside Hungary, only six leagues
from Vienna—an authorization from the Estates' Committee was

---

[3] Monsieur Otto was, as noted, in Prague.

required. Certainly, I could not help thinking, Europe—formerly so open to all travelers—has become, under the Emperor Napoleon's influence, like a great net which entangles you at every step. What problems, what stumbling blocks to the least movement! And just imagine how the unhappy governments oppressed by France console themselves by lording it over their subjects in a thousand ways with their meager vestiges of authority!

CHAPTER VIII

Departure from Vienna—Crossing into
Moravia; harassments by the governor—
Awkward position of the Austrian
government—The Archduke of Wurtzburg—
Galicia—Conduct of the Austrian police—
Excursion to a chateâu in ruins; the
goodness of the people—Departure for
Lanzut

As I was obliged to make a choice, I chose Galicia, which would
lead to the country I preferred, namely, Russia.[1] I convinced
myself that once I was far from Vienna, all these harassments,

---

[1] Itinerary upon leaving Vienna: Brunn in Moravia (she was in this city on
June 30, 1812), Wadovitz (July 7), Lanzut (home of Princess Lubomirski),
Léopol, where the women assembled to see her "just as the Queen of Sheba
came to pay homage to Solomon," and finally Brody, from which point she
entered Russia.

undoubtedly instigated by the French government, would cease. In any case I could leave Galicia if necessary, and get to Bucharest through Transylvania. The geography of Europe, as fashioned by Napoleon, is all too effectively demonstrated through misfortune: the detours made necessary in trying to avoid his power already amounted to nearly two thousand leagues, and now, setting out from Vienna, I had to go through Asiatic territory to escape from it. I left, after all, without having received my passport for Russia, hoping in that way to still the anxieties of the lower-level Viennese police concerning the presence of a person in disgrace with Emperor Napoleon. I asked one of my friends[2] to overtake me by traveling night and day as soon as the reply from Russia had arrived, and I set out on my journey. I was wrong to make this move, for in Vienna I was protected by my friends and by public opinion; from there I could easily address myself to the Emperor or to his principal minister, but once confined to a provincial town my only contact was Monsieur de Hudelist, who was trying to gain the French ambassador's favor through his clumsy maliciousness toward me. Here is how he set about it:

I stopped for several days at Brunn, the capital of Moravia, where an English captain, Mr. Mills, a man of perfect kindness and courtesy and—to use the English expression—completely "inoffensive," was detained in exile. He was made terribly unhappy owing to domestic problems. Apparently the Austrian Ministry believes it will derive an air of strength by turning persecutor. However, the discerning are not deceived and as a witty man said, their manner of governing where it touches on their police methods resembles the sentinels stationed on the half-destroyed citadel of Brunn, keeping a strict guard around ruins. Scarcely had I arrived in Brunn than I was subjected to all sorts of annoyances about my passports and those of my traveling companions. When I asked permission to send my son to Vienna to give the necessary explanations I was told that neither my son nor I was permitted to turn back a single league. Of course the Emperor of Austria, and even Monsieur de Metternich, was totally unaware of all these

---

[2] Note in the manuscript: "Monsieur Schlegel." Schlegel and Rocca in fact remained in Vienna to wait for the Russian passport.

absurdities, but in the officials at Brunn, I encountered, with few exceptions, men who were so afraid of compromising themselves that they were quite worthy of being present-day French officials. Yet one must admit that the French are afraid with good reason, for under Emperor Napoleon they run the risk of exile, imprisonment, or death.

The governor of Moravia, an estimable man in most respects, informed me that I had to proceed through Galicia as quickly as possible, stopping for no more than twenty-four hours at Lanzut, where I intended to go. Lanzut is the estate of Princess Lubomirski, sister of Prince Adam Czartoryski, Marshal of the Polish confederation, which the Austrian troops were going to support. Princess Lubomirski was much admired for her character, and especially for her charities. Moreover, her devotion to the house of Austria was well-known, and although she was Polish she had never supported the spirit of opposition to the Austrian government which has always persisted in Poland. Her nephew and niece, Prince Henry and Princess Thérèse, with whom I was intimately acquainted, are brilliant and delightful people. No doubt they were deeply attached to their native Poland, but they could scarcely be criticized for this opinion at a time when Prince Schwarzenberg was being sent with thirty thousand men to fight for its restoration. To what are these unfortunate princes not reduced when they are constantly being told that they must adapt to circumstances? Which amounts to advising them to pilot in any wind. Bonaparte's successes are envied by most of the German rulers, who like to think that they were defeated because they were too honest, whereas actually it was for not having been honest enough. If the Germans had been like the Spaniards, if they had said, "No matter what happens, we will not wear a foreign yoke," they would still be a nation, and their princes would not be languishing in drawing rooms, I do not say Emperor Napoleon's, but those of the least of his favorites.

The Archduke of Wurtzburg, formerly Grand Duke of Tuscany, was dining one evening with the princes Borghese. Also present were Madame Murat and Princess Elisa, now Grand Duchess of Tuscany, and therefore ruler of the beautiful country

which this same Archduke of Wurtzburg had lost. (If one were
to say no more, it would still be worthy of note that he was bearing
that loss so peaceably.) After dinner, these ladies, who in truth
had every reason to be gay, wanted to dance, and having learned
that the Archduke of Wurtzburg was a musician, they gave him
a violin, and there he was—the former Duke of Tuscany with his
elongated Hapsburg features, wearing his Austrian general's uniform, serving as musician so that the present grand duchess and
her two sisters could dance. The Emperor of Austria and his intelligent consort certainly maintain as much dignity as possible in
their present situation, but the essential falseness of the situation
cannot be overcome. Anything that the Austrians do for the
French must be attributed to fear: a muse who inspires the saddest
of songs.

I tried to point out to the governor of Moravia that if I were
continuously pushed toward the frontier, albeit with such polite
attention, I did not know what would become of me. Since I did
not have my Russian passport, and was unable either to retreat or
to advance, I would be forced to spend the rest of my life in Brody,
a frontier town between Russia and Austria, where the Jews have
settled in order to trade between the two empires. "What you say
is quite true," the governor replied, "but these are my orders." For
some time now governments have been persuading people that a
civil agent is subject to the same discipline as a military officer:
reflection on the part of the latter is forbidden, or at least it is
found but rarely. On the other hand, it would be difficult to convince men accountable to the law, as are all the English magistrates, that they may not question orders they receive. And what
is the result of this servile obedience? If it applied only to the head
of state, it might still be considered viable in an absolute monarchy, but in the absence of the king or his deputy a subaltern can
abuse at will the police measures—such an infernal invention of
arbitrary governments—which the truly great will never employ.

I set out for Galicia, and this time, I must say, I was completely
depressed. The phantom of tyranny haunted me everywhere. I
now viewed the Germans, whom I had formerly considered so
upright, as depraved by that fatal misalliance which, in mingling

the blood of their sovereign with a breed of African Corsican, seemed to have altered even the blood of the people themselves. It seemed to me that Europe no longer existed except beyond the seas or the Pyrenees, and I despaired of reaching an acceptable refuge. Nor did the sight of Galicia restore hope concerning the fate of the human race. The Austrians do not know how to endear themselves to their foreign subjects. When they were in possession of Venice, the first thing they did was to forbid the carnival, which was so well-known that it had almost become an institution. To govern this gay city, the Austrian Ministry chose the most inflexible man in the monarchy, with the result that those southern people would almost rather be pillaged by the French than lorded over by the Austrians.

The Poles love their country as they would an unfortunate friend. The landscape is dull and monotonous, and the people are ignorant and lazy. They have always wanted liberty, but have never known how to establish it. And yet the Poles believe they should and can govern Poland, which is very natural. However, education is so neglected, and every kind of industry is so foreign to them, that the Jews have monopolized all commerce and make the peasants sell the whole harvest of the coming year for a supply of brandy. The gulf between nobles and peasants is so great, and the luxury of the one is in such shocking contrast to the frightful misery of the other that the Austrian laws represent an improvement over those that previously existed. But a proud nation—and this nation is proud, even in its misery—does not wish to be humbled, even while receiving some benefits, and the Austrians have never failed in the art of humiliating people. They have divided Galicia into districts, each ruled by a German official. Sometimes a distinguished man accepts this post, but most often the holder is a kind of brute taken from subordinate ranks who despotically gives orders to the greatest nobles of Poland. The police who, at present, have replaced the secret tribunal, authorize the most oppressive measures. The police represent the most subtle and arbitrary power in the government. Now, just imagine what this power can be when entrusted to the gross hands of a district captain. At each post-stop in Galicia one sees three kinds of people quickly gathering around travelers' carriages: Jewish merchants, Polish beggars, and German spies. The country appears to be exclusively inhabited by these three kinds of men. The beggars, with their long beards and ancient Sarmatian costumes, inspire deep pity; it is true, of course, that if they wanted to work, they would no longer be in that state, but it is hard to evaluate whether it is pride or laziness that makes them disdain working on the subjugated land.

The highways are full of processions of men and women carrying the standard of the cross and singing psalms, and their faces are profoundly sad. I have seen them respond to gifts—not of money but of better than ordinary food—by looking at heaven in amazement, as if they did not believe themselves capable of enjoying such bounty. It is a custom of the lower classes in Poland to embrace the knees of the nobles when they meet them; you cannot take a step in a village without having women, children, and old people salute you in this way. In the midst of this spectacle of poverty you see a few men in shabby dress-coats spying on the misery of the others—for misery was all that there was to spy on. The district captains refused passports to Polish nobles out of fear that they would congregate together or go to Warsaw. They compelled the nobles to appear before them once a week, in order to prove their presence. By this kind of behavior the Austrians clearly showed that they knew they were detested in Poland. They divided their troops into two sections: one charged with maintaining Poland's interests outside the country, and the other employed in the interior to prevent the Poles from serving that same cause at home. No country has ever been more poorly governed—at least with respect to politics—than Galicia was at that time, and apparently it was to hide this sight from view that residence or even travel through the region was made so difficult for foreigners.

Here is how the Austrian police set about hastening my voyage. On this route, passports must be examined by each district captain, and at every third post-stop there was a district headquarters. In the police offices of each of these towns, placards had been posted saying that I must be closely watched when I passed through. Had it not been an extraordinary impertinence to treat a woman in this

manner—and a woman persecuted for having praised Germany—
one could not have refrained from laughing at a stupidity so excessive that it posted, in capital letters, police measures whose very
strength lay in secrecy. It reminded me of Monsieur de Sartines,
who had once suggested giving spies a livery. Apparently all this
is not because the director of all these absurdities is totally lacking
in intelligence, but rather that he is so anxious to please the
French government that he seeks above all to display his baseness as conspicuously as possible. This proclaimed surveillance
was carried out with as much finesse as had gone into its planning. A corporal or a clerk, or both together, came to look at
my carriage, puffing at their pipes, and after they had strolled
around it, they went on their way without even deigning to tell me
whether it was in good condition, which might, at least, have been
of some service.

I drove slowly, in order to wait for the Russian passport, which
was my only hope of salvation in these circumstances. One morning I turned off my route to visit a ruined château which belonged
to the princess whom I would see in a few days.[3] To get there, I
had to drive over roads the likes of which cannot be imagined
unless you have traveled in Poland. In the middle of a sort of
desert, which I was crossing alone with my son, a man on horseback greeted me in French. I wanted to answer him, but he was
already far away. I cannot describe the effect of hearing that dear
language at such a sad moment. Ah! if the French were to become
free, how one would love them! They themselves would be the
first to despise their present allies. When I alighted in the courtyard of this château, which was completely in ruins, the lodge-
keeper and his wife and children came forward and embraced my
knees. I had informed them through an inept interpreter that I
knew the princess. Her name was enough to reassure them and
they did not question what I said, even though I had arrived in a
very shabby carriage. They led me into a room that resembled a
prison cell, and just as I entered, one of the women came into it to
burn perfumes. They had no white bread and no meat, but they

---

[3] Princess Lubomirski.

did have an exquisite Hungarian wine. Everywhere, remnants of splendor existed side by side with the greatest poverty, a contrast often found in Poland, where there may be no beds in houses of the most exquisite elegance. In this country everything appears to be a preliminary sketch and nothing is finished, but what can never be too highly praised is the goodness of the people and the generosity of the nobles. Both are easily moved by all that is good and beautiful, and the agents Austria sends there seem like wooden men in the midst of this volatile nation.

At last my Russian passport arrived, and I will be grateful for it to the end of my life, so intense was the pleasure it gave me. Moreover, my friends in Vienna had succeeded in curtailing the malicious influence of those who had been trying to please France by tormenting me. This time, I thought I was entirely safe from new troubles, but I was forgetting that the bulletin ordering all district captains to keep me under surveillance had not yet been revoked, and that what I had received was advance information from the Ministry and a promise that these ridiculous torments would be made to stop. I thought I could follow my first plan and stop at Lanzut, Princess Lubomirski's château, which is so famous in Poland for its good taste and magnificence. It would be a pleasure to see Prince Henry Lubomirski again, whose company, with that of his charming wife, I had so enjoyed in Geneva. I planned to stay there for two days and then go quickly on my way since word had come that war had been declared between France and Russia. I do not quite see how my plan threatened Austria's peace and tranquillity or what harm could come of my relations with the Poles, who were then in the service of Bonaparte. Unquestionably—and I wish to emphasize this point—the Poles cannot be likened to the other nations dependent upon France. It is frightful to have to hope for liberty from a despot, and to seek national independence only through the enslavement of the rest of Europe. However, in support of this Polish policy the Austrian Ministry was more suspect than I, for it furnished troops, whereas I was devoting my meager strength to proclaiming the justice of the European cause, then defended by Russia. Besides, the Austrian Ministry and all the governments allied with Bonaparte no longer even know what constitutes opinion, conscience, or affection. All they have left as a result of their inconsistency and the skill with which Napoleon's diplomacy has entangled them is one single definite idea—power—and they do everything to gratify it.

CHAPTER IX

An Austrian commissioner–Visit to Lanzut–

Arrival at Léopol

It was early July when I arrived at the chief town of the district in which Lanzut lies. My carriage halted before the post-stop, and my son went to have my passport examined as usual. A quarter of an hour later, I was surprised that he had not returned, and I sent one of my companions to ask the reason for this delay. Both of them came back, followed by a man whose face I shall never forget as long as I live: an affable smile on stupid features gave him a most disagreeable expression. My son, almost enraged, told me that the district captain had said that I could not spend more than eight hours in Lanzut, and that to ensure my obeying this order one of his agents would follow me to the château, go in with me, and part from me only after I had left it. My son had pointed out to the captain that, overcome as I was with fatigue, I needed more than eight hours to rest, and furthermore, that in my weakened condition the sight of an agent could have a harmful effect on my health. The captain had replied with a kind of brutality that can only be found in German subalterns; only they can pass, without transition, from arrogance toward weakness, from obsequiousness toward power. Their minds resemble parade-day maneuvers; they take a half-turn to the right and a half-turn to the left, according to the order given.

The agent assigned to watch me tired himself out, therefore, with bows clear to the ground, but he had no intention whatsoever of modifying his instructions. He climbed into a *calèche* whose horses were practically touching the rear wheels of my *berline*. The idea of arriving with this escort at an old friend's—a place of pure delight where I looked forward to spending several days— was so painful that it made me terribly upset. I think the worst aspect of the situation was the knowledge of this insolent spy behind me, probably a very easy person to outwit, if one so fancied, but who was doing his work with an intolerable mixture of ped- antry and rigor.[1] I suffered a nervous attack in the middle of the journey, and had to be helped from my carriage and allowed to rest by a roadside ditch. The ridiculous agent thought it appro- priate to take pity on me, and without getting out of his carriage himself, he sent his servant to find me a glass of water. I cannot describe my anger at my own weakness. This man's compassion was a final insult which I would have liked to spare myself. He set out again when I did, and with him at my heels I entered the courtyard of the Château of Lanzut. Prince Henry, who had no idea of all this, came to meet me in the most hospitable manner. He was frightened by my pallor, and I immediately told him what sort of guest I had with me. From that moment on, his self-control, firmness, and friendship for me did not waver for an instant. But

---

[1] (Note of Auguste de Staël, edition of 1821.) To explain how acute and justifiable was my mother's anguish during this trip, I must say that the atten- tion of the Austrian police was not directed at her alone. Monsieur Rocca's description had been sent along the whole route, with an order to arrest him as a French officer, and although he had sent in his resignation, and his wounds had incapacitated him from continuing his military service, there is no doubt that if he had been delivered to France, he would have been treated with the utmost severity. Therefore he had traveled alone and under an assumed name, and it was at Lanzut that he had set a rendezvous with my mother. Having arrived there before her—and not suspecting that she might be escorted by a police agent—he came to meet her, full of joy and confidence. The danger to which he was exposing himself, without knowing it, froze my mother with terror. She barely had time to signal him to turn back; and without the gen- erosity and presence of mind of a Polish gentleman who gave Monsieur Rocca the means of escaping, he would unquestionably have been recognized and arrested by the commissioner.

Not knowing what might be the fate of her manuscript, and in what public or private circumstances she might ever publish it, my mother believed it a duty to suppress these details, which I may now make known.

can you imagine a state of affairs in which a police agent takes a seat at the table of a great lord such as Prince Henry, or even at anyone's table, without his consent? I am sure that I would have said to him, had he entered my house: "You have the right to take me to prison, but not to dine with me." After supper, the agent approached my son and said in that unctuous tone I particularly dislike when it is used to say offensive things: "According to my orders, I ought to spend the night in your mother's bedroom, to be sure that she has no private talks with anyone, but out of respect for her I will not do it."

"You can also say out of respect for yourself," my son replied, "for if you dare put one foot in my mother's room during the night, I will throw you out of the window."

"Oh, Monsieur le baron," was all that the agent responded, bowing lower than ever, for this threat with its feigned air of power did not fail to impress him. He went off to bed, and next day, at lunch, the prince's secretary managed him so well by giving him plenty to eat and drink, that I think I could have remained several hours longer, but I was ashamed of having been the cause of such a scene at my kind host's. I did not wait to see the beautiful gardens—which are patterned on those of the South, and have the same produce—nor to inspect the house where persecuted French émigrés have found refuge, and to which artists have sent their works in return for the many services rendered them by the mistress of the château.

The contrast between such fresh and vivid impressions and my own grief and indignation was intolerable. The memory of Lanzut, which I have so much reason to love, still makes me shudder whenever I think of it.

And so I departed in tears from that residence, not knowing what was in store in the fifty remaining leagues of Austrian territory. The agent conducted me to the border of his district, and when he left, asked me if I was satisfied with him. The man's stupidity disarmed my resentment. What is peculiar about all these harassments, which were never before characteristic of the Austrian government, is that they are executed so harshly and awkwardly. These once upright men carry out the base actions now required of them with all the scrupulous exactitude that they used to put into good ones, and their limited conception of this new and unfamiliar method of governing makes them commit a hundred blunders, either from ineptitude or clumsiness. They use Hercules' club to kill a fly, and during this useless exertion, matters of the greatest importance may elude them.

On leaving the district of Lanzut, I encountered grenadiers stationed from one post-stop to the next all the way to Léopol,[2] the capital of Galicia, to keep track of my progress. I would have regretted making these good men waste their time had I not thought it better for them to be there than with the unfortunate army which Austria was delivering to Napoleon. When I arrived at Léopol, I found old Austria again in the persons of the governor and the commanding officer of the province, both of whom received me with the greatest politeness and gave me what I wanted more than anything else, the permit for passing from Austria into Russia. So ended my stay in this monarchy, which I had formerly seen powerful, just, and upright. Its alliance with Napoleon, as long as it lasted, reduced it to the lowest rank among nations. Without doubt history will remember that Austria was very brave and aggressive in its long wars against France, and that its last effort to resist Bonaparte was inspired by a national enthusiasm worthy of real praise; but its sovereign, by trusting his advisers rather than his own judgment, completely destroyed that fervor. The unfortunate men who perished on the battlefields of Essling and Wagram so that there might still be an Austrian monarchy and a German nation could hardly have anticipated that three years later, their comrades-in-arms would be fighting to extend Bonaparte's empire to the borders of Asia and to deny any refuge in the whole of Europe—even a desert—to proscribed people, whether kings or their subjects; for such is the objective, and the sole objective, of France's war against Russia.

---

[2] Léopol or Lvov (in German, Lemberg).

CHAPTER X

Crossing the Russian frontier—

Volhynia—Napoleon and Monsieur de

Balachov—Advance of the French army;

Madame de Staël considers going to Odessa

One was hardly accustomed to thinking of Russia as the freest country in Europe, but the yoke that the Emperor of France has clamped on the whole Continent is enough to make any independent country seem like a republic to anyone escaping from Napoleon's tyranny. I entered Russia July 14, and this anniversary of the first day of the Revolution struck me particularly, because as far as I was concerned, the cycle of French history which had begun on July 14, 1789, was closed.[1] When the barrier between Austria and Russia was raised to let me pass, I swore never to set foot in any country which was in any way subject to Emperor Napoleon. I cannot help wondering if this oath will allow me ever to see beautiful France again.

The first person who met me in Russia was a Frenchman who

---

[1] (Note of Auguste de Staël, edition of 1821.) It was on July 14, 1817, that my mother was taken from us, and that God received her in His kingdom. Who would not be seized with a religious emotion in thinking about these mysterious parallels that human destiny offers!

was once a clerk in my father's offices, and who mentioned him with tears in his eyes. This incident seemed to me a happy omen. As a matter of fact, I have had only pleasant and inspiring impressions in this Russian empire, so falsely termed barbaric. I hope that my gratitude may bring still more blessings to this people and its sovereign! I entered Russia at a time when the French army had already penetrated deeply into Russian territory,[2] and yet no restraint or disturbance detained the foreign traveler for a moment. Neither I nor my companions knew a word of Russian; we spoke only French, the language of the enemies who were devastating the empire, and through a series of annoying accidents I did not even have with me a Russian-speaking servant. Had it not been for a German doctor (Doctor Renner), who very generously agreed to serve as our interpreter as far as Moscow, we would have truly deserved the name of *deaf and dumb* which the Russians gave to foreigners.[3] However, it is worth noting that even handicapped in this way, our voyage would have been quite safe and easy, so great is the hospitality of the Russian gentry and people! Right at the start we learned that the direct road to Petersburg was already occupied by the armies, and that to get there we had to go by way of Moscow. This meant another detour of two hundred leagues, but we had already gone fifteen hundred, and I now feel pleased at having seen Moscow.

The first province we had to cross, Volhynia, is part of Russian Poland; it is a fertile country, swarming with Jews like Galicia, but much less poverty-stricken. I stopped at the château of a Polish nobleman to whom I had an introduction, but he advised me to hurry on, because the French were marching on Volhynia and might be there in a week. Generally speaking, the Poles like the Russians better than the Austrians. The Russians and Poles are both of the Slavic race, and although they have been enemies, they respect each other, whereas the Germans, who are more ad-

---

[2] Madame de Staël's itinerary in Russia: Zhitomir, Kiev, Kursk, Orel, Toula, Moscow, Novgorod, Petersburg, Abo (in Finland). (Trans.)

[3] In Russian the verb *nement'* means "to become dumb." The noun *Nemets* means "a German," from the fact that the most frequently encountered non-Russian-speaking (and therefore mute) visitors to Russia were Germans. (Trans.)

vanced in European civilization than the Slavs, fail to appreciate them on any other terms. It was evident that the Poles in Volhynia did not dread the entry of the French, but although their attitude was known to the Russians, they were not subjected to those petty persecutions that only excite hatred and do nothing to hold it in bounds. However, it was, as always, distressing to see one nation subjugated by another. Centuries must elapse before the union is sufficiently established for the names of conqueror and conquered to be forgotten.

At Zhitomir, capital of Volhynia, I was told that the Russian Minister of Police had been sent to Vilna to learn the reason for Emperor Napoleon's aggression and to make a formal protest against his entry into Russian territory. One can hardly believe the countless sacrifices made by Emperor Alexander to preserve peace. In fact, far from Napoleon being able to accuse Emperor Alexander of having broken the treaty of Tilsit, Alexander could instead have been reproached for too scrupulous a fidelity to that dreadful treaty. Alexander would have had the right of declaring war against Napoleon for violating its terms, for while Russia was closing its ports to the English Emperor Napoleon was handing out licenses to import colonial produce into France. One can honestly say that the main aim of the war of France and Europe against Russia was to assure the firm of Bonaparte and Co. a trade monopoly in English merchandise. A fine reason for stirring up all the nations of the Continent!

In his conversation with the Minister of Police, Monsieur de Balachov, the Emperor of France indulged in inconceivable indiscretions which might be taken for carelessness if one did not know his trick of pretending to be completely sincere in order to heighten the terror he inspires. "Do you believe," he said to Monsieur de Balachov, "that I am concerned about these Polish Jacobins?" A letter actually exists—written some years ago by Monsieur de Champagny to Chancellor de Romanzov—which contains the proposal to strike out the names "Poland" and "Poles" from all European decrees. How unfortunate for this nation that Emperor Alexander has not taken the title King of Poland, thereby joining the cause of this oppressed people to that of all men of goodwill!

Napoleon asked one of his generals, in Monsieur de Balachov's presence, if he had ever been in Moscow and what the city was like. The general replied that it had looked like a large village rather than a capital. "And how many churches does it have?" continued the Emperor. "About sixteen hundred," he was told. "That is inconceivable," replied Napoleon, "at a time when no one is religious any more."

"Pardon me, Sire," said Monsieur de Balachov, "the Russians and the Spaniards still are." A splendid answer, foretelling, one could hope, that the Muscovites would be the Castilians of the North.

Nevertheless, the French army advanced rapidly, and since we are so accustomed to seeing the French triumph abroad—even though at home they cannot resist any kind of yoke—I had good reason to fear that I might even yet meet them on the road to Moscow. What a bizarre fate for me, first to be fleeing from the French—among whom I was born and who carried my father in triumph—and moreover to be fleeing from them to the borders of Asia! But after all, what destiny is there, great or small, which is not upset by that man destined to humiliate mankind? I thought I would have to go to Odessa, a city which had become prosperous under the Duke of Richelieu's enlightened administration, and from there to Constantinople and Greece. I consoled myself at the prospect of this long trip by thinking of a poem about Richard the Lion-Hearted that I still intend to write if my life and health permit. This poem will describe the customs and nature of the Orient and celebrate that great epoch in English history when enthusiasm for the Crusades gave way to enthusiasm for liberty. But since we can only describe what we have seen, just as we can only express what we have felt, I shall have to go to Constantinople, Syria, and Sicily, to follow in Richard's footsteps. My traveling companions, better able to judge my strength than I, dissuaded me from such an undertaking and assured me that if I hurried I could go by post-relay more rapidly than an army. You will see that in fact I did not have much time to spare.

CHAPTER XI

Kiev–Russian dress–The Dnieper–

The Greek religion–General Miloradovich

Having decided to continue my journey through Russia, I entered the Ukraine, whose capital is Kiev, formerly the capital of Russia, for this empire was originally centered in the south. At that time the Russians had uninterrupted communications with the Greeks of Constantinople and, in general, with all the peoples of the Orient, whose habits they have adopted in a variety of ways. The Ukraine is a very fertile country but not at all pleasing to the eye; you see great wheat plains which look as if they were cultivated by invisible hands, so sparse are the houses and inhabitants. When approching Kiev or most other so-called cities in Russia, you must not expect to find anything resembling the cities of the West. The roads do not get better nor do the country houses indicate a more populous region. The first thing I saw when I reached Kiev was a cemetery; that was how I realized I was nearing a concentration of people. Most houses in Kiev resemble tents, and from a distance the city has the appearance of a camp; it really looks as though the Tartars' nomadic dwellings served as models for these wooden houses, which hardly appear more solid. It takes only a few days to construct them, but they are frequently destroyed by fire, and then one orders a new house from the forest just as one orders winter provisions from the market. However, rising from the midst of these huts are palaces, and above all, churches, whose green and gilded cupolas make a singular impact on the eye. In the evening when the sun's rays strike these gleaming domes you think you are seeing festive illuminations rather than solid buildings.

The Russians never pass a church without making the sign of the cross, and their long beards add greatly to the pious expressions on their faces. They generally wear long blue robes, pulled in around their waists by red belts. The women's costume also has something Asiatic about it, and they seem to share the love of vivid colors characteristic of southern countries where the sun is so beautiful that people like to capture its brilliance in everyday objects. In a short time I acquired such a taste for these Oriental clothes that I did not like seeing Russians dressed like other Europeans. They then seemed to be on their way to succumbing to Napoleon's despotism, that great regulated system which first gives all nations the gift of conscription, then war-taxes, and finally the Napoleonic Code, in order to govern widely differing nations in the same manner.

The Dnieper—which the ancients called the *Borysthenes*—flows past Kiev, and a local tradition asserts that there was once a boatman who, while crossing it, found its waters so pure that he wanted to found a city on its banks. Actually, the rivers are the greatest natural beauties of Russia, though there are hardly any brooks, because the sand clogs them up. There is little variety in the trees; the melancholy birch appears endlessly in this monotonous landscape; one might even miss rocks and boulders, because one sometimes becomes so tired of seeing neither hills nor valleys, and of going on and on without meeting anything new. The rivers rescue the eye from this fatigue, and therefore the priests bestow their benedictions on these rivers. The Emperor, the Empress, and the whole court attend the ceremony of the blessing of the Neva, in the depth of winter. It is said that Vladimir, at the beginning of the eleventh century, declared all the waters of the Borysthenes to be sacred, and that immersion in them was sufficient to make a man a Christian, and since the Greek Orthodox baptism took the form of immersion, thousands of men went into this river to re-

nounce their idolatry. It was this same Vladimir who sent deputies
to various countries to learn which religion was best suited for him
to adopt. He chose the Greek ritual because of its ceremonial pomp.
Perhaps he had other motives as well, for the Greek faith, by ex-
cluding Papal authority, gives both spiritual and temporal powers
to the sovereign of Russia.

The Greek religion is of necessity less intolerant than the Roman
Catholic, for, being accused of schism, it can hardly complain of
heretics; and so all religions are permitted in Russia and the common fatherland unites men from the shores of the Don to those of
the Neva, even though their theological opinions may differ. The
priests are allowed to marry, but since noblemen almost never
enter this vocation, the clergy have very little political influence;
they have some effect on the people, but are very submissive to the
Emperor.

The ceremonies of the Greek religion are at least as beautiful as
the Catholic. The church music is heavenly, and everything in this
cult invites meditation. There is something poetical and sensitive
about it, but my impression is that it is better adapted to capture
the imagination than to regulate conduct. When the priest comes
out of the sanctuary, where he has remained secluded while par-
taking of the sacrament, it is almost like watching the portals of
daybreak open; the cloud of incense surrounding him, the silver,
gold, and precious stones glistening on his vestments and in the
church seem to come from a country of sun-worshipers. The con-
templative feelings inspired by Gothic architecture in Germany,
France, and England cannot in any way be compared to the effect
of Greek churches, which call to mind, rather, the minarets of the
Turks and Arabs. Nor should one expect to find, as in Italy, the
splendor of the fine arts; their most remarkable ornaments are
virgins and saints crowned with diamonds and rubies. Magnificence characterizes everything one sees in Russia; neither man's
genius nor nature's gifts account for this beauty.

Russian baptism, marriage, and burial ceremonies are noble and
touching; in them one sees traces of Greek paganism, but only in
those which are unconcerned with dogma and can heighten one's
emotional responses to life's three great dramas: birth, marriage,

and death. Russian peasants still observe the custom of addressing the dead person before parting from him forever. "Why have you left us?" they say to him. "Were you unhappy on this earth? Wasn't your wife beautiful and good? Then why have you left her?" The dead person does not reply, but the value of existence is thus proclaimed in the presence of the living.

In Kiev, visitors are shown catacombs rather like those in Rome, and pilgrims come there on foot from as far away as Kazan and other cities bordering on Asia. However, these pilgrimages are less costly in Russia than anywhere else, although the distances are much greater. It is characteristic of this nation to fear neither fatigue nor physical pain. They unite the most striking contrasts —patience and vigor, gaiety and melancholy—and this entitles us to expect great things from them, for ordinarily only superior beings possess opposing qualities; the masses are, for the most part, all of one color.

At Kiev, I had proof of Russian hospitality. The governor of the province, General Miloradovich, overwhelmed me with the most agreeable attentions. He was an aide-de-camp of Suvorov, and just as intrepid, and he greatly increased my confidence in Russia's military prospects. Before then I had met only a few officers, and they were of the German school, having nothing of the Russian character. I perceived a true Russian in General Miloradovich, impetuous, brave, confident, and wholly free of that spirit of imitation which sometimes robs his countrymen of even their national character. He told me some anecdotes about Suvorov which prove that he studied a great deal, although without losing his natural instinct for judging men and affairs. He concealed his studies in order to impress his troops by seeming always to act on inspiration.

In my opinion the Russians have much more affinity with the nations of the South—or rather, those of the Orient—than with those of the North. What is European in them is limited to court manners, which are much the same in all countries, but their nature is Oriental. General Miloradovich told me that a regiment of Kalmuks had been garrisoned in Kiev, and that the prince commanding these Kalmuks came to him one day to tell him how much he suffered from having to spend the winter in a city. He wanted permission to camp in the forest nearby. Such a simple pleasure could hardly be denied him, and so he and his troops went out into the snow to live in their wagons, which also served as their huts. Russian soldiers bear fatigue and privation, whether from the climate or from war, equally well; and people of all classes have such scorn for obstacles and physical suffering that they can rise to great heights of accomplishment. This Kalmuk prince who considered wooden houses too elaborate, even in the middle of winter, gave diamonds to the ladies who caught his fancy at a ball. Because he could not make himself understood, he substituted presents for compliments, just as they do in India and other taciturn Eastern countries where speech has less importance than with us. General Miloradovich invited me to a ball at the residence of a Moldavian princess, the very evening of my departure. I felt genuine regret at being unable to go. All these names of strange countries, of nations that are hardly European, have an extraordinary effect on the imagination. In Russia one feels on the threshold of another continent close to that Eastern world from which so many religious faiths have come and which still enfolds in its bosom unbelievable treasures of perseverance and intellectual depth.

CHAPTER XII

Route from Kiev to Moscow—Gentleness of

the Russian people—Monotony of the

country—Cossacks—Madame de Staël's

fears—Russian hospitality—Luxury in

Russia—Gigantic character of the Russian

people

About nine hundred versts[1] still remained between Kiev and Moscow. My Russian coachmen drove with lightning speed, singing songs whose words, I was told, were compliments and encouragements to their horses: "Go along, my friends," they sang to them. "We know one another, run quickly." I have seen nothing barbaric in this people; on the contrary, their manners have an elegance and gentleness that one finds nowhere else. A Russian coachman never passes a woman, of any age or class, without saluting her, and the woman responds with a nod that is always dignified and graceful. An old man, who could not otherwise make me understand him, pointed to the earth and then to the sky to show that for him the

---

[1] A verst is 3500 feet, or slightly less than seven-tenths of a mile. (Trans.)

one would soon be the road to the other. Of course, one may well object that there have been shocking atrocities in Russian history; but, in the first place, I would indict the boyars rather than the nation itself. The boyars were depraved by the despotism that they inflicted on the people, and again by the despotism they suffered from the state. Moreover, political discords everywhere and at all times pervert national character, and history offers nothing more deplorable than the succession of Russian rulers elevated and then overthrown by crime. Such is the inevitable condition of absolute power on earth. The lower levels of the bureaucracy, and all who seek their fortunes through cunning or intrigue are not at all typical of the rural population; I am aware of their bad reputation, which is in large part justified, but to appreciate the character of a warrior nation, one must look to its soldiers and the class from which soldiers are drawn: the peasantry.

Although I was driven along at great speed, the country was so monotonous that I hardly seemed to be advancing. Sandy plains, a few birch forests, and villages far removed from each other— made up of wooden houses all built on the same model—were the only sights to see. I experienced something like the kind of nightmare in which one is forever walking and never getting anywhere. It seemed to me that this country was the image of infinite space, and that eternity was needed to cross it. Continually one saw couriers travel by at incredible speed; they were seated on a wooden bench placed across a small cart drawn by two horses, and nothing stopped them, even for a minute. Violent jolts would throw them two feet in the air, but they always landed with astonishing coordination, shouting *forward*, in Russian, with an energy like that of the French on a battle day. The Slavic language is especially sonorous; I am tempted to say that it has a metallic quality; you could be hearing brass struck when the Russians pronounce certain letters of their alphabet that are entirely different from those of Western languages.

We saw reserve units hastening toward the theater of the war. Cossacks were joining the army one by one, without order or uniform, carrying long lances and wearing a grayish garment with whose ample hood they cover their heads. I had had an entirely different notion of these people; they live beyond the Dnieper, independently, like savages, but in wartime they obey the government absolutely. We are used to seeing the most formidable armies in fine uniforms of brilliant colors. The somber clothing of these Cossacks induces another sort of fear; they are like ghosts who swoop down upon you.

Halfway between Kiev and Moscow we were already near the armies, and post-horses became harder to procure. I began to fear being detained in my journey at the very moment when haste was essential. One of my companions,[2] who was greatly impressed by the rapid advance of the French, was intensely worried in case I should be caught without horses as the armies advanced, and when I had to wait for five or six hours in front of a post-station —there was seldom a room one could go into—I thought, trembling, about this army that might overtake me at the very limits of Europe and make my position both tragic and ridiculous. For that is what happens when one fails in an enterprise of this kind: not understanding the circumstances that had forced me into it, people would have wondered why I had left my home—even though it had been made my prison—and some, with the best of intentions, would not have failed to say with an air of compunction that it was indeed unfortunate, but that I would have done better to stay where I was. If tyranny had only its direct followers on its side, it could never maintain itself. The astonishing thing, and the one most revealing of human weakness, is that most ordinary men are docile toward events; they lack the ability to look beyond immediate facts, and when an oppressor has triumphed and a victim is ruined, they hasten to justify—not exactly the tyrant—but the destiny whose instrument he is. Weakness of mind and character no doubt causes this servility, but there is also a certain need in human nature for saying that fate is right, whatever it may be, as if this were a way of living at peace with it.

I finally reached the part of my route which removed me from the theater of war, and I arrived in the provinces of Orel and Toula, which have since figured so prominently in the bulletins

---

[2] Monsieur Rocca.

of the two armies. I was received with perfect hospitality in these desolate places (for Russian provincial towns are desolate indeed). Several noblemen of the area came to my inn to compliment me on my writings, and I confess I was flattered to find that I had a literary reputation this far from home. The governor's wife received me in the Asiatic style, with sherbet and roses; her apartment was elegantly furnished, with musical instruments and paintings. One notices riches contrasting with poverty everywhere in Europe, but in Russia, for some reason, neither the one nor the other attracts attention. The nation is not poor; when necessary, the nobles know how to lead the same life as the people. What characterizes this country is the mixture of the most rigorous privations with the most exquisite pleasures. While traveling from place to place, these same nobles, whose homes contain extraordinary luxuries, live on much worse food than our French peasants, and they can endure great physical hardships in everyday life as well as in wartime. Because of the severe climate, the marshes, forests, and deserts that comprise a great part of the country, man is engaged in a constant struggle with nature. Fruits, and even flowers, are grown only in greenhouses, vegetables are not generally cultivated, and there are no vineyards. The way of life of an average French peasant can be achieved in Russia only at very great expense. The necessities of the one are the luxuries of the other, with the result that when luxuries are unobtainable one has to do without necessities. What the English call *comfort*, and what we mean by *l'aisance*, is almost never found in Russia.

A French general requested for his bed-curtains a material so magnificently embroidered that it was impossible to obtain the necessary amount. "Very well," he said, "since this material cannot be found, put a bundle of straw over there in the corner. I will sleep quite well on it." This story holds good for the great Russian noblemen. You could never find anything rich enough to satisfy their imaginations completely, but in the absence of this dream of perfection, they drink hydromel, sleep on a board, and travel night and day in an open carriage, without seeming to miss what you thought was their accustomed luxury. They like wealth more for its magnificence than for the pleasures it makes possible, resembling—again—the Orientals, who are hospitable to strangers, overwhelm them with presents, and yet frequently neglect their own everyday comforts. This is one of the explanations for that fine courage with which the Russians endured the losses caused by the burning of Moscow. More accustomed to outward show than to care for their persons, they have not been softened by luxury, and having to sacrifice money satisfies their pride as much as—or more than—the magnificence with which they spend it. In every way, there is something gigantic about this people: ordinary dimensions do not apply to them at all. I do not mean by this that they lack true grandeur and stability, but their boldness, their imaginativeness knows no bounds. With them, everything is colossal rather than well-proportioned, audacious rather than reflective, and if they do not attain their goals, it is because they exceed them.

CHAPTER XIII

Appearance of the country—Russian

peasant women; character of the people—

Public spirit in Russia—Russians and

French—Slavery

I was approaching nearer and nearer to Moscow, but nothing yet indicated a capital. The wooden villages were just as far apart; no greater movement on the vast plains that are called major roads was visible; there was no additional noise to be heard; and country houses were not more numerous. There is so much space in Russia that everything is lost in it, even the châteaux, even the population. You might suppose that you were crossing a country whose inhabitants had just abandoned it. The absence of birds adds to this silence, and livestock, too, is rare, or kept far from the road. The vast expanse makes everything disappear except the expanse itself, which haunts the imagination like certain metaphysical ideas that one cannot dislodge from one's mind once they take possession of it.

On the eve of my arrival in Moscow, at the end of a very warm day, I stopped in a rather pleasant meadow; some peasant women, dressed in their picturesque local costume, were returning from work, singing those Ukrainian songs which praise love and liberty with a kind of melancholy, tinged with regret. I asked them to dance, and they consented. I know of nothing more graceful than these native dances, which have all the originality that nature gives to the fine arts; a certain modest sensuality is noticeable in them, too; Indian dancing girls must have something analogous to this mixture of indolence and vivacity, the charming feature of Russian folk-dances. This indolence and vivacity express reverie and passion, two elements in their temperaments which civilization has as yet neither formed nor subdued. I was struck by the sweet gaiety of these peasant girls, as I had been, in different degrees, by that of most of the common people with whom I had come in contact in Russia. I can readily believe that they are terrible when their passions are aroused, and as they have no education, they do not know how to control their violence. As a result of this same ignorance they have few moral principles, and theft is very frequent in Russia, but so also is hospitality. They give as easily as they take, depending on whether they are in the mood for cunning or generosity, for either can excite their imagination. There is something in their mentality that is reminiscent of savages; but it seems to me that nowadays European nations lack vigor unless they are either what may be called barbarous—in other words, not enlightened—or unless they are free. But nations which have only acquired from civilization an indifference to any form of yoke, provided their own fireside is not disturbed; nations which have only learned from civilization the art of justifying power and rationalizing slavery—these nations are made to be conquered. I often try to picture what must have become of those places—so serene when I visited them—of those amiable young girls, those peasants with long beards who were so peacefully enduring the fate that Providence had marked out for them: they have surely perished, or fled, for not one has entered the service of the conqueror.

One noteworthy aspect of Russia is its pronounced public spirit. The reputation for invincibility earned by the nation's many victories, the natural pride of the nobles, the loyalty characteristic of the people, their religion, with its depth and power, and their hatred of foreigners—which Peter I tried to destroy in order to

enlighten and civilize his country, but which is in the blood of the
Russians, and reasserts itself when the occasion arises—all these
causes combine to make this a most energetic nation. Some unfavorable anecdotes about preceding reigns, some Russians who
contracted debts in Paris, and a few of Diderot's quips gave the
French the idea that Russia consisted of nothing more than a
corrupt court, dignitaries of the royal household, and a population
of slaves. This is a great mistake. It is true that under ordinary
circumstances this nation cannot be understood without a lengthy
investigation; but during my visit conditions were such that everything was thrown into sharp relief; a country can never be seen
more clearly than at a time of misfortune and courage. What cannot be too often repeated is that this nation consists of the most
striking contrasts. Perhaps the explanation is to be found in the
mixture of European civilization with the Asiatic character.

The Russians are so easy to approach that from the very first
day you would think you were on intimate terms with them, and
yet after ten years this might still not be the case. Russian reticence is altogether extraordinary; this reticence is uniquely reserved for things in which they are intensely interested. Otherwise, they talk as much as one could wish, but their conversation
informs you of nothing but their politeness; it reveals neither
their feelings nor their opinions. They have frequently been compared to the French, a totally inaccurate comparison it seems to
me. The flexibility of their vocal organs makes imitation very
easy for them, and they can be English, French, or German, according to the circumstances, while never ceasing to be Russians:
that is to say, both impetuous and reserved, more capable of passion than of friendship, more proud than considerate, more de-
vout than virtuous, more brave than gallant, and so violent in
their desires that nothing can restrain them. They are much more
hospitable than the French, but society does not consist—with
them as with us—of a circle of intelligent men and women who
take pleasure in conversation. They assemble as we would for a
festival, to be with other people, to enjoy fruit and rare products
from Asia or Europe, to hear music, to amuse themselves; in
short, to experience strong emotions from external stimuli rather

than from the mind and heart: they reserve the latter two for action, not for social gatherings. Besides, since they are usually poorly educated, and find little pleasure in serious conversation, they do not seek to satisfy their egos by displaying intellectual prowess. Poetry, eloquence, and literature are simply not to be found in Russia; luxury, power, and courage are the chief objects of pride and ambition; all other ways of seeking distinction still seem effeminate and vain to this nation.

But the people are slaves, it will be said; what individuality can they be expected to have? Surely I do not need to tell you that all enlightened Russians want the people freed from this condition, and probably no one wants it more than Emperor Alexander. But Russian slavery does not resemble in its effects the institution familiar to Western Europeans.[1] These are not conquerors who have imposed harsh laws on the conquered, as in feudal times; the relationship between the nobles and the people is more like what the ancients called "the family of slaves" than like European serfdom. There is no middle class in Russia, which is a great disadvantage as far as literature and the arts are concerned, for enlightenment usually develops in that class; but the absence of an intermediary between the aristocracy and the people makes for a greater mutual sympathy between them. The gap between the two classes appears greater because there are no degrees between the two extremes, although in fact they are in closer contact for not being separated by a middle class. This kind of social organization is quite unfavorable to the enlightenment of the upper classes, but not to the happiness of the lower. Moreover, in countries where there is no representative government—in other words, where the sovereign still promulgates the laws he is to execute—men are often more degraded, even to the extent of damage to their reason and character, than in this vast empire where a few simple ideas of religion and country guide the masses with the help of a few leaders. Also, because of Russia's vastness, despotism does not oppress the people in small matters. Finally—most important—the religious and military spirit is so dominant in the nation that a great many

---

[1] One feels in this whole passage that Madame de Staël is experiencing some embarrassment in speaking about the enslaved condition of the Russian people.

failings can be overlooked for the sake of these two great sources
of noble actions. A very intelligent man once said that Russia resembled Shakespeare's plays, where all that is not faulty is sublime,
and all that is not sublime is faulty, a remarkably apt observation. But during the great crisis Russia was undergoing when I
was there, one could only admire that nation's energetic resistance and its resignation to sacrifices, and in the presence of such
virtues one hardly dared to notice what one might have criticized
at other times.

CHAPTER XIV

Moscow—Preparations for war—Churches

and palaces; the Kremlin—Asiatic

character of Moscow—Madame de Staël's

feelings—Visit to Count Rostopchin—

Primitive nature of the Russians—What

Russian literature must become

Golden cupolas announce Moscow from afar; however, since the surrounding country is one immense plain—as is all of Russia—one can arrive in the great city without particularly noticing its size. Someone rightly said that Moscow was more like a province than a city. In fact, you see there huts, houses, palaces, an Oriental bazaar, churches, public buildings, stretches of water, woods, and parks. The diversity of customs and peoples in Russia was apparent in this vast place. I was asked, do you want to buy cashmere shawls in the Tartar quarter? Have you seen the Chinese town? Asia and Europe were blended in this immense city. There was more freedom than in Petersburg, where the court necessarily exercises greater influence. The aristocracy of Moscow did not seek public office, but they proved their patriotism by enormous gifts to the state, either for public institutions during peacetime, or for military aid in time of war. Their colossal fortunes are used to support all kinds of collections, to undertake business enterprises, and to organize festivals modeled after the *Thousand and One Nights;* and their fortunes are also frequently lost because of their own unbridled passions.

When I arrived in Moscow, the only subject of conversation was the sacrifices being made for the war. A young Count Momonov raised a regiment for the State, and would only serve in it as a second-lieutenant. A Countess Orlov, hospitable and wealthy in the Oriental tradition, contributed a quarter of her income to the government. When I passed before palaces surrounded by gardens, which used city space as extravagantly as if they were in the middle of the countryside, I was told that the owner of one superb residence had just given a thousand peasants to the State; another, two hundred. I had some difficulty in getting used to the expression *to give men;* but the peasants themselves volunteered their services with ardor, and in this war their lords were only intermediaries.

As soon as a Russian becomes a soldier, his beard is cut off, and from that moment on, he is free. It was felt that all who had served in the militia should also be considered free, but in that case the entire nation would have been free, for it was almost completely mobilized. Let us hope that this emancipation, so keenly desired, can be achieved without violence, but until that happens, it would be nice if the beards could be kept, for they add so much to the strength and dignity of the face. Russians with long beards never pass a church without making the sign of the cross, and their faith in the visible trappings of religion is very touching. Their churches filled with ornaments of gold, silver, and rubies bear the imprint of that Asian taste for luxury. The story is told that a Russian had suggested making an alphabet of precious stones, and then writing the Bible with them. He understood the best way to interest the Russians in reading. Their interest has so far not been devoted to the fine arts or to poetry. They rapidly reach a certain point in all fields but do not go beyond it. Some impulse makes them take the

first step, but the second requires reflection, and the Russians—
who are so unlike a northern people—have so far shown little
aptitude for meditation.

Some palaces in Moscow are made of wood, to cut down on
building time, and to make it easy for the nation's natural inconstancy in all things—other than religion and patriotism—to be
satisfied by frequent changes of residence. Several of these beautiful structures were built for festive occasions; they were designed
to enhance the splendor of a single day, but the rich lavishness of
the decorations has made them last up to this period of universal
destruction. A great many edifices are green, yellow, or pink, and
are as ornately sculptured as dessert decorations.

The Kremlin—the citadel in which Russian emperors defended
themselves against the Tartars—is surrounded by a high crenel-
lated wall and flanked by towers with odd shapes, reminiscent of
Turkish minarets rather than fortresses of the kind seen in the
West. But although the external appearance of the city's buildings
is Oriental, the influence of Christianity is visible in the multitude
of venerated churches, which attract the eye at every step. In seeing Moscow, one was reminded of Rome, not—of course—because
the monuments are in the same style, but because the combination
of empty surrounding countryside and magnificent palaces, together with the grandeur of the city and the infinite number of its
churches, gives Asiatic Rome some resemblance to European
Rome.

It was early August when I was taken to see the interior of the
Kremlin. I entered by the same staircase which Emperor Alexander had ascended a few days before, surrounded by an immense
crowd, who blessed him and promised to defend his empire at all
costs. These people have kept their word. I was first shown the
rooms in which the armor of ancient Russian warriors was kept:
other European countries have more interesting arsenals of this
type. The Russians did not participate in the age of chivalry, nor
did they take part in the Crusades, because they were constantly
at war with the Tartars, Poles, and Turks, so their military spirit
was formed in the midst of all sorts of atrocities produced by the
barbarism of Asiatic nations and of Russia's own tyrants. It is

not, therefore, the gallant fearlessness of the Bayards and Percys, but rather a dauntless, fanatical courage which has been exhibited in these countries for several centuries. In their social relationships, which are still rather new to them, the Russians are not chivalrous in the way that Western peoples are; but they have always been ferocious against their enemies. So many massacres have taken place in Russia, up to the reign of Peter the Great and even later, that the nation's moral conscience, and especially the aristocracy's, must have suffered severely. These despotic governments—restrained only by occasional assassinations of their despots—destroy all principles of honor and duty in men's minds; but their love of country and attachment to religious beliefs have been maintained in full force amidst all the wreckage of their bloody history, and the nation which preserves such virtues may yet astonish the world.

From the ancient arsenal I was conducted to the apartments formerly occupied by the Czars, where their coronation robes are kept. These apartments are not handsome, but they are well suited to the hard life the Czars led, and still lead. The greatest magnificence is evident in Alexander's palace, but he himself travels in the rough manner of a Cossack officer and sleeps on the ground.

In the Kremlin I was shown a divided throne which was first used by Peter I and Ivan his brother. Their sister, Princess Sophia, would place herself behind Ivan's chair and tell him what to say; but this borrowed strength was not enough to withstand the native strength of Peter I for long, and soon he ruled alone. From this reign onward, the Czars ceased wearing Asiatic dress. The great wig of the age of Louis XIV was introduced by Peter I, and without offense to this great man's memory, one cannot help noticing a certain disagreeable contrast between the ferocity of his genius and the ceremonial conformity of his dress. Was he right in attempting to efface his nation's Oriental ways? Was he right to place his capital in the north, at the edge of his empire? These are great questions not yet answered. Centuries alone can provide a proper commentary on such thoughts.

I climbed to the cathedral belfry, called *Ivan-Veliki*, which commands a view of the whole city. From there I saw the palace of the Czars who conquered the crowns of Kazan, Astrakhan and Siberia. I listened to singing from the church where the *Catholicos*, Prince of Georgia, conducted a service for the Muscovites and formed a Christian union between Asia and Europe. Fifteen hundred churches attested to the piety of the Muscovite people.

The commercial establishments in Moscow had an Asiatic character; men in turbans, and others dressed in the different costumes of all the Eastern nations displayed the rarest merchandise: furs from Siberia and woven materials from India offered all the refinements of luxury to the great nobles, whose imaginations are equally stirred by the Samoëns' sables or the Persians' rubies. Here, the Razoumovski garden and palace contained the finest plants and minerals collection; there, a Count Boutourlin had spent thirty years collecting a fine library, among whose books were several with notes in Peter I's handwriting. Little did that great man suspect that the very European civilization he so desired to emulate would come to destroy the schools he had founded in the middle of his empire, with the aim of stabilizing through study, the Russians' impetuous spirit.

Farther on was the Foundling Home, one of the most inspiring institutions in Europe; in other parts of the city hospitals for all classes of society could be seen; in short, everywhere there were signs of great wealth or benevolence, buildings suggesting luxury or charity, and palaces or churches, all of which spread splendor or happiness on a large portion of the human race. One could see the meanderings of the Moscow river, which had not, since the last Tartar invasion, carried blood in its waters. The day was superb; the sun seemed to take delight in casting its rays upon the glittering cupolas. I thought of old Archbishop Platon, who had just written a pastoral letter to Emperor Alexander. Its Oriental style had deeply moved me. He sent a likeness of the Virgin to the borders of Europe in order to exorcise from Asia the man who wished to impose on Russia the whole weight of the nations chained to his steps. For a moment it occurred to me that Napoleon might yet walk on this same tower from which I was admiring the city which his presence would destroy. For a moment I thought that he would glory in replacing—in the palace of the

Czars—the chieftain of the Great Horde, who also succeeded in seizing it for a while; but the sky was so beautiful that I put aside this fear. A month later this splendid city was in ashes, so that it might be said that every country which had allied itself with this man would be destroyed by the fires at his disposal. But how gloriously have the Russians and their monarch redeemed this error! The very misery of Moscow has regenerated the empire, and this religious city perished like a martyr whose spilled blood gives new strength to the brothers who survive him.

The famous Count Rostopchin, mentioned so often in the Emperor's bulletins, came to see me, and invited me to dine with him. He had been Minister of Foreign Affairs under Paul I. He was a witty conversationalist, and one could easily perceive that his strength of character would show itself in no uncertain terms if circumstances so required. Countess Rostopchin was kind enough to give me a book that she had written about the triumph of religion, very pure in style and moral tone. I went to visit her in her country house, actually located within the limits of Moscow; one had to cross a lake and a wood to get there. This is the house— one of the most pleasant residences in Russia—that Count Rostopchin himself set fire to when the French army was approaching. Surely, such an act should arouse a certain admiration, even on the part of enemies. Nevertheless, Emperor Napoleon compared Count Rostopchin to Marat, forgetting that the governor of Moscow sacrificed his own property, while Marat set fire to the houses of others, which after all does make a considerable difference. What Count Rostopchin could have been reproached for was having concealed for too long the news of the army's reversals, either because he was deceiving himself or because he believed it necessary to deceive others. With that admirable rectitude which distinguishes all their actions, the English publish as truthful an account of their reverses as they do of their victories, and their enthusiasm is sustained by the truth, whatever it may be. The Russians cannot yet attain this moral perfection, which is the result of a free constitution.

No other civilized nation has retained as much of the primitive as the Russian people; and while their nobles possess energy, they also combine the defects as well as the qualities of this unbridled nature. Diderot's famous quip—"The Russians became rotten before they matured"—has been much praised. I cannot think of anything more false. Their very vices, with few exceptions, are not the result of corruption but of violence. A Russian desire, said an eminent man, is capable of blowing up a city; fury and ruse possess them in turn when they want to accomplish whatever they have resolved upon, be it good or evil. The nature has not been changed by the rapid civilizing, which was given them by Peter I; up to now, that has only trained them in manners; fortunately for them, they are still what we call barbarians; in other words, they act from instincts that are often generous but always involuntary, which permit them to reflect only on the choice of means, and not on their objective: I say fortunately for them, not because I wish to praise barbarism, but because I wish to designate by this word a certain primitive energy which is the only substitute nations have for the concentrated strength of liberty.

In Moscow I met the most enlightened men of science and letters, but there, as in Petersburg, nearly all professorships are held by Germans. In Russia there is a great dearth of educated men in all branches of learning. For the most part young men only go to the university in order to enter the military profession more quickly. Civil offices, in Russia, confer a rank corresponding to a grade in the army. The nation's thoughts are entirely on war; in everything else, administration, political economy, public instruction, and so forth, other nations of Europe have thus far surpassed the Russians. Nevertheless they are making efforts in literature, for the sweetness and resonant sonority of their language are noticed even by people who do not understand it: it should be well-suited to music and poetry. But the Russians—like so many other continental nations—make the mistake of imitating French literature, which, even with all its beauty, is appropriate only to the French. I think that the Russians ought to derive their literary studies from the Greeks rather than from the Latins. The Russian alphabet, which is similar to the Greek, the historic links between the Russians and the Byzantine empire, and their future destinies which will perhaps lead them toward the illustrious monuments of

Athens and Sparta; all this should turn the Russians to the study of Greek, but above all, their writers must draw poetry from the deepest inspiration of their soul. Their works thus far have something about them that is forced and artificial, and so passionate a nation can never be stirred by such thin harmonies.

CHAPTER XV

Route from Moscow to Petersburg—

Novgorod

I left Moscow with regret. Near the city, I stopped for a short while in a wood where the people come on holidays to dance and enjoy the sun, whose splendor is of such short duration, even in Moscow. What is it like to go even farther north? Those eternal birch trees, which are so monotonous in their sameness, become very rare, it is said, as one approaches Archangel. Up there they are preserved with the care one gives to orange trees in France. The country from Moscow to Petersburg is at first sandy, then all swamp. When it rains the ground becomes black, and one can no longer find the main road. However, the peasants' houses show signs of modest affluence; they are decorated with columns, and the windows are encircled with arabesques carved in wood. Although it was summer when I traveled through the country, I sensed the menacing winter hiding behind the clouds; the fruit that I was offered was bitter because it had been forced to ripen; a rose aroused my emotions—a reminder of our beautiful provinces —but the flowers seemed to hold their heads less proudly, as if the icy hand of the North were already on the point of seizing them.

I proceeded through Novgorod, which six centuries ago was a republic allied with the Hanseatic cities, and which has long preserved a spirit of republican independence. People like to say that the demand for liberty in Europe did not arise until the last century; rather, it is despotism which is a modern invention. Even in Russia, peasant slavery was introduced only in the sixteenth century. Up to the reign of Peter I, the formula for all edicts was: *the Boyars have advised, the Czar will decree.* Although in many respects Peter I did infinite good for Russia, he curbed the nobles and united temporal and spiritual power in his own person in order to remove all obstacles to his designs. Richelieu acted similarly in France, which is why Peter I admired him so greatly. On being shown his tomb in Paris, he cried, "Great man! I would give half my empire to learn from you how to govern the other half." On this occasion the Czar was too modest, for in the first place he had the advantage over Richelieu of being a great warrior, and furthermore, he was the founder of his country's navy and commerce, whereas Richelieu merely governed tyrannically at home and with cunning abroad. But to return to Novgorod: Ivan Vasilievich took possession of it in 1470. He destroyed the city's liberty, and removed and sent to Moscow—into the Kremlin—the great bell called *viechevoy kolokol* in Russian, at whose ringing the citizens used to assemble in the marketplace to deliberate on matters of public interest. With the loss of its freedom, Novgorod saw its population, commerce, and wealth gradually disappear, so withering and destructive is the breath of arbitrary power, says Russia's best historian! Even today Novgorod has a singularly melancholy aspect: a vast walled enclosure indicates that the city was once great and populous, but now you see only scattered houses whose inhabitants seem to be placed there like figures weeping over tombs. Perhaps that is how the beautiful city of Moscow looks today;[1] but public spirit will rebuild it, as it has reconquered it.

---

[1] Written in 1812, after the burning of Moscow.

CHAPTER XVI

Saint Petersburg—Madame de Staël's

impressions—Statue of Peter the

Great—Meridional character of the

Russians—Notre Dame of Kazan; Saint

Alexander Nevski—Visit to Monsieur de

Romanzov; Lord Tyrconnel; Admiral

Bentinck—Reception at Count Orlov's—

Russian conversation

From Novgorod to Petersburg there is almost nothing but marshes, and so you arrive in one of the world's most beautiful cities just as if—with the wave of a wand—a magician had made all the wonders of Europe and Asia burst forth from the heart of a desert. The founding of Petersburg offers the greatest proof of that Russian strength of will which refuses to believe anything impossible. The surroundings are totally unimpressive; the city is built on a marsh, and even its marble rests on pilings, but on seeing these superb edifices one forgets their fragile foundations and cannot help thinking about the miracle that such a beautiful city was built in such a short time. This people, who can only be described with contrasts, possesses extraordinary perseverance against nature or enemy armies. Under stress the Russians have always been patient and invincible, but in the ordinary course of life they are very flighty. The same men, the same masters, do not inspire their enthusiasm for very long. Reflection alone can guarantee the duration of feelings and opinions through extended periods of everyday existence, and the Russians, like all people subjected to despotism, are more capable of dissimulation than reflection.

On arriving in Petersburg, my first impulse was to thank heaven for bringing me to the seacoast. Over the Neva I saw the English flag waving, a symbol of liberty, and I felt that by entrusting myself to the ocean, I would be under the direct power of the Deity; one cannot resist the illusion that one is more safely in the hands of Providence when at the mercy of the elements than when one is dependent upon men, and especially upon that particular man who seems to be a revelation of the principle of evil on this earth.

Across from the house where I lived in Petersburg was the statue of Peter I; he is on horseback, climbing a steep mountain in the middle of serpents who try to stop his progress. These serpents, it is true, are put there to support the enormous weight of horse and rider, but the concept is not a happy one, for in fact envy is not what a sovereign must fear, nor are his enemies those who crawl, and Peter I, especially, had nothing to fear during his lifetime except the Russians, who regretted the abandonment of their country's ancient customs. Nevertheless the persistence of admiration for him is proof of the good he accomplished for Russia, for despots no longer have flatterers a century after their deaths. On the pedestal of the statue, one reads: *To Peter the First, Catherine the Second*. This simple yet proud inscription has the merit of truth. These two great people have done a great deal to enhance Russian pride and to teach a nation that it is invincible is to make it so—at least within its own borders—for conquest is a gamble which probably depends more on the faults of the conquered than on the genius of the conqueror.

It is rightly claimed that you cannot say of a woman in Petersburg that she is as old as the streets, for the streets themselves are so new. The buildings are still a dazzling white, and at night, in the moonlight, seem like great white phantoms staring motionlessly upon the Neva. I do not know what is so particularly beautiful about this river, but never has any other water seemed so clear to me. A succession of granite quays thirty versts in length border it, and this magnificent example of man's labor is worthy of the transparent water it adorns. Had Peter I organized similar projects in the south of his empire, he would not have obtained what he wanted—a navy—but perhaps he would have better conformed to his nation's character. The Russian inhabitants of Petersburg have the look of a southern people condemned to live in the north, struggling with a climate at variance with their nature. Northern residents for the most part lead an indoor life, and dread their perpetual enemy, the cold. The Russian lower classes have none of these habits; during winter coachmen wait for ten hours at the gate without complaining. They sleep on the snow under their carriages, transferring the customs of Neapolitan beggars to the sixtieth degree of latitude. They can be seen, installed on the steps of staircases like Germans in their eiderdowns; sometimes they sleep standing, their heads propped against a wall. By turns indolent and impetuous, they deliver themselves alternately to sleep and to unbelievable toils. Some get drunk, and in that they differ from southern peoples, who are very temperate; but the Russians are also temperate in a manner beyond belief when the hardships of war require it.

The great Russian noblemen show—in their own way—the same tastes as inhabitants of the South. Visitors to Petersburg should not fail to see the different country residences they have built on an island formed by the Neva, in the very center of the city. These dwellings are beautified by plants from the South, perfumes from the Orient, and divans from Asia. Immense greenhouses, where fruits of all countries ripen, create an artificial

climate. The owners try not to waste a single ray of the sun when
it appears on their horizon; they treat it like a friend who is about
to depart, whom they formerly knew in a more fortunate region.

The day after my arrival I dined with one of the city's most
esteemed merchants, who entertained in the Russian manner; that
is to say, he placed a flag on his rooftop to announce that he was
dining at home, and this was an invitation to all his friends to join
him. We were served in the open air, to make the most of these
last poor days of summer, for there still remained a few, although
we would hardly have called them summer in the south of Europe.
The garden was very pleasant, embellished by trees and flowers,
but four paces from the house were wasteland and marsh. In the
environs of Petersburg, nature is like an enemy who takes possession as soon as man ceases, for a moment, to struggle with him.

Next morning I went to the church of Notre Dame of Kazan,
built by Paul I with Saint Peter's of Rome as a model. The interior
of this church—decorated with a great number of granite columns
—is extraordinarily beautiful; but the building itself is displeasing, precisely because it reminds one of Saint Peter's and yet somehow differs from it all the more for being an imitation. One does
not accomplish in two years what cost the world's foremost artists
a century of labor. The Russians wanted, through swiftness, to
overcome time as they do space; but time preserves only what it
has founded, and the fine arts—although their principal source
seems to be inspiration—cannot, however, dispense with reflection.

From Notre Dame of Kazan I went to the monastery of Saint
Alexander Nevski, a place consecrated to one of Russia's hero
sovereigns, who extended its conquests to the banks of the Neva.
The Empress Elizabeth, daughter of Peter I, had a silver coffin
made for him upon which it is customary to place a coin, as a
pledge of your vow to the saint. Souvorov's tomb is in this monastery, but his name is its only decoration. It is enough for him, but
not for the Russians, to whom he rendered such important services.
What is more, this nation is so warlike that it takes less notice
than others would of achievements of this kind. The most distinguished families of Russia have erected tombs for their relatives
in the cemetery belonging to the Nevski church, but none of these

monuments is noteworthy, for they are not beautiful as works of art, and they do not fire the imagination with any great inspiration. It is true that the idea of death has little effect on the Russians—whether from courage or from inconstancy of feelings, lasting sorrows are hardly characteristic of them—they are more susceptible to superstition than to emotion. Superstition relates to this life, religion to the next. Superstition is linked to fatality, while religion is to virtue. It is through the intensity of earthly desires that we become superstitious, and it is—on the contrary—through the sacrifice of these same desires that we are religious.

Monsieur de Romanzov,[1] the former Russian Minister of Foreign Affairs, was extremely courteous to me, and it was with regret that I thought how, as one who had been closely associated with Emperor Napoleon's system, he had been obliged, like an English minister, to retire when that system was rejected. No doubt in an absolute monarchy the master's will explains everything; but the dignity of a prime minister perhaps requires him not to make contradictory statements. The sovereign represents the State, and the State may change policies whenever circumstances require it; but the minister is only a man, and a man, on questions of this importance, ought to have but one opinion in the course of his life. No one could have better manners than Monsieur de Romanzov, or receive foreigners more handsomely. I was at his house when the English envoy, Lord Tyrconnel, and Admiral Bentinck [2]—both men of distinguished appearance—were announced. They were the first Englishmen to reappear on the Continent, from which they had been banished by the tyranny of one man. After ten years of frightful conflict, ten years during which the English—through

---

[1] Nicholas Petrovich, Count Romanzov, born in 1754, died in 1826. He had been Minister of Foreign Affairs in 1807. Hostile to England and friendly to France, he accompanied the Czar to Erfurt in 1808. When Napoleon, whom he admired, invaded Russia, he retired from public life. Nesselrode replaced him in Alexander's confidence.

[2] George, Count Tyrconnel, Irish peer, born in 1788; he volunteered for military service in Russia and died at Vilna, December 10, 1812, as a result of over-fatigue in the pursuit of the French army. Admiral Bentinck, of the family of the Dukes of Portland; he is mentioned in a note from Madame de Staël to Galiffe, August 14, 1812; she writes that she will bring "the admiral" to the ball given by the banker, Rall.

good fortune and bad—had remained faithful to their guiding principle, conscience, they finally returned to the country which was the first to free itself from universal monarchy. Their accent, their simplicity, and their pride rekindled one's passion for truth in all things, which Napoleon has managed to obscure for those who have only read his press and listened to his agents. I do not even know if Napoleon's adversaries on the Continent, perpetually bombarded and dazed by false opinions, can even trust their own instincts without becoming confused. If I may judge by my own experience, I know that often, after having listened to all the counsels of prudence or cowardice with which one is engulfed in Napoleon's milieu, I no longer knew how to form my own opinion. My instinct told me not to renounce it, but my reason was not always sufficient protection against so many sophisms. Blessed is the country where I can hear again the voice of that England with which one is almost always sure to agree when one seeks to merit the esteem of honorable men as well as one's own self-respect.

The next day Count Orlov invited me to visit the island that bears his name. It is the most pleasant of all the islands formed by the Neva: oak trees—rare in this country—shade the garden. Count and Countess Orlov use their fortune to receive foreigners with ease and magnificence, and one is as comfortable with them as in a country retreat, while enjoying all city luxury. Count Orlov is one of the most learned noblemen in Russia, and his love of country is so strong that one cannot help being moved by it. On my first day there, peace with England had just been proclaimed. It was a Sunday, and in his garden, which was open that day to strollers, we saw a great number of those bearded Russian merchants who still wear the muzhiks' costume, in other words, peasant attire. Several gathered to listen to Count Orlov's delightful music; we heard the English tune "God Save the King," the song of liberty in a country where the king is its chief guardian. All of us were moved, and we applauded this national song for the sake of all Europeans, for there are only two kinds of men in Europe, those who serve tyranny, and those who have learned how to hate it. Count Orlov went up to the Russian merchants and told them that peace between England and Russia was being celebrated. They immediately made the sign of the cross, and thanked heaven that the sea was again open to them.

The Orlov Island is in the midst of all those which the great nobles of Petersburg—and even the Emperor and Empress—have selected for their summer residences. Nearby is the Strogonov island; its wealthy owner has brought Greek antiquities of great value to it. His house was open every day during his lifetime, and anyone who had once been presented there could return. He never invited anyone to dine on a particular day, for it was understood that once admitted one was always welcome. Frequently, he did not know half the people who were dining at his table, but this lavish hospitality pleased him as did any other kind of magnificence. In Petersburg the same practice, or something resembling it, prevails in many houses; from that, it is easy to conclude that what we in France mean by the pleasures of conversation cannot be found there: the company is much too numerous for an interchange of any interest ever to take place. In the best society everyone has perfect manners, but there is neither sufficient education among the nobles, nor sufficient confidence among people living under the perpetual influence of a despotic court and government, to allow for the charms of intimacy.

Most of the great Russian nobles express themselves with so much elegance and propriety that one is frequently deceived at first about the extent of their wit and knowledge. Their opening remarks are almost always those of a man or woman of great intelligence, but sometimes too—in the long run—one finds nothing more than the opening remarks. In Russia they are not accustomed to speaking from the bottom of their heart or mind. Until recently there was such fear of their masters that they have not yet learned to feel comfortable with the sensible liberty that they owe to Emperor Alexander.

Several Russian gentlemen have tried to distinguish themselves in literature, and have given proof of considerable talent; but knowledge is not yet sufficiently diffused for there to be a public judgment formed by individual opinions. The Russian character is too passionate to like ideas that are the least bit abstract. Facts alone amuse them. They have not yet had the time nor the inclination to reduce facts to general ideas. Moreover, every significant idea is always more or less dangerous at a court where everyone observes everyone else, and where more often than not envy is the predominant feeling.

The reserve of the East is here transformed into pleasant words, but words which generally never penetrate to the root of things. For a while one enjoys this brilliant atmosphere, which so, but in the long run nothing is learned, one does not develop one's mental faculties, and the men who spend their lives in this manner never acquire any capacity for study or business. Parisian society was not like this: men could be found whose education was largely derived from the stimulating or serious conversations made possible by assemblages of nobles and men of letters.

CHAPTER XVII

The Imperial Family: Empress

Elizabeth–Conversation with Emperor

Alexander; memorable words–Russian

despotism–Empress Marie; the Taurida

Palace

At last I saw the famous monarch, absolute by law and custom, yet so moderate by his own choice. I was first presented to Empress Elizabeth, who seemed to me to be the guardian angel of Russia.[1] Her manner is extremely reserved, but what she says is full of warmth and vitality, as if her sentiments and opinions are drawn from some inner source of noble thoughts. While listening to her, I was affected by something inexpressible which was a result, not of her grandeur but of the harmony of her soul. It had been a long time since I had witnessed the union of power and virtue.

As I was conversing with the Empress the door opened, and the Emperor Alexander honored me by coming to speak with me. What first struck me about him was his expression of kindness

---

[1] Czarina Elizabeth was a princess from Baden-Durlach; her mother was born Princess of Darmstadt; the Grand Duchess of Saxe-Weimar was her aunt.

and dignity: the two were inseparably joined, as if he had made a single quality of them. I was also very impressed, from the start of our conversation, by the imposing simplicity with which he discussed the great interests of Europe. The fear of serious discussion that has been instilled in most European sovereigns has always seemed to me to be a sign of mediocrity. They are afraid to say anything that has real meaning. Emperor Alexander, on the contrary, talked with me just as English statesmen—who rely on inner strength rather than on protective barriers—would have done. Emperor Alexander—whom Napoleon has tried to misrepresent—is a man of remarkable intelligence and education, and I do not believe that he could find in his whole empire a minister more capable than himself in all that pertains to the judgment and direction of public affairs. He did not hide from me the admiration to which he had yielded in his relations with Napoleon. Alexander's grandfather had felt a similar great enthusiasm for Frederick II. In illusions of this kind, inspired by an extraordinary man, there is always a generous motive, whatever may be the errors that result from it.

Nevertheless, Emperor Alexander very shrewdly described the impression these conversations with Bonaparte had had on him, in which Bonaparte said the most contradictory things, as if each statement were so amazing on its own that one would never realize they were contradictory. He also told me about the lessons in Machiavellism that Napoleon had seen fit to give him. "You see," Napoleon said to Alexander, "I am careful to keep my ministers and my generals at odds with each other, so that they will reveal each other's faults to me. I maintain continual jealousy by the way I treat my associates. One day one thinks he is the favorite, the next day another, so that no one is ever certain of my favor." What a vulgar, vicious theory! One can only hope that sometime there will be a man superior to this one, who will demonstrate its futility. What the sacred cause of morality needs is to demonstrate in a striking manner that it leads to great success in this world; anyone who fully appreciated the dignity of this cause would gladly sacrifice to it any other success; but the presumptuous, who mistake defects of character for profundity of thought, must still be taught that if there is sometimes cleverness in immorality, there is genius in virtue.

While convincing myself of Emperor Alexander's good faith in his relations with Napoleon, I was also satisfied that he would not follow the example of Germany's unfortunate sovereigns and would not sign a peace treaty with a man who is as much the enemy of people as of kings. A noble soul cannot twice be deceived by the same person. Alexander gives and withdraws his confidence only after the most careful thought. At the beginning of his reign his youth and physical advantages alone were enough to make people suspect him of shallowness, but he is as serious as only a man who has known misfortune can be. Alexander told me of his regrets at not being a great captain. My response to this noble modesty was to say that a sovereign is rarer than a general, and that to sustain his nation's public spirit by his own example was to win the greatest victory, the first of this kind ever to have been won. The Emperor spoke enthusiastically about his country and what it was capable of becoming. He expressed his desire—which all the world knows he has—to better the lot of the peasants still subject to slavery. "Sire," I said to him, "your character is a constitution for your empire, and your conscience is its guarantee."

"Even if that were the case," he replied, "I would never be more than a fortunate accident." [2] Noble words, and the first of their kind, I believe, to be pronounced by an absolute monarch! It takes tremendous virtue to judge despotism while being a despot! Also to avoid its abuse, when the nation being governed is almost incredulous at such moderation!

In Petersburg especially, the great nobles are less liberal in their principles than the Emperor himself. Accustomed to being absolute masters of their peasants, they want the monarch, in his turn, to be all-powerful in order to maintain the hierarchy of despotism. The bourgeois class does not yet exist in Russia; nevertheless, it is beginning to take shape: the sons of priests and merchants, and

---

[2] This remark has already been cited in *Considérations sur la Révolution française*, but it merits being repeated. All this, moreover, I must remind you, was written at the end of 1812. (Auguste de Staël's notes.) Cf. *Considérations*, part VI chap. X.

some peasants who have obtained permission from their masters to become artists, may be considered a third order in the state. The Russian nobility, moreover, bears no resemblance to the German or French. A man becomes a noble in Russia as soon as he obtains a military rank. No doubt the great families—such as the Narishkin, the Dolgoruki, the Galitzin, and others, will always enjoy precedence in the empire; but it is also true that the advantages of aristocracy belong to some men who were made nobles overnight because it suited the monarch's pleasure, and the principal ambition of the bourgeois is to have their sons made officers, so that they may belong to the privileged class. The result is that young men finish their education at fifteen years of age, they rush into military service as soon as possible, and everything else is neglected. This is not the time, certainly, to criticize a system which has produced such splendid resistance. In a calmer period, one might truthfully say that in respect to civil relations, there are great deficiencies in Russia's internal administration. The nation has energy and grandeur, but order and enlightenment are in many respects still lacking, both in government and in private behavior. By Europeanizing Russia, Peter I certainly gave it great advantages through the agency of despotism prepared by his father and which he consolidated. Catherine II, on the contrary, tempered the use of absolute power, of which she was not the author. If the political state of Europe should ever be restored to peace, in other words, if a single man no longer dispensed evil to the world, we would see Alexander solely occupied in improving his country, and he himself would seek to establish laws, guaranteeing for Russia the happiness which can, at present, only be assured during his lifetime.

From the Emperor's, I went to the home of his worthy mother, a princess whom no one has ever been able to accuse of any sentiment other than loyalty to her husband, her children, and the family of unfortunates whom she protects through her charities. I plan to tell more about the story of her management of this empire of good works in the midst of her son's all-powerful empire. She lives in the Taurida palace, and to get to her apartment one has to cross a huge hall built by Prince Potemkin. This is a chamber of incomparable grandeur. A winter garden occupies a part of it, and you see plants and trees through the columns that surround the middle enclosure. Everything in this residence is colossal, for the prince who built it had fantastically monumental conceptions. He had towns built in the Crimea solely so that the Empress might see them while passing by, and he ordered an assault on a fortress to please a beautiful woman—Princess Dolgoruki—who had disdained his homage. His sovereign's favor made him what he was. There is, also, something fantastic, violent, and also ironic in most of the great men of Russia, such as Menshikov, Souvorov, Peter I himself, and—going further back—Ivan Vasilievich. Intelligence was a weapon for them rather than a joy, and they were guided by imagination. Generosity, barbarism, unbridled passions, and religious superstition could all be found in the same person. To this day, civilization in Russia has not yet penetrated beneath the surface, even among the great nobles. Outwardly, they imitate other peoples, but all are Russian at heart, which is what gives them their strength and originality, love of country being—next to love of God—the finest sentiment men can experience. A country must be markedly different from its neighbors to inspire such a strong attachment. Nations which gradually become indistinguishable from one another, or which are divided among several separate states, never devote themselves with real passion to the contractual association to which they have given the name of *patrie*.

CHAPTER XVIII

Customs of the great Russian nobles:

Monsieur Narishkin–Strange music–

Songs of the Ukraine–A toast–

Kalmuks–Promenade in the park;

Russian mountains–Love in Russia–

Drawbacks of despotism

I spent a day at the country residence of Monsieur Narishkin, Grand Chamberlain of the court, an amiable, accommodating, and cultivated man, but a man who cannot live without a party of some kind. In his company one learns what is really meant by the violent enthusiasms which explain both the defects and qualities of the Russians. It is always open house at Monsieur Narishkin's, and when he has only twenty guests at his country residence, he becomes bored with this philosophical retreat. He is kind to foreigners, always on the move, yet perfectly capable of the discernment needed for proper conduct in court circles. Avid for pleasures of the imagination, he finds them only in things, and not in books. He is impatient everywhere except at court, witty when it is ad-

vantageous to be so, imposing rather than ambitious, and in everything seeking a certain Asiatic grandeur where fortune and rank
count for more than the superiority of the individual. His estate is
as pleasant as a man-made natural setting can be. All the surrounding country is barren and swampy, so this residence is an oasis.
From the terrace, the Gulf of Finland is visible, and in the distance,
the palace which Peter I had built on its shore,[1] but the space
between the sea and the palace is almost a wasteland, and only
Monsieur Narishkin's park delights the eye. We dined in the
Moldavian house, or rather, in a room built in the Moldavian style.
It was constructed so as to avoid the heat of the sun; a rather need-
less precaution in Russia. However, one's imagination is so impressed with the idea that one is living in a nation that is in the
North only by accident, that it seems natural to find the customs
of the South there, as if the Russians might some day bring the
climate of their former country to Petersburg. The table was laden
with fruits of all countries, according to an Oriental custom of
having only the fruit visible, while a throng of servants brought
meat and vegetable dishes to each guest.

We were entertained with a concert of horn music of a type
peculiar to Russia and often described by travelers. Each of the
twenty musicians plays one and only one note every time it occurs;
thus each man bears the name of the note he plays. On seeing one
of them pass, people say, "Here comes Monsieur Narishkin's *sol*,
mi, or *re*." The horns get bigger from row to row, and this music
has rightly been called a *living organ*. At a distance, the effect is
very beautiful. The precision and purity of the harmony inspire
the most noble thoughts, but when one approaches these poor
musicians, who are there like pipes giving out sounds, quite unable
to participate emotionally in the effect produced, the pleasure
grows cold. No one likes to see the fine arts transformed into
mechanical arts, to be learned compulsorily, like a drill.

Some people from the Ukraine, dressed in scarlet costumes, next
sang us some of their region's songs, which are singularly beautiful, sometimes gay, sometimes melancholy, or both at the same

---

[1] Peterhof, which Peter I built upon his return from France, between Oranien-
baum and Petersburg.

time. These songs occasionally break off in the middle of the melody, as if the composers had tired of what had pleased them at first, or found it more piquant to suspend the music's charm at the moment of its greatest power. The Sultana of the *Thousand and One Nights* always breaks off her story in the same way, when its interest is liveliest.

In the midst of these varied pleasures Monsieur Narishkin proposed a toast to the success of the combined Russian and English forces, and at that moment gave a signal to his artillery, which responded with a salute worthy of a king. All the guests were intoxicated with hope. As for me, I was bathed in tears. Was it my fate that a foreign tyrant should make me want the French to be beaten? "I wish," I said then, "for the downfall of the man who is oppressing France as well as Europe, for those who are truly French will triumph if he is defeated." First Monsieur Narishkin, and then the English and Russian guests praised my impulsive statement, and the word France, until then like the name Armida,[2] was once more favorably received by the knights of the East and of the sea, who were going to fight against her.

A few Kalmuks with flat features are brought up in the homes of the Russian nobility, as if to preserve a specimen of the Tartars whom the Slavs conquered. In the Narishkin palace two or three of these half-savage Kalmuks were running around. They are rather winsome in childhood, but after the age of twenty, they lose all their youthful charm. Although they are slaves, they are obstinate, and they amuse their masters by their resistance, like squirrels struggling with the bars of a cage. These debased specimens of humanity were painful to watch: I seemed to glimpse, in the midst of all the pomp of luxury, an image of what man can become when he derives no dignity from either religion or the laws, and this spectacle was humbling to any pride inspired by the enjoyment of splendor.

After dinner we went for a drive in the park in long promenade carriages drawn by the most beautiful horses. It was the end of

---

[2] One of the heroines of *Jerusalem Delivered*, by Torquato Tasso. Armida fell in love with one of the knights of the First Crusade and was converted to Christianity. (Trans.)

August, but the sky was pale and the grass almost an artificial green, for it was preserved only by dint of great care. Even the flowers seemed an aristocratic pleasure, because it was so expensive to grow them. One did not hear birds warbling in the woods, for they did not trust this momentary summer, nor were there cattle in the meadows: one would not dare let them graze among plants so difficult to cultivate. The water barely flowed—and then only by means of machines which diverted it into the gardens— where nature itself looked like party decorations which would be removed when the guests had left. Our carriages stopped before a part of the garden made to look like a Tartar camp. There all the reassembled musicians began to play again. The noise of horns and cymbals was quite intoxicating. And to complete the diversion, the Russians imitated, in summer, the swift-moving sleighs which console them for their winter; they made a game of riding with the speed of lightning from the top of an artificial mountain made of wood.[3] This sport charmed the women as well as the men, giving them a small share in the exhilarating wartime sensations of rapid movement and awareness of danger. So the time passed, for almost every day saw a renewal of what to me seemed like a continual festival.

With few differences, most of the great houses of Petersburg lead this kind of life. It should be clear that there can be no question of any serious conversation, and in this kind of society education is of no benefit. When such efforts are made to bring together a great number of people in one's home, entertainments are, after all, the only means of preventing the boredom which crowds in drawing rooms always produce.

In the midst of all this tumult, is there any room for love? This is the question that would be asked by Italian women, who scarcely have any interest in society other than the pleasure of meeting the one by whom they wish to be beloved. I spent too short a time in Petersburg to have a true idea of family relationships. It appeared to me, however, that on the one hand there was more domestic virtue than was said to exist, but on the other hand there was little

---

[3] This is the pastime called *Russian mountains*.

romantic love. One effect of the Asiatic customs that are everywhere encountered is that women never interfere in domestic affairs; all these are directed by the husband, and the wife merely
adorns herself with his gifts and receives his guests. Respect for
morality is much greater now than it was in Petersburg in the time
of those emperors and empresses who corrupted morals by their
own examples. The two present empresses are models of virtue,
and have increased the public's esteem for these qualities. However, in this as in many other respects moral principles are not
firmly established in the minds of Russians. The ruler's influence
has always been so strong that all maxims on any subject can be
changed from one reign to the next. The Russians, both men and
women, generally bring to love their characteristic impetuosity,
but their penchant for change also makes them quick to renounce
their choices. A certain disorderliness of imagination keeps them
from finding happiness in continuity. Cultivation of the mind,
which increases sensibility through familiarity with poetry and
the fine arts, is very rare among the Russians, and in these capricious and vehement natures love is more of an entertainment or an
ecstasy than a profound and thoughtful affection.

Consequently good society in Russia is a continual whirlwind;
and perhaps because a despotic government teaches people extreme
prudence, the Russians prefer not to be exposed, in the excitement
of conversation, to speaking on subjects that might have any consequence whatever. To this reserve—which, under different reigns,
has been only too necessary—we must attribute their reputation
for untruthfulness. In all countries civilization's refinements alter
sincerity of character, but when a sovereign possesses unlimited
power to exile, to imprison, to send to Siberia, and so forth, this
power is too strong for human nature. One might have encountered men proud enough to disdain favors, but to brave persecution
heroism is required, and heroism cannot be a universal quality.

None of these reflections, we know, applies to the present government, since its head is perfectly just as an emperor, and extraordinarily generous as a man. But subjects retain the defects of
slavery long after the sovereign himself would like to remove them.
Nevertheless, we have seen in the course of this war what great

virtues even the Russians of the court possess. While I was in Petersburg, practically no young men were to be seen; even married men, only sons, or nobles with immense fortunes were in the army serving as simple volunteers, and when they saw their lands and houses ravaged they thought of these losses only to avenge them, and never of capitulating to the enemy. Such qualities overshadow all the abuses, disorders, and defects that a still faulty administration, a new civilization, and despotic institutions may have produced.

CHAPTER XIX

The natural history collection—The

church of Saint Peter and Saint Paul:

tomb of the Czars—Tsarskoe Selo—

Taking of Smolensk by the French; Madame

de Staël's discouragement; depressing

symptoms—Saint Catherine's Institute;

gracious attention of the Czarina—Lack

of learning in Russia—A Russian

tragedy—The nation's patriotism

We went to see the natural history collection, which is notable for its articles from Siberia. Siberian furs have aroused the cupidity of the Russians just as Mexican gold mines did that of the Spaniards. There was a time in Russia when the medium of exchange consisted of sable and squirrel skins, so universal was the need for protection against winter frosts. The most curious thing in this Petersburg museum is a rich collection of bones of antediluvian animals, and especially the remains of a gigantic mammoth found almost intact in the Siberian ice. From geological observations it appears that the earth's history dates from much further back than we had suspected. Infinity creates fear in all things.

At present the inhabitants and even the animals of this outermost limit of the inhabited world are almost penetrated with the cold, which causes all nature to die, a few leagues beyond their country. The coloration of the animals becomes indistinguishable from the snow, and the ground seems to disappear in the ice and fog which mark the earthly limits of the creation. I was struck by the faces of the inhabitants of Kamchatka, which are perfectly reproduced in the Petersburg museum. Their priests, called "shamans," are a race of improvisors. Over their tunics of tree bark they wear a sort of steel net to which several pieces of iron are attached, which makes a very loud noise when the improvisor moves; he has moments of inspiration which resemble nervous attacks, and he impresses the people more by sorcery than by skill. In these rather dreary lands imagination is hardly noteworthy except where fear is involved, and the earth itself seems to repel man by the terror it arouses in him.

Next I visited the fortress within which is the church containing the coffins of all sovereigns from the time of Peter the Great.[1] These coffins are not enclosed in vaults but are exhibited just as they were on the day of the funeral ceremony, and one imagines oneself quite close to these dead, separated from the living by only a simple plank. When Paul I came to the throne, he had the remains of his father—Peter III—crowned, because without that honor, which he had not received in his lifetime, he could not be placed in the citadel. By order of Paul I, the burial ceremony for his father and his mother, Catherine II, was repeated. Again, both lay in state; again, four chamberlains guarded their bodies as if they had died the night before, and the two coffins are there, side by side, forced to live in peace in the empire of the dead. Among

---

[1] The church of Saint Peter and Saint Paul.

the sovereigns who have held the despotic power handed down by Peter I, several were toppled from the throne by bloody conspiracies. The same courtiers, who do not have the strength of character to tell their master the simplest truth, know how to conspire against him. The most profound duplicity inevitably accompanies this kind of political revolution, for they must overwhelm with respect the ruler they wish to assassinate. And yet what would become of a country governed despotically if a lawless tyrant had nothing to fear from daggers? A horrible alternative, and one which suffices to show the true nature of institutions where crime must be reckoned in the balance of powers.

I paid homage to Catherine II by going to her country residence (Tsarskoe Selo). This palace and garden are artistically and magnificently arranged, but the weather was already very cold, although we were barely into September, and it was a strange contrast to see those flowers from the south agitated by the wind from the north. Everything one learns about Catherine II as a sovereign inspires admiration for her, and I wonder if the Russians are not indebted to her—rather than to Peter I—for their fortunate conviction of invincibility: a conviction which has contributed so much to their success. A woman's charm tempered her exercise of power and mingled chivalrous gallantry with the successes for which she was paid homage. Catherine II had a superbly developed talent for governing. A more brilliant mind than hers would have resembled genius less, and her superior intelligence inspired deep respect in the Russians, who mistrust their own imagination and want someone to guide it with prudence. Close to Tsarskoe Selo is Paul I's palace, a charming residence, because the Dowager Empress and her daughters have furnished it with masterpieces reflecting their talent and good taste. This place is a reminder of the admirable patience of that mother and her daughters, whom nothing has been able to divert from their domestic virtues.

I was indulging myself in the pleasures which my daily visits to new objects gave me, and I had somehow forgotten the war, on which Europe's fate depended. It was so satisfying to hear everyone express the sentiments I had so long stifled, that it seemed to me that there was nothing more to fear, and that such truths became all-powerful merely for having been expressed. Neverthe-less, a succession of reverses had taken place without the public being informed of them. A man of wit said that everything was a mystery in Petersburg although nothing was a secret; and in fact, one finally does discover the truth, although the habit of silence among Russian courtiers is so strong that they conceal today what must surely be known tomorrow, and only reveal what they know unintentionally. A foreigner told me that Smolensk had been captured,[2] and that Moscow was in grave danger. Discour-agement seized me. I thought I was seeing a repetition of the deplorable history of the Austrian and Prussian peace treaties which were the result of the conquest of their capitals. It was the same trick being played for the third time, but it might succeed again. I did not notice any public reaction. The fluctuations of Russian sentiments made them impossible to gauge. Despondency had frozen all minds, and I did not then know that in men of such strong feelings, despondency is the forerunner of a terrible awak-ening. In the same way you notice an incredible laziness in the lower classes up to the moment when their energy is aroused; then it knows no obstacle, fears no danger, and seems to triumph equally over men and the elements.

I knew that the country's internal administration, in matters of war as well as of justice, frequently fell into the most venal hands, and that because of embezzlements by subordinate employees it was impossible to form an exact idea either of the number of troops or of the measures taken to provision them, for lying and theft are inseparable. In a country where civilization is so recent the middle class has neither the simplicity of the peasantry nor the grandeur of the boyars, and no public opinion as yet exists to restrain this new third class, which has lost the naïveté of popular faith without having learned the meaning of honor. A growing spirit of rivalry was also apparent among military leaders. It is in the very nature of despotic government to spawn—even in spite of itself—jealousy among those in high positions. Since one man's whim can com-pletely change any individual's fate, fear and hope are too wide-

---

[2] Smolensk had been captured by Ney and Davout after a bloody battle (August 17–18, 1812). On withdrawing, the Russians set fire to the city.

spread not to be continually stirring up this jealousy, which is also aroused by another emotion: the hatred of foreigners. The general in command of the Russian army, Monsieur Barclay de Tolly, was not a Slav,[3] although born in Russia, and that was enough to prevent him from leading the Russians to victory. Moreover, he was more interested in systems of encampments, positions, and maneuvers than in attacking, which is the military tactic best suited to the Russians. To make them retreat—even as a result of wise and rational calculations—is to cool their impetuosity, the source of their strength.

The omens for the campaign were therefore particularly inauspicious, and the official silence surrounding this subject was even more alarming. The English newspapers give a detailed account —man by man—of the wounded, the prisoners, and those killed in each engagement: noble candor of a government that is as sincere toward the nation as toward its monarch, recognizing in both the same right to know the truth concerning public affairs. Sadly, I walked about the beautiful city of Petersburg which might fall to the conqueror. When I returned from the islands in the evening and saw the citadel's golden spire, seeming to flash like a ray of fire, while the Neva reflected the marble quays and palaces surrounding it, I imagined all these wonders tarnished by the arrogance of a man who would come to say, like Satan on the mountaintop: "The kingdoms of the earth are mine." All that was beautiful and good in Petersburg seemed to be threatened with impending destruction, and I could not enjoy any of it without being haunted by this painful thought.

I went to see the schools founded by the Empress, and there even more than in the palaces my anxiety was redoubled, for a whiff of Bonaparte's tyranny is sufficient to spoil the purity of institutions devoted to improving the human race. Saint Catherine's Institute is composed of two houses, each containing two hundred

---

[3] Barclay de Tolly was a descendant of a Scottish family which had settled in the Baltic province of Courland, and for this reason was viewed with a certain hostility by the Russians. He advised delaying tactics, to draw the French into the interior of Russia. This policy was opposed by Prince Bagration, a Georgian who was jealous of Barclay and was a believer in a military offensive.

and fifty young ladies of the nobility or bourgeois class. They
are educated under the Empress's supervision, with a degree of
care surpassing even the education a wealthy family could give
to its own children. Order and elegance are clearly evident in
even the smallest details at this institute, and one is conscious of
the purest religious and moral influences presiding over an excellent training in the fine arts. Russian women have so much natural
grace that on entering the room where all the young ladies greeted
us, I did not see a single one who failed to express perfect politeness and modesty in her curtsy. The young girls were asked to
show us their special talents, and one of them, who knew some
selections from the best French writers by heart, recited several
of the most eloquent pages of my father's *Course in Religious
Morality*.[4] This very delicate attention may have been suggested
by the Empress herself. I was greatly moved on hearing those
words which for so many years had had no other sanctuary than
my heart. In every country beyond Bonaparte's empire, posterity
begins and justice is done to those who—even in the tomb—have
been subjected to his imperial slanders. The young girls of Saint
Catherine's Institute sang psalms before sitting down at table;
the great choir of pure, sweet voices filled me with tenderness
mixed with regret. I could not help wondering what would be the
war's effect on peaceful establishments such as this. Where could
these doves flee from the conqueror's weapons? After the meal the
young ladies assembled in a superb hall, where they all danced
together. There was nothing striking in their features but their
grace was extraordinary. They were daughters of the East, with
all the decorum that Christian manners have introduced among
women. First they performed an old dance, to the tune of "Long
live Henry the Fourth, Long live this valiant king!" What a long
time has elapsed between the age this song recalls and the present! Two little plump ten-year-old girls ended the ballet with a
Russian dance: this dance sometimes assumes the voluptuous
sensuality of love, but when executed by children of that age it

---

[4] Necker's *Cours de morale religieuse* was published in 1800.

mingled innocence with national originality. These gentle arts, encouraged by the delicate generosity of a woman and sovereign, were indescribably appealing.

An institute for deaf-mutes, and another for the blind are also under the Empress's direction. For his part, the Emperor pays great attention to the Cadet School, which is directed by an outstanding man, General Klinger. All of these institutions are truly useful, though they might be criticized for being overly magnificent. It would at least be desirable to establish—in different parts of the empire—less polished schools which would still give the people some elementary learning. In Russia, everything has begun in luxury, and the roof has—so to speak—preceded the foundation. There are only two large cities in Russia, Petersburg and Moscow. The others scarcely deserve mention, and moreover they are separated by very great distances. Even the châteaux of the great nobles are so far from each other that their owners can hardly communicate with one another. In a word, the inhabitants of this empire are so dispersed that it is almost impossible for the knowledge of some to be of use to the others. The peasants can reckon only by means of a calculating machine, and even post-office clerks use the same method. The Greek Orthodox priests are not as well educated as Catholic curates or—more particularly—as Protestant ministers; as a result the Russian clergy is not capable of instructing the people, as in other European countries. The nation is united by religion and patriotism, but there is no seat of learning to extend its influence to all parts of the empire, and the two capitals are so far unable to share what they have acquired in the way of literature and the fine arts with the provinces. If this country could have remained at peace, it would have experienced all kinds of improvements under Emperor Alexander's benevolent reign. But who knows if the virtues developed by wars such as this one may not be precisely those needed to regenerate nations?

Until now, the Russians have had men of genius only in the military. In all other spheres they are only imitators; printing— after all—was only introduced here a hundred and twenty years ago. The other European nations became civilized at almost the same time, and have been able to blend their natural talents with acquired knowledge, but for the Russians, this mixture has not yet taken place. Just as two rivers, after their juncture, flow in the same channel without mingling their waters, nature and civilization have been brought together in the Russians without fusing; and depending on the circumstances, the same man may seem at times to be a European who consists of nothing but social graces, and at other times, a headstrong Slav, guided only by violent passions. They will only achieve genius in the fine arts, and especially in literature, when they have found a way to express their true nature in words as they now do in actions.

I saw a Russian tragedy performed whose subject was the deliverance of the Muscovites when they drove the Tartars beyond Kazan.[5] The Prince of Smolensk appeared in the ancient boyar costume, and the Tartar army was called the "Golden Horde." This play was written almost entirely according to the rules of French drama; the rhythm of the verses, their recitation, and the division into scenes were all French, and only one situation was derived from Russian customs: the profound terror that a father's curse inspired in a young girl. Paternal authority is almost as strong among the Russians as among the Chinese. However, it is always among the common people that authentic national character must be sought. Good society is the same in all countries, and nothing is less appropriate than that elegant world for furnishing subjects for tragedy. Of all those offered by Russian history, one particularly impressed me: Ivan the Terrible, who was already old, was besieging Novgorod. Seeing how enfeebled he was, the boyars asked him if he would not turn over the command to his son. This proposal enraged him so that nothing could appease him; his son prostrated himself at his feet, but he repulsed him with a blow of such violence that two days later the unfortunate son died. Then the father, in despair, grew indifferent to the war and to power, and survived his son by only a few months. This revolt of an aged despot against the passage of time has something

---

[5] Probably the poet Ozerov's tragedy, *Dmitri Donskoi*, which was first performed in 1807. In 1812 the invasion of Russia by the French gave it a topical revival.

grand and solemn in it. The tenderness that succeeds the fury in
that ferocious soul represents man as he comes from the hands of
nature, sometimes driven by egoism, sometimes restrained by affection.

A Russian law inflicted the same penalty on the person who
maimed a man's arm as on the one who killed him. It is true that
a Russian is principally valued for his military strength. All other
kinds of energy are derived from manners and institutions which
Russia has not yet developed. However, the women in Petersburg
seemed to be imbued with the kind of patriotic pride that constitutes the moral power of a state. Princess Dolgoruki, Baroness
Strogonov, and several others of equally high rank knew that
they had lost a part of their fortunes when the province of Smolensk was devastated, yet they appeared not to think about it except to encourage their peers to make sacrifices as they had. Princess Dolgoruki told me that an old bearded man, seated on a hill
overlooking Smolensk, said, weeping, to his little grandson whom
he was holding on his knee: "Once, my child, the Russians went
to the ends of Europe to win victories. Now foreigners come to
attack them at home." The old man's grief was not in vain, and
we shall soon see how his tears have been redeemed.

CHAPTER XX

Interview at Abo—Madame de Staël's

further conversation with Emperor

Alexander—Madame de Staël and Prince

Kutusov—Foreigners in Petersburg:

Robert Wilson, Stein, Tyrconnel, Bentinck,

Alexis de Noailles, Dörnberg—Entry into

Finland: appearance of the country—

Madame de Staël embarks at Abo;

difficulties of the crossing

The Emperor left Petersburg, and I learned that he had gone to Abo, where he was to meet with General Bernadotte, Crown Prince of Sweden.[1] This meant the end of doubt as to the stand

---

[1] The conference in Abo, Finland, between Alexander and the Crown Prince of Sweden took place from August 27–30, 1812. Madame de Staël wrote from Stockholm, January 12, 1813, to the Grand Duchess of Saxe-Weimar: "The Abo conference allied the three powers permanently, and Emperor Alexander spoke to me about his great esteem for the Prince of Sweden."

the Prince had decided to take in the present war, and nothing was more important at that moment for the safety of Russia, and consequently, of Europe. The influence of this decision will become more obvious during the course of this narrative. News of the French entry into Smolensk arrived during the interview between the Prince of Sweden and the Emperor of Russia, and it was then that Alexander made the commitment, to himself and jointly with his ally the Crown Prince, never to sign a peace treaty. "If Petersburg should be captured," he said, "I would withdraw into Siberia. There I would resume our ancient customs and—like our bearded ancestors—we would return to reconquer the empire."

"Your resolution will liberate Europe!" cried the Prince of Sweden, and his prediction is beginning to come true.

I saw Emperor Alexander a second time upon his return from Abo, and our conversation convinced me so thoroughly of his determination that in spite of the capture of Moscow and the many reports that followed, I firmly believed that he would never yield. He volunteered the information that after the capture of Smolensk the French Marshal Berthier had written to the Russian commander-in-chief about some military matters, and had concluded his letter by saying that Emperor Napoleon still retained the most affectionate friendship for Emperor Alexander, an insipid mockery which the Emperor of Russia accepted in the spirit it deserved. Napoleon had given him some lessons in politics and war, indulging himself, in the first, in the quack remedies of vice, and in the second, in the pleasure of exhibiting a disdainful unconcern. He had been mistaken about Emperor Alexander; he had mistaken his idealism for trickery. He had not been able to perceive that if the Emperor of Russia had let himself go too far in his enthusiasm for him, it was because he believed him to be a partisan of the basic principles of the French Revolution, which agreed with his own opinions. Alexander had never thought of associating himself with Napoleon in order to subjugate Europe. Napoleon believed, in this circumstance as in all others, that he could blind a man by appealing to his interest, falsely interpreted; but here he encountered a conscience and all his calculations were frustrated, for conscience is an element with whose strength he is unacquainted, and which never enters his schemes.

Although Monsieur Barclay de Tolly was highly regarded as a military leader, he had experienced setbacks at the start of the campaign, and public opinion wanted him replaced by a general of great renown, Prince Kutusov. He took command fifteen days before the French entered Moscow, but was unable to reach the army until six days before the great battle which took place at Borodino almost at the gates of Moscow. I went to see him the night before his departure. He was an old man with charming manners and an expressive face, despite the loss of an eye from one of the many wounds he had received in the course of fifty years of military service. Looking at him, I was afraid he was not strong enough to oppose the rough powerful men who were assaulting Russia from all corners of Europe, but although the Russians are courtiers in Petersburg, they become Tartars again in the army, and we have seen, in the case of Souvorov, that neither age nor honors can weaken their physical and moral energy. I felt quite moved on leaving this illustrious Marshal Kutusov. I did not know whether I was embracing a conqueror or a martyr, but I saw that he fully understood the grandeur of the cause he was serving. It was a question of defending—or rather, reestablishing—all the moral virtues that man owes to Christianity, all the dignity he derives from God, and all the independence that nature allows him. It was a question of rescuing all these possessions from the clutches of one man—for the French can no more be accused than the Germans and Italians who were following Bonaparte—of the crimes of his armies. Before leaving, General Kutusov went to say a prayer in the church of Notre Dame of Kazan, and the crowds who were following him cried out to him to save Russia. What a moment for a mortal being! His age gave him no hope of surviving the fatigues of the campaign, but there are moments when a man must face death in order to satisfy his soul.

Certain of the generous views and noble conduct of the Prince of Sweden, I was more than ever determined to arrange for the

return of my sons to their father's native land by putting them in
Sweden's military service. I left Petersburg toward the end of
September to go to Sweden by way of Finland. My new friends—
those who had drawn close to me because we shared the same
feelings—came to bid me good-bye: Sir Robert Wilson, who was
going to seek an opportunity to get into the fighting and to arouse
his friends to do the same; Monsieur de Stein, a man of old-style
virtues, who lives only in the hope of seeing his country liberated;
the Spanish envoy; the English minister, Lord Tyrconnel; witty
Admiral Bentinck; Alexis de Noailles, the only French émigré
from imperial tyranny and the only other person who was there,
like me, to bear witness for France; Colonel Dörnberg, that intrepid Hessian whom nothing has diverted from his objective; and
several Russians whose names have since been celebrated for their
exploits.[2] Never had the fate of the world been exposed to greater
dangers; no one dared to say so, but everyone knew it. I alone—
as a woman—was not endangered, but what I had suffered
counted for something. In saying good-bye to these worthy
knights of the human race, I did not know which of them I would
ever see again, and already two of them are dead. When men's
passions turn them against each other, when nations attack each

---

[2] Robert Wilson, an English general, had distinguished himself in Portugal
at the head of the Lusitanian Legion in the battle of Talaveyra and had supported Wellington when Masséna invaded Portugal. In 1812 he was sent to the
headquarters of the Russian army as the military representative of Great
Britain. It was he who, in 1815—with two other English officers—prepared for
the invasion of Lavalette.

Lord Cathcart was the English minister at Petersburg.

Count Alexis de Noailles had in 1809 taken part in the opposition to the imperial government by circulating the bill of excommunication put forth by the
Pope against Napoleon. Arrested, he was set at liberty only because of the
appeals of his brother Alfred. He left France, joined Louis XVIII at Hartwell,
and received from him several missions to foreign governments. In 1814 he
returned to France with the Count of Artois.

For Tyrconnel and Bentinck, see chapter XVI.

Baron Stein was the well-known Prussian minister who was obliged to resign
in November, 1808, and whom an imperial decree had declared "enemy of
France and of the Confederation."

The Hessian Colonel Dörnberg, having entered Prussian military service,
was made prisoner at Lübeck in 1806; later a colonel in the guard of the King
of Westphalia, he attempted an uprising (1809) which failed. Condemned to
death for high treason, he entered the free corps of the Duke of Brunswick, and
then the Russian army under the command of Wittgenstein.

other with fury, one generally recognizes human destiny in the misfortunes of humanity. But when a single being, comparable to the idols of the Lapps, which are worshiped through fear, spreads torrents of misery over the earth, one experiences a superstitious fear which leads one to consider all honorable men as his victims.

On entering Finland, you know immediately that you are in another country and that the people are a different race from the Slavic. The Finns, it is said, come straight from the north of Asia, and their language has no relation to Swedish, which is somewhere between English and German. However, for the most part the faces of the Finns are entirely Germanic. With their blond hair and fair complexions they lack Russian expressiveness, but their manners are also gentler: the common people have a sober probity, the result of Protestant teaching and purity of customs. On Sundays you can see the young girls returning from church on horseback, with the young men following them. The pastors of Finland are most hospitable, for they consider it their duty to lodge travelers, and the welcome extended in these families is genuine and pleasant. There are hardly any castles or great lords in Finland, and so in general the pastors are the country's most important men. In several Finnish songs, young girls assure their lovers that they would even sacrifice the pastor's house for their sake if they should inherit it. This reminds me of the young shepherd who said: "If I were king, I would guard my sheep on horseback." Even in imagination one seldom goes beyond what is familiar.

The Finnish landscape is very different from the Russian. Instead of the marshes and plains around Petersburg, there are rocks, low mountains, and forests. After a time these mountains and forests, composed of the same trees—pine and birch—become monotonous. The enormous blocks of granite scattered throughout the fields and along the highways give the country an appearance of vigor; but there is very little life around them, and vegetation begins to thin out from the latitude of Finland to the farthest point of the inhabited world. We crossed a forest half consumed by fire. The north winds, which spread the flames, make disasters from fire very frequent, both in towns and in the country. In all ways, man finds it difficult to struggle against nature in these frigid climates.

There are few towns in Finland, and those that exist are thinly populated. There is no center, no rivalry, nothing to say, and very little to do in a northern Swedish or Russian province, and during eight months of the year all living nature sleeps. Emperor Alexander took possession of Finland after the treaty of Tilsit,[3] at a time when the deranged faculties of the Swedish king, Gustavus IV, rendered him incapable of defending his country. This prince had an estimable moral character, but from childhood he himself had recognized that he could not hold the reins of government. The Swedes fought courageously in Finland, but without a warlike leader on the throne a small nation could not triumph over a powerful enemy. Emperor Alexander became master of Finland by conquest and by treaties based on force, but one must do him the justice of saying that he treated this new province very well and respected its liberties. He allowed the Finns to retain all their privileges relative to the raising of taxes and men. He sent generous assistance to the cities destroyed by fire, and his favors compensated to a certain extent for what the Finns had formerly possessed as rights, if indeed free men can ever voluntarily accede to that sort of exchange. Finally, according to one of the dominant ideas of the nineteenth century—that of natural boundaries— Finland was as necessary to Russia as Norway was to Sweden, and one can truthfully say that wherever such natural boundaries have not existed, there have been perpetual wars.

I embarked at Abo, the capital of Finland. There is a university in that city, and some attempts are made to cultivate the mind, but the presence of bears and wolves during the winter makes the task of ensuring tolerable physical existence the first necessity. In the northern countries these problems consume a great part of the time

---

[3] Napoleon had encouraged Alexander to take Finland in order to involve him more deeply in his system. On February 15, 1808, twenty thousand Russians entered Finland. Profiting by the arrest of the Russian ambassador, Monsieur d'Alopéus, in Stockholm, Alexander proclaimed the joining of Finland to his empire. It was definitively ceded to him by the peace treaty of Fredrikshamn (September 17, 1809).

which elsewhere is devoted to the enjoyment of the creative arts. On the other hand, the very difficulties with which nature confronts men contribute greater firmness to their character and shield them from the disorders caused by idleness. Nevertheless, I constantly longed for the rays of the southern sun, which had penetrated to my very soul.

The mythological beliefs of the northern peoples are forever providing them with ghosts and phantoms; the day is as propitious for apparitions as the night: for something about the pale, cloudy atmosphere seems to summon the dead to return to earth and breathe the air—cold as the tomb—which surrounds the living. In these countries, the two extremes are more generally the rule rather than the intermediate degrees: one is either solely occupied with a physical struggle against nature, or the workings of the mind become mystical, drawing everything from within the self and finding no inspiration in exterior objects.

Since I have been so cruelly persecuted by the Emperor, I have lost all confidence in destiny. However, I have an even stronger belief in the protection of Providence, though not in the form of earthly happiness. The result is that every decision frightens me, and yet exile often obliges me to make decisions. I was afraid of the sea, but was constantly told, "Everyone makes this crossing, and nothing happens to anyone." Speeches like this reassure almost all travelers, but the imagination is not permanently lulled by this kind of consolation, and the vast depths of the ocean, from which one is separated by such a frail object, continue to torment one's thoughts. Monsieur Schlegel saw how frightened I was about the fragile craft that was to take us to Stockholm.[4] He showed me the prison near Abo in which one of the most unfortunate kings of Sweden, Eric XIV, had been confined for some time before he died in another prison near Gripsholm. "If you were in there," he said, "how you would long for the crossing of this sea, which now so terrifies you!" This ac-

---

[4] In fact it was only a fishing boat. "Madame de Staël arrived from Abo fifteen days ago on a fishing boat and fell like a bomb on Stockholm . . ." (Letter addressed to Monsieur de Ribbing in Paris from Stockholm, October 20, 1812. Translated from the Swedish, Archives des Affaires Étrangères, Suède).

curate observation turned my thoughts in a different direction, and the first days of our voyage were rather pleasant for me. We made our way between islands, and although there is greater danger near the shore than on the open sea, one is never as terrified with land in sight as when the waves seem to touch the sky. I made myself look at the land on the horizon, for as long as possible: infinity is as fearful to our sight as it is pleasing to our soul. We passed Aaland island, where plenipotentiaries of Peter I and Charles XII negotiated a peace and tried to set limits to their ambitions in this frozen land, which only the blood of their subjects had been able to warm for a moment. We hoped to reach Stockholm the next day, but a decidedly contrary wind obliged us to cast anchor by the side of a rocky island with a few trees hardly higher than the stones which surrounded them. We hastened, however, to take a walk on this island, in order to feel solid ground under our feet.[5]

I have always been very subject to boredom, and, far from knowing how to occupy myself during these completely empty moments, which seemed destined for study . . . [Here the manuscript breaks off.]

Auguste de Staël's note to the edition of 1821

After a crossing which was not without danger, my mother disembarked in Stockholm. She was received with great kindness in Sweden, and spent eight months there, and that was where she wrote the journal which you have just read. Shortly afterward she departed for London, and there published her work *On Germany*, which the Imperial police had suppressed. But because her health —already cruelly impaired by Bonaparte's persecutions—had been affected by the fatigues of a long journey, my mother felt obliged to undertake the history of Monsieur Necker's political life with-

---

[5] She wrote to Princess Kutusov, September 29, from Stockholm: "My own exploits have been limited to a very difficult sea crossing, and since I had just learned about Prince Kutusov's victory, I would have found it very sad to be drowned." The archipelago of Aaland forms a group of about eighty islands belonging to Russia since 1809. It is on the direct route from Stockholm to Abo. The sea is rough in these regions. In winter, a great part of the crossing must be made on ice.

out delay, and to postpone all other work until she had finished what her filial affection made her regard as a duty. She then conceived the plan for *Considerations on the French Revolution*. She was unable to finish even this work, and the manuscript of her *Ten Years of Exile* remained in her portfolio in the state in which I now publish it.

Works Cited in Gautier's Footnotes

Archives des Affaires étrangères, Suède. Dépêche de M. de Cabre du Octobre 1812, adressée de Stockholm à M. de Ribbing, à Paris.

Chaptal, Jean Antoine Claude, Comte de Chanteloup. *Mes Souvenirs sur Napoléon.* Paris, 1893.

Chateaubriand, François Auguste René. *Mémoires d'outre-tombe.* Édité par Edmond Biré. Paris, 1898.

Fontanes, Louis Jean Pierre, Marquis de. *Parallèle entre César, Cromwel* (sic), *Monk et Bonaparte.* Fragment traduit de l'Anglais. 1800.

Gautier, Paul. *Madame de Staël et Napoléon.* Paris, 1903.

Golovkin, Fédor Gavrilovich, Graf. *La Cour et le Règne de Paul Premier.* Paris, 1905.

Jung, Th. *Lucien Bonaparte et ses mémoires, 1775–1840, d'après les papiers déposés aux Archives étrangères et d'autres documents inédits.* Paris, 1882–1883. 3 volumes.

Napoléon I. *Mémorial de Sainte-Hélène, ou Journal où se trouve consigné, jour par jour, ce qu' a dit et fait Napoléon durant dix-huit mois, par le Comte de Las Cases.* Paris, 1823. 8 vols.

Necker, Jacques. *Cours de morale religieuse.* 1800. Genève.

———. *Dernières vues de politique et de finance, offertes à la nation française.* An X (1802).

Remacle, L., Comte. *Bonaparte et les Bourbons; relations secrètes des agents de Louis XVIII à Paris, avec une introduction et des notes par le Comte Remacle.* Paris, 1899.

Reynier, Jean Louis. *De l'Egypte après la bataille de Héliopolis.* Paris, 1802.

Rémusat, Claire Elisabeth, Comtesse de. *Mémoires de Madame de Rémusat, 1802–1808*. Publiés (sic) par son petit-fils, Paul de Rémusat. Paris, 1880. 3 volumes.

Rovigo, Anne Jean Marie René Savary, Duc de. *Mémoires du Duc de Rovigo* [M. Savary]. Écrits de sa mains (sic), pour servir à l'histoire de l'Empereur Napoléon. Paris, 1828. 4 volumes.

Staël-Holstein, Anne Louise Germaine Necker, Baronne de. *Considérations sur les principaux événemens* (sic) *de la Révolution française*. Paris, 1818. 3 volumes.

————. *Lettres inédites de Madame de Staël à Henri Meister*. Publiées par MM. Paul Usteri . . . et Eugène Ritter. Paris, 1803.

————. *Des Circonstances actuelles qui peuvent terminer la Révolution, et des Principes qui doivent fonder la République en France*. Paris, Bibliothèque Nationale, Manuscrits, Nouvelle acquisition française. 1300, Folio 121 et suivant.

————. *Dix années d'exil* . . . Formant le tome XV des Oeuvres complètes de Madame de Staël publiées par son fils. Paris, 1821.

Ambigu, variétés atroces et amusantes, volumes 1–58, 1803–1818. Edited by J. G. Peltier. London.

Journal de l'Empire, January 14, 1808. [Arrival of Madame de Staël in Vienna.]

Revue de Paris, December 1, 1903. L. Pingaud, Madame de Staël et le Duc de Rovigo.

Revue des Deux Mondes, November 1, 1899. [Article by Paul Gautier on Madame de Staël and the censoring of newspapers.]

Revue des Deux Mondes, October 1, 1903. "Chateaubriand et Madame de Staël."

Archives Nationales, Paris. F⁷ 6331. [Letter from the Prefect of Léman to the Minister of Police, October 27, 1810.]

Works by Madame de Staël

(Where there are many editions, only the earliest has been cited.)

1786   *Sophie, ou les sentiments secrets.* Paris.

1788   *Lettres sur les ouvrages et le caractère de J. J. Rousseau.* 2 volumes.

      In English: *Letters on the Works and Character of J. J. Rousseau.* Translated from the French. London, 1789.

1790   *Jane Gray.* Paris, Desenne.

1793   *Réflexions sur le procès de la Reine.* Londres, Imprimerie de T. Spilsbury et Fils.

1795   *Réflexions sur la paix adressées à M. Pitt et aux Français.* Genève.

      Réflexion sur la paix intérieure. (Unpublished.)

      Recueil de morceaux détachés. Lausanne. (The short writings of her youth, and *Epître au malheur*, *Zulma*, *Essai sur les fictions*.)

1796   *De l'Influence des passions sur le bonheur des individus et des nations.* Lausanne, J. Mourer. 2 volumes.

1800   *De la littérature considérée dans ses rapports avec l'état moral et politique des nations.* Paris, Maradan. 2 volumes.

      In English: *A Treatise on Ancient and Modern Literature.* From the French of the Baroness de Staël. London, printed by G. Cawthorn, 1803. This was published in 1813 under the title *The Influence of Literature upon Society.* Boston, W. Wells and T. B. Wait & Co.

1802 *Delphine*. Genève, J. J. Paschoud. 4 volumes.

In English: *Delphine*. Philadelphia, E. L. Cary & A. Hart, 1836. 3 volumes.

1804 *Du Caractère de M. Necker et de sa vie privée*. Paris.

In English: *Memoirs of the Private Life of My Father*, by the Baroness de Staël-Holstein. To which are added, *Miscellanies*, by M. Necker. London, H. Colburn, 1818.

1807 *Corinne, ou, l'Italie*. Paris, H. Nicolle. 2 volumes.

In English: *Corinne, or Italy*. Translated by Isabel Hill; with metrical versions of the odes by L. E. Landon. New York, Derby & Jackson, 1857.

1809 *Lettres et pensées du Prince de Ligne*. Paris, J. J. Paschoud.

In English: *The Prince de Ligne: His Memoirs, Letters, and Miscellaneous Papers*. With preface by Madame de Staël-Holstein. 1899.

1813 *De l'Allemagne*. London. 3 volumes.

In English: *Germany*. Translated from the French. London, J. Murray, 1813. 3 volumes

Réflexions sur le suicide. London.

In English: *Reflections on Suicide*. Translated from the French. London, Longman, Hurst, Rees, Orme and Brown, 1813.

Zulma et Trois nouvelles, with *Essai sur les fictions*. London.

In English: *Zulma and Other Tales. To Which is Prefixed an Essay on Fiction*. Translated from the French. London, 1813. 2 volumes.

An Appeal to the Nations of Europe against the Continental System. Published at Stockholm, by authority of Bernadotte, in March, 1813. London, J. M. Richardson; Boston, S. H. Parker, 1813.

1818 *Considérations sur les principaux événemens* (sic) *de la Révolution française*. Paris, Delaunay. 3 volumes. (Posthumous.)

In English: *Considerations on the Principal Events of the French Revolution*. Posthumous work of the Baroness de Staël. Edited by the Duke de Broglie and the Baron de Staël. Translated from the original manuscript. London, Baldwin, Cradock and Joy, 1818; New York, James Eastburn, 1818.

1821   *Dix années d'exil, fragments d'un ouvrage inédit composé dans les années 1810 à 1813.* (Volume XV of *Oeuvres complètes de Mme de Staël publiées par son Fils.*) Paris, Treuttel et Wurtz, 1821.

In English: *Ten Years of Exile, or, Memoirs of That Interesting Period of the Life of the Baroness de Staël-Holstein, Written by Herself, During the Years 1810, 1811, 1812 and 1813, and Now First Published by Her Son.* Translated from the French. New York, Collins and Co., 1821. 2 volumes.

1820–1821   *Oeuvres complètes.* Paris, Treuttel et Wurtz.

Oeuvres inédites. Londres, Treuttel et Wurtz.

1904   *Dix années d'exil. Édition nouvelle d'après les manuscrits, avec une introduction, des notes et un appendice par Paul Gautier.* Paris, Plon-Nourrit.

Selected References

Andrews, Wayne. *Germaine: A Portrait of Madame de Staël.* New York, Atheneum, 1963.

Balayé, Simone. *Les Carnets de voyage de Madame de Staël.* Genève, Droz, 1971.

Berry, Mary. *Extracts of the Journals and Correspondence of Miss Berry.* London, Longmans, Green and Co., 1866.

Blennerhasset, Lady Charlotte. *Madame de Staël, Her Friends and Her Influence in Politics and Literature.* London, Chapman and Hall, 1889. 3 volumes.

Castelot, André. *Napoleon.* Harper & Row, 1971.

Clarke, Isabel Constance. *Six Portraits.* London, Hutchinson, 1935.

Connelly, Owen. *The Gentle Bonaparte: A Biography of Joseph, Napoleon's Elder Brother.* New York, Macmillan, 1968.

Constant de Rebecque, Benjamin. *Adolphe and the Red Notebook* (With an Introduction by Harold Nicolson). Indianapolis, Bobbs-Merrill, 1959.

————. *Journaux intimes. Édition intégrale des Manuscrits autographes publiée pour la première fois.* Paris, Gallimard, 1952.

————. *Oeuvres.* Paris, Gallimard, 1957.

Delderfield, Ronald Frederick. *Retreat from Moscow.* New York, Atheneum, 1967.

Forsberg, Robert J. *Madame de Staël and the English.* New York, Astra Books, 1967.

Gautier, Paul. *Madame de Staël et Napoléon.* Paris, Plon, 1903.

Haussonville, Gabriel, comte de. *Madame de Staël et l'Allemagne.* Paris, Calmann-Lévy, 1928.

Hawkins, Richmond L. *Madame de Staël and the United States.* Cambridge, Harvard University Press, 1930. Kraus reprint, no date.

Herold, J. Christopher. *Mistress to An Age: A Life of Madame de Staël.* Indianapolis, Bobbs-Merrill, 1958.

Jasinski, Béatrice W. *L'Engagement de Benjamin Constant: Amour et politique, 1794–1796.* Paris, Minard, 1971.

Lefebvre, Georges. *Napoleon.* Volume I: *From 18 Brumaire to Tilsit, 1799–1807.* Translated from the French by Henry F. Stockhold. Volume II: *From Tilsit to Waterloo, 1807–1815.* Translated from the French by J. E. Anderson. New York, Columbia University Press, 1969.

Levaillant, Maurice. *The Passionate Exiles: Madame de Staël and Madame Récamier.* Translated from the French by Malcolm Barnes. New York, Farrar, Straus & Cudahy, 1958. Freeport, New York, Books for Libraries Press, 1971.

Luppé, Robert de. *Les idées littéraires de Madame de Staël et l'heritage des lumières (1795–1800).* Paris, J. Vrin, 1969.

Madame de Staël et l'Europe. Colloque pour la célébration du deuxième centenaire de la naissance de Madame de Staël (1766–1966). Paris, Klincksieck, 1970.

Markham, Felix Maurice. *Napoleon.* New York, New American Library, 1966.

Massin, Jean. *Almanach du Premier Empire, du neuf Thermidor à Waterloo.* Paris, Club Français du Livre, 1965.

Napoleon I, Emperor of the French. *The Mind of Napoleon: A Selection from His Written and Spoken Words.* Edited and translated by J. Christopher Herold. New York, Columbia University Press, 1955.

Napoléon et l'Empire, 1769, 1815, 1821. Sous la direction de Jean Mistler. Paris, Hachette, 1968. 2 volumes.

Nicolson, Harold. *Benjamin Constant.* New York, Doubleday and Co., 1949.

Nolde, Baroness Elisabeth de. *Madame de Staël and Benjamin Constant. Unpublished Letters, Together with Other Mementoes from the Papers Left by Madame Charlotte de Constant.* Edited by Madame de Constant's Great-Granddaughter, Baroness Elisabeth de Nolde. Translated from the French by Charlotte Harwood. New York, G. P. Putnam's Sons, 1907.

Sorel, Albert. *Madame de Staël*. London, T. Fisher Unwin, 1892.

Staël-Holstein, Anne Louise Germaine Necker, Baronne de. *Choix de Lettres (1778–1817) présenté et commenté par Georges Solovieff* (Préface de la Comtesse Jean de Pange). Paris, Klincksieck, 1970.

————. *De Staël–DuPont Letters; Correspondence of Madame de Staël and Pierre Samuel DuPont de Nemours and of Other Members of the Necker and DuPont Families.* Edited and translated by James F. Marshall. Madison, University of Wisconsin Press, 1968.

————. *Madame de Staël on Politics, Literature and National Character.* Translated, edited, and with an introduction by Morroe Berger. London, Sedgwick & Jackson, 1964.

Stevens, Abel. *Madame de Staël, a Study of Her Life and Times, the First Revolution and the First Empire.* New York, Harper & Brothers, 1881. 2 volumes.

Thompson, J. M. *Napoleon Bonaparte.* New York, Oxford University Press, 1952.

Whitford, Robert C. *Madame de Staël's Literary Reputation in England.* Urbana, University of Illinois, 1918; Johnson Reprint, 1968.

Index